Anxiety in the Era of Uncertainty

Anxiety in the Era of Uncertainty

An Interdisciplinary Reading of Lacan's Seminars

EDITED BY

Ali Chavoshian AND
Jung Eun Sophia Park

☛PICKWICK *Publications* · Eugene, Oregon

ANXIETY IN THE ERA OF UNCERTAINTY
An Interdisciplinary Reading of Lacan's Seminars

Pickwick Publications
An Imprint of Wipf and Stock Publishers
199 W. 8th Ave., Suite 3
Eugene, OR 97401

www.wipfandstock.com

PAPERBACK ISBN: 979-8-3852-1010-7
HARDCOVER ISBN: 979-8-3852-1011-4
EBOOK ISBN: 979-8-3852-1012-1

Cataloguing-in-Publication data:

Names: Chavoshian, Ali, editor. | Park, Jung Eun Sophia, editor.

Title: Anxiety in the era of uncertainty : an interdisciplinary reading of Lacan's seminars / edited by Ali Chavoshian and Jung Eun Sophia Park.

Description: Eugene, OR : Pickwick Publications, 2025 | Includes bibliographical references and index.

Identifiers: ISBN 979-8-3852-1010-7 (paperback) | ISBN 979-8-3852-1011-4 (hardcover) | ISBN 979-8-3852-1012-1 (ebook)

Subjects: LCSH: Lacan, Jacques, 1901–1981—Criticism and interpretation.

Classification: BF173 .A679 2025 (paperback) | BF173 .A679 (ebook)

VERSION NUMBER 03/18/25

"*Anxiety in the Era of Uncertainty* is a critical, spiritual, psychological collection of Jacque Lacan's theory and work edited by Ali Chavoshian and Jung Eun Sophia Park. The volume is rich with diverse contributors covering important topics such as anxiety, practical ministry, Lacan in the clinic, and Lacanian psychoanalysis.

—GRACE JI-SUN KIM, professor of theology,
Earlham School of Religion

"*Anxiety in the Era of Uncertainty* by Ali Chavoshian and Jung Eun Sophia Park is a remarkable interdisciplinary and intercultural study distilling contributions from Jacques Lacan's influential psychoanalytic, cultural, and political ideas to contemporary discussions of postcolonialism, race, gender, and late capitalism in Hong Kong, the U.S., Korea, Iran, China, and Europe. Authors from around the globe (with a strong emphasis on Asia) repristinate Lacan insights on anxiety, uncertainty, Neo-Freudian object-relations theory, intersubjectivity, women's sexuality, and 'the Real' (among many others) for a new generation, including people of color and non-western discussions of culture, ministry, theology, biblical studies, social science, and the body. The product of an intensive nine-year international seminar, each author draws challenging new fruits from Lacan's Seminars, beginning in 1951 post-war France while a member of the Paris Psychoanalytic Society and concluding in 1980, just over two years before the January 1, 1983, U.S. Defense Data Network adoption of the TCP/IP protocol created the internet. Accessible to experts and beginners, this book will challenge every reader!"

—ROBERT LASSALLE-KLEIN, professor emeritus of
religion and philosophy, Holy Names University

Contents

Introduction

ALI CHAVOSHIAN AND JUNG EUN SOPHIA PARK

THE IDEA OF THIS book emerged from nine years of teaching close readings of Jacques Lacan's texts, which we offered to a diverse group of people. In this reading seminar, we opened up to people from various professional fields: Lacanian analysis trainees, theologians, artists, therapists, ministers, and any intellectuals drawn to Lacan's discourse. Ali Chavoshian's pioneering idea, that the training should always follow the Lacan text and fully embrace other intellectual people who have examined the text, unfolded into an inter-disciplinary and global reading seminar. This book is an edited volume of interdisciplinary readings of *Lacan's seminars,* with each chapter signifying the author's location and situation. The contents listed in this book include their life experiences and socio-political situations, and the way each author engages and even struggles with the Lacan texts, delving into life-transforming meanings.

Lacan's scholarship and discourse were primarily European and male-centered until recently, when they were extended. They now include, but is not limited to, Lacan's capitalist discourse. Many social critics have widely utilized Lacanian discourse to critique the current late capitalism with a slight modification of Karl Marx's critique of capitalism. Furthermore, with an interest in gender study and feminist thought, Lacan's comprehension of feminine sexuality, emphasizing the position of the female and not an ontological difference, and even giving an advantage to women's position of "not all," has supported an alterity, resisting the male-centered framework of human society and mental composition. His notion of feminine sexuality has extended into the concept of gender fluidity. For example, Judith Butler contends that "performativity acts" as a way to elaborate the gender role as being fluid, and her theory juxtaposes Lacan's position of female sexuality. However, Butler does not cite him directly in her work.

Remarkably, the Lacan discourse on identification extends into Black and Latinx Studies and concerns of race and identification in postcolonial reality and identification.[1] Unconscious bias, a deeply seated human psyche, is analyzed and identity politics can be examined through Lacan's lens. It has developed into an implication on postcolonial discourses.

CHARACTERISTICS OF THIS BOOK

Along with this direction, this book first provides readings of the primary texts from a global context, emphasizing an intersectionality in which postcolonialism, race, gender, and late capitalism are all interconnected and interrelated. Intensive, critical readings and applications are located worldwide, in places such as in Hong Kong, US, Korea, Iran, and China, focusing on current global and diasporic life and reality. Each reading's diverse setting, such as a university, prison ministry, Asian diaspora, local Presbyterian Church, spiritual direction, and psychoanalysis in practice, provides rich flavors of the joy of reading volumes of the Lacan Seminar. Fully embracing the theoretical level of Lacan discourse, this book features the current era of anxiety and uncertainty in revisiting and reinvigorating the texts. In Lacan's discourse, we do not often hear Asian voices or those of the Asian diaspora or global ministry. In this volume, we bring more diverse voices, frequently unheard, and other cultural contexts.

Second, in the literature of Lacan's discourse, one of the most apparent aspects is interdisciplinarity. Lacan explicitly stresses the importance of an interdisciplinary approach: "I mean directly geared into a reality accessible to us through other disciplines and other human sciences. The interdisciplinary approach has to be done to properly situate our domain and find our bearings within it."[2] Lacan himself was an interdisciplinary intellectual, engaging with various disciplines such as philosophy, theology, linguistics, and many other fields. This book manifests primary text

---

1. See George and Hook, *Lacan and Race*; Marriott, *Lacan Noir*.

2. Lacan, *Object Relation*, 244–45.

readings with modern tools from multiple disciplines, such as popular culture, pastoral ministry and theology, and body discourse.

This work is an effort of interdisciplinary open intellectual work, which began between a Lacanian psychoanalyst and a scholar of Christian Spirituality, through the frame of *Lacan's Seminar*. Jung Eun Sophia Park's interest began with her interdisciplinary approach within her home discipline of Christian spirituality, which explores the human experience and then searches for the meaning of human desire. Often, Lacan's seminars challenge theologians with his knowledge and insights on theology, Biblical Studies, Buddhism, and Eastern Philosophies.

Ali Chavoshian, a senior Lacanian psychoanalyst, deeply understands Islamic Mysticism and Western Philosophy. His passion for depth ignited an intellectual desire to read with others with more diverse backgrounds. Out of some initial conversations, we created a reading group and expanded our comprehension of Lacan's psychoanalysis. As Lacan engaged with numerous scholarly works, such as those of Levi Strauss, Ludwig Wittgenstein, and Maurice Merleau-Ponty, we engaged Lacan's texts with diverse expertise. Thus, these collected essays, on the one hand, comprehend the text through close readings. On the other hand, they investigate possible meanings from their various academic areas and lived experiences.

Last but not least, we must pay attention to the clinical aspect of Lacan's seminars. Even though Lacan emphasizes his work as clinical, the discourse has been heavily theoretical. Lacan's seminar began in 1951, when he was a member of the Paris Psychoanalytic Society, with weekly Wednesday meetings at his apartment. The following year, they moved to Sainte-Anne Hospital and continued until 1964, when he was excluded from the International Psychoanalytical Association. Nevertheless, he resumed his seminar in 1965, which continued until 1980.[3]

Since then, his series of seminars has been translated into many languages and his theory has flourished. Lacan's text fascinates us in that he often talks abstractly, but this talk always reflects—and is based on—clinical cases. For example, when Lacan explains phobia, he utilizes the clinical case of Little Hans by Freud. He also examines polyvalent ways through several consecutive seminars in Seminar IV, *Object Relation*.[4]

---

3. For the history of Lacan seminars, see Lacan, "Excommunication," 1–16.

4. See Lacan, *The Object Relation*.

Our book includes explicit examples of Lacanian psychoanalysis, bearing the fruits of Chavoshian's decades of teachings and practice.

PRINCIPLE OF READING THE LACAN TEXTS

Contributors listed in this volume come from different backgrounds: psychoanalysis, clinical psychology, psychology, spirituality, Ethics, and pastoral ministry. The original idea of a reading group followed some ground rules: that is, they should stay within the texts and Lacan's theory and practice as the only source from which to interpret other disciplines. It emphasized that various humanistic disciplines should be read from Lacan's theoretical point of view, not the other way around.

Also, since Lacanian theory comes from the clinic, we committed ourselves to staying within the proximity of praxis. To do so, we read the texts line by line to find clinical relevance. Lacan's Seminar has been translated into English by a few Lacanian psychoanalysts, and the most accessible ones are by Cormac Gallagher and Jacques-Alain Miller. An Irish Lacanian, Gallagher translated eighteen seminars from unpublished French manuscripts,[5] while Miller, Lacan's son-in-law, edited and published translations from official public manuscripts and translators.[6]

For this reading group, we set up a curriculum to understand the development of Lacan's theory, particularly the structurization of the human subject from the Imaginary to the Symbolic and the Real. This developed from the early seminars to the middle and final ones, which respond respectively to the Imaginary, the Symbolic, and the Real.

To explain how the nine-year reading course has evolved, we post the list of readings. When Chavoshian designed the course "An Introduction to Lacan" in 2016, he introduced Lacan's writings: the Case of Aimee, Family Complex in the Formation of Individuals, the Mirror Stages, and the early writings from *Écrits*. The chronology of our yearly curriculum seminars based on the Lacan texts, which began in 2017, is as follows:

2017 Selected chapters from *Écrits: The Early Writing*.

2018–2019 Reading the first two seminars of all books from Ghallager's list.

---

5. We accessed Cormac Gallaher's collected translations and papers on his website, "Jacques Lacan in Ireland" (http://www.lacaninireland.com).

6. Jacques-Alain Miller edited and published through Norton and Polity.

2019 *L'envers: The Other Side of Psychoanalysis—Lacan Four Discourses*

2020 *The Ethics of Psychoanalysis*

2021 *Encore: On Feminine Sexuality*

2022 *The Foundations of Psychoanalysis: Four Fundamentals*

2023 *Anxiety* and *The Object Relation*

2023–2024 *Identification*

We recognize that Lacan founded a reading group named "The Lacan Cartel" at the beginning of the training. He encouraged members to develop a writing project on psychoanalytic practice, theory, and technique. He also formed a group called "Plus One," composed of a supervisor or an analyst invited from the outside, who was unknown to the group, to sit in the class.[7] Having the plus one was to prevent members from developing a mixed identity with other organizations or their own.

Also, Lacan tried to open a personal space of formation in which each member paid attention to one's desires and dread. Practically, the personal space allowed the members to develop a desire to listen, to contain their anxiety, and to speak with the unconscious. It gave them the *savoir,* truthful knowledge, or a science of the unconscious from the analytic experience of a close reading of the Lacan texts. Furthermore, true knowledge provided insight into how to apply the experience to their writing project.

In the spirit of Lacan's Cartel, our undertaking of such a project has been challenging. Close readings of Lacan's primary texts require a capacity to hold one's anxiety, damage one's narcissism, remove deeply seated judgmental lenses, and face the fear of the unknown. It means confronting one's ego in the unconscious of the Other as one speaks about the texts, following the ethics of the unsayable with one's desire to write as a speaking subject with authenticity. Otherwise, the reading and writing processes remain replicative and paranoid, which are dangers one may encounter. Paranoiac knowledge, for instance, memorizing concepts or mechanical comprehension, occurs because of one's inability to hold anxiety while reading the text. When we read Lacan's text, the text also reads us, meaning that the fear of not knowing brings out our

7. Lacan, "Cartel."

obsessional neurosis for confabulation, cut and paste, censorship, and paranoid addiction.[8]

To avoid the trap of paranoiac knowledge, our reading group members encountered their unconscious through a full analytic reading. During the last nine years, they have stayed with the ambiguity and complexity of the texts, and through this, they have found their voices and desires to write and be scholars of psychoanalysis. Their works will remain incomplete, like any scholarly work suffering from the signifier of lack. However, due to the Cartel, the project has generally become a signifier of lack. It demonstrates the singularity formation of a personal desire for the unsayable within the praxis of writing.

Finally, to ensure each member's wish for a writing formation that reflects the singularity of their desires, we followed the tradition of psychoanalysis training to do a palimpsest exercise and do a passage through which the person experiences transformation while tracing one's process. The palimpsest, from the Greek, "scraped again," is writing and rewriting which includes marks from the previous writing on the papyrus.

The assumption signifies that a project is an impossible gift that will never be complete; instead, it always follows a signifier of lack. This openness allows for the transmission of knowledge and the quest for further search within the reading and writing community. Our contributors exercised their palimpsest by presenting a pilot study of their works at a conference in Seoul, South Korea, in 2021. In the post-conference discussion, the contributors expressed their wish to pursue their project further. The conference provided an opportunity for a passage presentation; they expressed their desire to publish as a group. This book is a rewriting as a part of the writing process, which continues to evolve.

CONTENTS

This book, composed of four parts, focuses on the theme of anxiety in the era of uncertainty as a fundamental human condition, which could manifest as phobia, fantasy, and intense emotions and reactions. Part I is a collection of current culture and its critique through Lacan's theory. Part II deals with praxis, including practical ministry, engaging with people and seeking to deepen their understanding of people. Part III reads Lacan's text concerning the body discourse in the contemporary

8. Mills, "Lacan on Paranoiac Knowledge," 30–51.

global world. It includes the body of a Medieval mystic woman and a woman character in the Bible, as well as the COVID and the Church as the Body of Christ. Part IV is titled "Clinical Lacan" and deals with Lacan in the clinic. This part provides three intense clinical cases of Lacanian psychoanalysis.

Part I. Culture and Anxiety

Part I deals with popular culture, emphasizing contemporary society and the prevalence of anxiety. This part mainly includes the role of fantasy in finding one's subjectivity amid angst. It also involves the concern of an AI sex doll, whether it can satisfy human sexual desire, as well as the Christian moral paradox, which results in anxiety.

Taking the lead is Jung Eun Sophia Park's chapter, which explores the function of fantasy through the analysis of *The Phantom of the Opera*. Her analysis demonstrates the function of the imagination in subjects, being caught by symbolic domains in the development of the human mind. Her analysis of *The Phantom of the Opera* is like the discourse of analysis and treatment, where subjectification takes place through the journey of traversing the fantasy and accepting the impasse as the nature of one's desire.

Fantasy is the unconscious that motivates humans toward an indefinite search in life. You cannot eliminate fantasy, rather you must take it in. Lacan states that the analysand must go on to "traverse the fundamental fantasy." Based on Lacan's Seminars, especially *Book IX: Identification* and *Book IV: The Object Relation,* Park argues that in the dynamic of the phantasmatic, each main character of this story finds subjectivity or at least moves into an approximate genuine subjectivity and the *jouissance* of sublimation.

In chapter 2, Levi Checketts examines the frustration and the impossibility of the masculine desire projected on AI sex robots. As a Lacanian ethicist of science and technology, Checketts refers to Lacan's seminars on *Desire and Its Interpretation* (1958–1959) and *Encore: Feminine Sexuality* (1972–1973), explaining the impossibility and the impotency of male sexuality. The impossibility or frustration is rooted in the concept of moiety, where the man assumes a woman as his half. Women who do not follow this moiety, the position of not all, can deal with this impossibility.

Also, he analyzes the nature of AI as Metaphor, not Metonymy, as a limit to understanding the human psyche based on permutation.

Also, in chapter 3, Checketts raises a critical question on Christian moral teaching, regarding the paradox of a desire for moral order, which we cannot fulfill due to the fundamental human condition of lack and consequent anxiety. The impasse that exists between ourselves and the Other creates a desire to cover over our anxiety with strict adherence to the law. Engaging Lacan's theory of anxiety, object relation, and identification, Checketts manifests that the radical message of Christianity, embedded in the Church's teachings and interpretations of the Bible, is a resignation to anxiety rather than an insistence upon a solid moral order. Then, he suggests that we should understand Christian ethics as a paradoxical insistence on a law that Christ has done away with because, without the Symbolic order, we cannot exist.

Part II. Praxis

In the second part, this book deals with a practical matter called praxis. In Ancient Greek society, the word praxis (πρᾶξις) referred to activity engaged in by free people, emphasizing the process of learning and practice. We now use the term praxis as a dialectical process, not necessarily opposed to theory, but one of learning and practice. Although all Lacanian practices are action-oriented, this part emphasizes practical application to a specific practice of spiritual direction, prison ministry, and being in the ministry as a pastor's wife concerning identity.

In chapter 4, Ali Chavoshian and Jung Eun Sophia Park are concerned with spiritual direction in the context of immigrant life and spirituality. They pursue an alternative explanation of an apophatic God, using Lacan's concept of the Real of God, as something which could help those living in the twenty-first-century global world of immigration. By examining Lacan's theory of the Real, the negative way of approaching God finds a more contemporary explanation. In addition, as an application of the concept of the Real of God, this chapter manifests importance of the director's role in understanding the directee's spiritual struggle over language, which could bring oppression and anxiety. Later works of Lacan that emphasize the concept of the Real through *Joyce and Sinthome* (1975–1976), *RSI* (1974–1975), and *Encore* (1972–1973) are discussed.

Chapter 5 deals with prisoners' anxiety by exploring the Lacanian gaze, through self-portraits drawn in a prison in Peru. This chapter is composed of a dialogue between Jung Eun Sophia Park and Miyoung Sung, an expressive art therapist who served as a part of the prison ministry, elaborating how the prison population in Peru encounters the gaze and experiences subsequent anxiety. Sung's ministry experience and analysis of the prisoners' paintings, based on Lacan's *Seminar X: Anxiety*, *Seminar XI: Four Fundamentals of Psychoanalysis*, and *Écrits*, are provocative. She explains that the prisoners internalize the rules and laws of the group and become their watchers. The watcher's gaze is internalized so that each prisoner becomes one's watcher. She concludes that the more they recognize the Other, such as watchers or God, the more they are alienated from who they are.

The subsequent chapter has a uniquely self-implicating nature. As a pastor's wife in a Korean American Christian congregation, the author Nuri Park explains her struggle to gain subjectivity, exploring Lacan's four discourses of University, Master, Hysteric, and Analytic. She examines the dialectical progression of the pastor's wife in terms of her identity, anxiety, and desire, which move toward finding her independence and subjectivity. Then, in dealing with her identity, she employs the analytical discourse, embracing the given role as a pastor's wife, opening new spaces for other realms of identity, which manifest as multiple and sometimes conflicting. Through this dialectical process of reading Lacan's *The Other Side of Psychoanalysis Lacan's Four Discourses* and *The Desire and Interpretation*, she explains how she gains subjectivity. While fully aware of its nature of impossibility, she analyzes her identity formation.

Part III. Body in the Global World

The third part comprises various topics related to the body in the global world in relation to Lacan's body discourse. The body can be a site of social phenomena and sharply indicates the human struggle for identity, acceptance, and social location. In this part, the authors cover broad topics related to the body, from the COVID-Body to women's defying bodies, to challenge the social norm. Also, in this global world, the Church body is cross-cultural.

In chapter 7, Chavoshian explains the crisis of COVID-19, exploring science in all its complexity and its interactions with politics, economics, and the spiritual or religious culture. To pursue this thesis, first, he describes Lacan's psychoanalytic theory of body formation, which emphasizes that the body is constituted from the outside, referring to the Symbolic world. In this chapter, he elaborates on the Lacanian Symbolic world in its three contingency domains: economics, politics, and spiritual or religious culture. Chavoshian, in this chapter, implies the need to reconstruct social order.

In chapter 8, Jiyoung Ko, by juxtaposing the character of Antigone, investigates the peculiar spirituality of Mary of Bethany, as presented in the Gospel of John (12:1–8). Ko mainly employs Lacan's seminar, *Ethics of Psychoanalysis*, using significant terms such as the pleasure principle, death drive, *das Ding*, sublimation, etc. If we consider Antigone as a figure of the death drive, autonomous and indifferent to the law, Ko argues that Mary of Bethany is Antigone's double. Through a narrative-critical approach, Ko investigates how the spirituality of this mysterious character in John's Gospel (Mary of Bethany) rejects conforming to the Judaism of her time by refusing the desire of the Other, which was forced on many women. As a result, Mary finds her own genuine desire.

In chapter 9, Heejung Cho is concerned with the body of the Church, which claims to be diverse and equal. She examines how the subject, an Asian theologian, should positions herself within the body of the Roman Catholic Church and its discourse and claim her owns desire, rather than the desire of the body of the Roman Catholic church, which is often a Western voice. Cho develops her argument based on Lacan's statement, "There is no Other of the Other," and the concept of "the double negation of the subject," where the subject is negated twice, once on a personal level and then in relationship with the Other.

Cho argues that Western theologians must recognize that all discourse is engulfed and spoken by the Other, the body of language, the impossibility. This chapter is a reminder to existing Western-centered discourses within the Roman Catholic Church that affects Asian theology, and the author envisions a dialogue grounded on a mutual understanding of impossibility and a postcolonial reality.

Jiyoung Ko, in chapter 10, analyzes the body of Margery Kempe, an English lay woman mystic who is often described as crazy and hysterical, from the perspective of Lacanian ethics of psychoanalysis. Kempe damaged norms and trespassed the prohibitions of the Symbolic order through constant unpredictable behaviors in public, bringing shame upon her, while creating a hole (crack) within the hegemonic cultural and religious systems. In this way, she made a new path of access to higher holiness within a secularized lay woman's body. Ko emphasizes alternative ways to achieve subjectivity through a full embrace of a sense of shame and bodily senses. Kempe's struggle through her troubled body signifies the ethics of psychoanalysis, emphasizing a knowledge of one's desire, which is limited and barred.

Part IV. Clinical Lacan

In part IV, we involve clinical cases of Lacanian psychoanalysis in terms of anxiety. Contrary to the DSM-5-TR, which defines psychopathology in terms of symptoms, Lacanian psychopathology is the structural analysis of the human mind. The structure includes three categories: Neurotic, Perversion, and Psychotic. These structures are formed at the beginning of childhood, and the degree of separation of children from their primary caretakers and the intensity of parental authorities impact the structures. As a result, further development toward inculturation and socialization can take place in the children on their way toward adulthood.

In his seminar on *Psychosis* (1955–1956), Lacan argues that children's early attachment toward their primary caretakers is gradually waned out/ cut by the Name-of-the-Father. Within the first category of neurotic structure, which includes anxiety, phobia, obsession, and compulsion, neurotics accept the cut but hold a grudge and a feeling of discontent toward this cut, and the feeling continues to haunt them for the rest of their adult lives. In the perverse structure, the subject displays sexual fetishism, but not necessarily all the symptoms are sexual disorders, and tends to disavow the Name-of-the-Father and feels that one can perform the function of the Father. Within the psychotic category, psychotics, including paranoia, psychoses, and schizophrenia foreclose the Name-of-the-Father and deny its existence. In this part, Chavoshian presents Lacan's three categories of structure through an analysis of his patients.

Chapter 11 provides an analysis of a perverse patient with a fetishistic object and its treatment while helping the patient manage his anxiety. In the Lacanian practice of psychoanalysis, the perverse structure would be equal to the disavowal of the Name-of-the-Father. In this case, the male patient suffers from depression, anxiety, and somatization disorders. Specifically, he feels suffocated with preoccupation with a body part (foot fetish) and inanimate objects (shoe and piece of underwear) in which sexual excitement occurs. He explains that the fetish is a symbolic substitute for the missing phallus of the mother, emphasizing that fetishism takes place in the preoedipal stage within the triad of mother-child-phallus. Rather than treating the fetish as perverse symptoms and sexual deviations, Chavoshian explains that the structural analysis of the perversion approaches it as an ontological symptom in which the subject deals with problems of alienation, separation, castration, and putting limits on one's *jouissance.*

In chapter 12, Chavoshian introduces the clinical case of a sixty-year-old devout Muslim woman who is suffering from Melancholia and depression. She was preoccupied with her daughter's homosexuality and obsessive thoughts of the death of her mother, which occurred ten years ago. Chavoshian analyzes the speech of the patient in terms of several paradoxes: open vs. closed circuit and matrix, limit and indefiniteness, disjunction and conjunction, and disjointment and jointment, engaging with Freud's classic paper, "Mourning and Melancholia."

In chapter 13, Chavoshian illustrates the clinical case of Richard, who fears bugs coming into his room. Richard's paranoia is the result of his psychotic structure, which is one of the three structures in the human mind, with delusion and hallucination. Although Lacanian psychoanalysts are skeptical about treating psychotic patients, Chavoshian argues that there is tremendous theoretical enrichment brought in through the discussion of Lacan's psychotic structure. The author emphasizes the importance of the modality of listening to the speech of psychosis in recognizing the difference between psychotic transference and neurotic transference.

In summary, readers will find that this book has diverse and different perspectives, with each author's unique interest and context. Also, in this edited volume, seasoned and emerging scholars explore fundamental themes of anxiety and uncertainty in Lacan's teachings, from an enhanced global perspective. Readers will find that Lacan's texts supply alternative and transformative meaning for marginalized subjects, and each author's analysis or critique provides a global perspective and diverse context for a new readership. Collectively, these writings explore new contexts, including prison, Church, and spiritual direction, and aim to bring Lacanian discourse to an expanded global audience, using the critical lenses drawn from various discourses, such as culture, ministry, theology, biblical studies, and the body.

This book shows a distinct approach, emphasizing praxis for people around the globe. Fully embracing the theoretical level of Lacan discourse, authors are driven by questions that are sensitive to the many crises facing the planet. The themes of anxiety and uncertainty tie together these writings as the authors revisit and reinvigorate Lacan from multiple perspectives and diverse contexts. Opening up authorship to new generations, people of color, and non-western countries—these themes across critique will change and challenge readers. This project is the fruit of nine years-long reading seminar on Lacan's primary text, composed of academics and clinical workers, stressing intersubjectivity, post-coloniality, and diversity in geography, gender, and age, each of which will provide a unique perspective.

Part I

Culture and Anxiety

1

The *Phantom of the Opera*

Fantasy in the Real

Jung Eun Sophia Park

One of the most evocative and well-known Gothic stories is *The Phantom of the Opera*, which was originally written in French in 1910 by Gaston Leroux (1868–1927). As a Gothic novel, this story manifests characteristics of fantasy and accents a level of anxiety through mysterious settings, and romance. Gothic literature, including the currently resurging theme of *zombies*, or the living dead, as a haunted self-image, emphasizes the invisible or unknowable nature of the Real[1] which, by appearing and disappearing in the symbolic world order, causes anxiety.

As many popular stories are, this story has been revised, adapted, and changed through the years by various authors. The first adaptation of the novel was featured as an American silent horror film directed by Rupert Julian in 1925, and attained high popularity. More recently, *The Phantom of Opera* as a musical stage production became internationally renowned, playing to over 160 million people in 46 countries and 193 cities, and in 21 languages.[2] In the US, *The Phantom of the Opera* was one the most popular repertoires on Broadway, and ran for 35 years until

1. Wilson, "Anamorphosis of Captial," 164–69.
2. https://uk.thephantomoftheopera.com.

17

its closure in 2013. Its dramatic and enticing music, along with the final scene of the disappearing phantom left great impression on the audience.

The book includes numerous psychoanalytic aspects. First, the "underground," which implies the unconscious, is the main space and topic of the novel, which descends into the depths beneath the Paris Opera. Along with the motive to move underground, the three characters also move around. Christine takes an initial journey with Erik down to his lair and maternal bedroom, Raoul seeks her by descending into the underground, and finally Erik disappears and the two ascend. In the verse of the upside down, the whole setting clearly indicates a psychoanalytic dimension.

Also, in this story, there are multiple actions which operate in ways that are far from ordinary, and transformations occur as parts of subliminal desires, like the ones described in Freud's *Interpretation of Dreams*.[3] Magical events, such as the chandelier falling during the opera and certain voices behind the wall haunting the protagonist, etc., happen. This story clarifies what exactly happens, but there still remain several ways to interpret the story. Finally, imagination and fantasy haunt the readers and the audience with a blurred nature of being in-between imagination and reality, and in crossing boundaries of two domains. In certain performance of the musical in San Francisco, some characters appeared from the audience and went onto the stage.

Thus, this chapter reads, in a psychoanalytical way, the original story of *The Phantom of the Opera* as a gothic novel—not excluding the musical genre—exploring the role of fantasy as "object petit a" which functions as a leverage to move forward characters' psychosexual development. In so doing, I utilize Lacan's theory of fantasy, object petit a, the Name of the Father, and the death drive or sublimation.

THE PHANTOM OF OPERA AS GOTHIC NOVEL

Gothic literature, which was generally dominant in the nineteenth century in the West, describes anxiety as a human condition and social critique, presenting monsters such as vampires and ghosts and signifying the advent of modernity with a scientific world view, as well as the decline of aristocracy along with the increased agency of women.[4] For example, Mary Shelley's novel *Frankenstein* presents a monster, a lonely being abandoned

3. Wolf, *Essential Phantom of Opera*, 6.

4. Sharoni, *Lacan and Fantasy Literature*, 35.

by the creator, conveying the social and cultural anxiety of the scientific time in Europe. Remarkably, as a frontier of feminism, many Gothic novels deal with women's experiences, especially expressed as anxiety in struggling to gain a sense of agency. For example, Elizabeth Gaskell's *The Grey Woman*, which was published in 1861, manifests a woman's fundamental anxiety and strong sense of horror within a violent environment of marriage, and the process of her gaining agency. In that sense, *The Phantom of the Opera* fits perfectly in the category of Gothic novels.

First of all, it reflects the societal mood in relation to anxiety. When this novel was written in 1910, France (and especially Paris) was in turmoil. The whole of society was suffering anxiety with political upheavals such as the Paris Commune and the subsequent conflicts regarding civic order. In addition, the novel manifests the social identity of the middle class, which was created within urban culture during the time. The boundary between the noble class and commoners becomes blurred through the desire of love and union. This story also fundamentally reflects social reality and the woman's sense of agency in life in France, and in Paris in particular.

As a matter of fact, the author Gaston Leroux was a journalist who had investigated the former Opera House, presently the House of the Paris Ballet. Thus, the undertone of the Gothic novel comes from the architecture of the Gothic Opera House building, which historically contained basement cellars which held the prisoners of the Paris Commune. In fact, actual hidden passages were linked to the wall behind the room of the fictional Christine, with which the Phantom could reach her.

Underneath the building is an underground lake (in reality, a cistern), which is connected to the mysteriously standing tall building of the Paris Ballet. This strange structure of the building stimulates human anxiety in imagination, and guides us into the world of fantasy. In the novel, by adding a whole description of the Opera House, Leroux tries hard to give the impression that it is a detective novel of a crime which could be resolved through the scientific approach, aligned with its contemporary time, a time of science. Nevertheless, in the whole mood of the novel—and more dominantly in the film and opera adaptations—the role of fear, imagination, and fantasy remains strong.

Leroux employs a "reportage" style in that the narrator, "I" in the novel, investigates the mysterious story of the Opera Ghost who resides in the Opera House. He wants to solve questions such as: is the ghost real?; who is the ghost?; and what really happened? The novel unfolds the mystery and, in so doing, reveals a deep human psyche of anxiety and fantasy in romantic love. More deeply, it tackles the drive which is moving toward *the objet petit a*.

A prominent scholar of Gothic theory, Jerold E. Hogle, points out that the Opera Ghost living in an under-terrestrial space signifies the other and/or othering process of Western civilization.[5] As well, I comprehend additional main characters as the other who struggles to be an authentic sense of subject, emphasizing that they handle their alienation as a barred subject through fantasy.

In the story, the narrator investigates anyone who may be familiar with the Opera House or any rumors about a ghost. While interviewing people, he encounters an old Persian man who seems to know the whole story. As the other of the Other in this novel, the Persian shows enormous power in knowing the truth, along with the Ghost, who is the typical other.[6] This other, who comes from difference, is supposed to have knowledge and power—he is fetishized. The Persian, fascinating and desirable as "the other," can tell the narrator about another "other," the Ghost whose name is Erik, who resides in the basement because of his ugly face. His appearance is like a "death," a skull covered with thin skin, a kind of living dead who is socially forbidden and has no social access.

As the story unfolds, Erik falls in love with Christine, a new opera singer. He lures her through his voice, even giving her music lessons from the other side of the wall. He ultimately seduces her into his dungeon through his haunting voice. According to Lacan, the voice is one of the fundamental partial objects which attracts the subject—the barred subject—with a lack. The voice, along with the gaze, causes great anxiety because of the mask.[7] As the title of the novel suggests, the voice here operates as *the objet petit a*, the object of desire which is, most importantly, empty. Lacan uses the French word *manqué*, which means "unfulfilled" or "missed," in describing the object. In English translations the word lack is often used. Thus, the object could suggest a state of being lost and an active sense of yearning for the missed object.

Christine, who has lost her father, is attracted to the voice, *the objet petit a*. The charming voice is the father *manqué*, or the sound of music that her father made through the violin. Christine obsessively wants to be

---

5. Hogle, *Undergrounds of the Phantom of Opera*, 5.

6. Edward Said emphasizes that the role of the other, or the Oriental, exists only to serve the Occidental (Said, *Orientalism*, 158).

7. Lacan, *Anxiety*, 325.

with her father, to go back in time to be with him. The novel depicts her desire by describing how Christine would visit her father's grave and experiences *jouissance* with the voice of the ghost of the opera. It is a reunion in fantasy through the voice of the ghost singing. It is obvious that Erik and Christine act as doubles in the context of fantasy, seeking lost things or desires in each other. Also, it is remarkable, according to the nature of *the objet petit a*, that each one operates at least in the mode of fantasy.

Of course, this scene is very dreamy and fantastic by nature, and the only moment that it can be real is in the gaze of third person but it is unclear what the third person is dreaming or witnessing. Here, the witness is Vicomte Raoul de Chingy—a young solider of a noble class, who also loves Christine. His is a burning romantic love that crosses borders between aristocrats and commoners. The young Raoul chases Christine when she disappears during the opera performance, reminding us of Orpheus who went to the netherworld to look for Eurydice. In the midst of this chase adventure to save or gain his love object Christine, he who is not equipped with a knowledge of the building cannot solve the all tricks created by Erik; Raoul fails and is powerlessly captured by Erik.

After being held captive in the underground habitat of Erik, Christine is forced to decide whether to marry Erik on the condition that everyone will remain safe, including Raoul. Upon deciding to become Erik's wife, she unmasks him and kisses him on the forehead. The narrative describes this moment almost religiously: Christine is calm and like a nun. She cries over his ugliness. Having never being kissed before, by even by his mother, Erik resolves his anger, resentment, and fury, and decides to disappear into nothingness.

Obviously, this final scene is a moment of courtly love, or Christine's Agape love, not a carnal one or one of the flesh, thereby reflecting an impossibility. Lacan emphasizes the nature of courtly love, employing the concept of the *objet petit a,* as an impossible love to reach or achieve. He explains that courtly love exists in sublimation, which is in essence *empty*.[8] This imaginary (empty) union of a marriage emphasizes a more phantasmic aspect of love between Erik and Christine. Then, in a manner of courtly love, Erik sends Christine away so that she could be united with Raoul. As the musical's climax, the Opera Ghost disappears, leaving behind his mask. The novel concludes that Erik later dies while Christine and Raoul live together far away, but the real truth remains hidden.

---

8. Lacan, *Ethics of Psychoanalysis,* 128–29.

MOVING OBJECTS IN FANTASY

In this story, the three characters of Erik, Christine, and Raoul manifest as those who chase desirable things, as *the objet petit a,* whose nature is fundamentally phantasmic and empty. Lacan emphasizes the moving state of *the objet petit a,* which is never the real matter, such that it cannot complete the subject's unfulfilled desires. Lacan analyzes *The Purloined Letter,* "the repetition automatism (*Wiederholangszwang*) finds its basis in what we have called the insistence of the signifying chain, and it stands as a correlate of the ex-sistence (or: eccentric place) in which we must necessarily locate the subject of the unconscious."[9] In the story of *The Purloined Letter,* no one knows the content of the letter, and the letter as *the objet petit a* is circulated, creating a great level of anxiety.

Here, in *The Phantom of the Opera,* the moving object operates through the three main characters in the dominant format of fantasy, in conjunction with anxiety. The spookiness functions as an open access to the audience, luring it to the world of the imaginary, with an emphasis on the strong emotions of phantasy. Lacan says, "in the scoptic relation, the object on which depends the phantasy from which the subject is suspended in an essential vacillation is gaze."[10] The three characters operate as the object petit a, and thus this tri-relation creates an anxiety which is greatly felt by the audience, who sees itself through the characters.

Erik for Christine as the Substitute of Mother

One of the main characters is in this story, Erik, who lives in an invisible space. He is himself invisible and not an object of being gazed, but rather a subject who obsessively gazes at others—particularly Christine. The ghost is not supposed to be seen, and so the inconsistency of his appearance and disappearance causes deep anxiety and horror; he is somewhat of a living dead. In the beginning of the novel, some characters claim that they have seen the ghost, but ghosts do not reside in the symbolic order in a civilized world.

The symbolic order is composed of the word, the language, and signification which can be actualized in law, logic, and civility. It is a resemblance of the cosmos. In this story, the Phantom embodies the nature of

---

9. Lacan, "Seminar on *The Purloined Letter,*" 11.

10. Lacan, *Four Fundamental Concepts,* 83.

the anti-civic order and, as such, he is considered a monster. People panic when the Opera Ghost, revealing a lack of the symbolic order, appears during their parties or passes by the stage. The moment of anxiety caused by these encounters creates a space to realize that the symbolic world has hole in it. In this story, the invisible being acts out, seemingly manifesting demonic powers, a manipulation of scientific knowledge, in chasing *the objet petit a*, Christine.

As a way to achieve what he desires, he acts out all manners of behavior, including committing crimes. First, Erik tries to force the current prima donna to resign: he manipulates her voice to sound horrible, and let the chandelier fall down, killing some of audience. In this way, Christine becomes the prima donna and commits herself to the music or the Spirit of Music, meaning that she should reject Raoul's proposal. At the climax, Erik abducts her and finally demands she marry him. In other words, he wants to make a union with the embodiment of desirability projected beyond something, which results in a movement to the death drive.[11] In it, death signifies the state of being tensionless because the subject achieves what the ego is supposed to want, be, or be acknowledged.[12] Death is expressed as he disappears or releases Christine, especially in the musical.

When analyzing Erik, it is obvious that he carries a deep lack of love. He is abandoned because of his ugliness, even by his mother. Gaston Leroux works hard to prove that the ghost is a real living man, not just a supernatural being. At the end of the novel, readers are told that he was born deformed:

> Erik was born in a small town not far from Rouen. He was the son of a master-mason. He ran away at an early age from his father's house, where his ugliness was a subject of horror and terror to his parents.[13]

He is deprived of the primary time of fantasy, or the mirror stage, wherein the infant imagines the mother as being one. Without this process of identification, the subject cannot have *einziger Zug*,[14] the primary trail to create identity, even though it is imaginary and based on a fantasy with the mother.

---

11. Lacan, *Ethics of Psychoanalysis*, 212–14.
12. See Carrigan, "Choose Life."
13. Leroux, *Phantom of the Opera*, 374.
14. Lacan, *Identification*, 33.

His being is invisible or remains only as running drive. His whole being is like a lamella, a lump, which is on the move and embodies an unfulfilled desire or a lack. This can be called lack in the Real.[15] When Christine is lured or kidnapped to his mansion, the chamber resembles the chamber of his mother, where Erik was supposed to have been loved. Instead, Erik's lack of the original desirable object—the breast of the mother—is replaced here by tears, a feminine liquid.[16] Employing Lacan, when Erik completes his lack by being united with the object, he is not a lamella anymore, and he is in the state of the death drive: there is no movement of the object. Erik is supposed to die or, at least, to disappear.

Christine for Erik, as the Angel of Music

The other main character is Christine Daaé, a newcomer to the opera team. The story begins when she is by herself in her room, surrounded by a mirror. Raoul watches her debut Opera and then runs to her room after the show. However, he overhears a man's voice and jealously wonders if Christine has a secret lover.

In the novel, Christine debuts successfully as Marguerite in the opera *Faust*. The narrator describes the superhuman notes that she gave forth in the prison scene and the final trio in FAUST, which she sang in the place of La Carlotta, who was ill. No one had ever heard or seen anything like it.[17] People wondered how she could sing so well, with an angelic voice, presumably without any voice lessons.

Christine, an innocent and charming girl, surprisingly does not seem to enjoy her fame or success. Her thoughts run only toward the Angel of Music, the voice or the phantom, who guides her into the fantasy that she is still with her father. For her, *the objet petit a* is not fame or success, but the voice, which represents her late father.

In the story, Christine is fascinated by the voice of the Opera Ghost and receives voice lessons. In the musical, the lyrics of the Angel of Music depict Christine's fascination with the voice:

---

15. Lacan, *Four Fundamental Concepts*, 89.
16. Hogle, *Undergrounds of the Phantom of the Opera*, 12.
17. Geroux, *Phantom of the Opera*, 24.

Father once spoke of an angel
I used to dream he'd appear
Now as I sing, I can sense him
And I know he's here

Here in this room, he calls me softly
Somewhere inside, hiding
Somehow I know he's always with me
He, the unseen genius.[18]

Her fantasy reaches a level where her father and the Angel of Music are one. She is almost sexually excited by the invisible voice. Yet, at the same time, she feels a great amount of anxiety about the unknown. Christine feels lost because her father, a violinist and her music teacher, has passed away. Her father, the first one who had a phallus, is gone, and now the voice becomes the substitute for her father, which is represented by the Angel of Music.

Through music, she and her father are united. For her, the voice, actually the invisible master of music, is a substitute for the father as *the objet petit a*. The attractive and invisible being is more a pull—through voice and music—to the imagined and exalted father, rather than to Erik in any erotic way. Hogle, in his fascinating book, *The Undergrounds of the Phantom of the Opera,* argues that the erotic Oedipal fantasy of Erik parallels Christine's desire for Erik as her dead father.[19]

In the novel, Christine goes to her father's gravesite and falls into a state of *jouissance* with the fantasy of her dead father. Hogle emphasizes this fantasy and her Oedipal desire to be with her late father. The narrator says that it seems as if " Daaé has been interred with his violin" and Christine's "ecstasy" has come from making a kind of love with his buried body and its most seductive instrument.[20] This is obvious a scene of phantasma, in which Christine is with the lost object, her father.

In this sense, the voice, the hidden figure of Erik, as the partial object, haunts Christine. Thus, it is almost impossible to say that she is kidnapped by Erik. Rather she is lured by the voice, the Angel of Music, as a substitute in her longing for her father. In the early part of the story, she receives a voice lesson from an invisible teacher, the Opera Ghost, who has fallen in love with her. The room is composed of mirrors, which

18. Webber et al., "Angel of Music."
19. Hogle, *Undergrounds of the Phantom of the Opera,* 10.
20. Leroux, *Phantom of the Opera,* 122.

reminds us of the mirror stage, in which the infant begins to create identity through images in the mirror. Her identity of a successful singer is created by the sounds behind the mirror, and, in this fantasy, she identifies with her I, the ideal ego, the successful prima donna.

In the story, Christine is often described as an innocent girl, but her desire to be a good singer is not completely clear. It is also unclear whether she loves her suitor Raoul, an aristocrat from one of the powerful families in France. She seems restless, not knowing her desire, and being drawn to moving objects. As such, the only thing that compels her to move is the Angel of Music, whom she believe has been sent by her father. However, it is also possible to argue that she could fulfill her own desire to be a successful singer through the fantasy in which she receives voice lessons and boosts up her musical confidence.

Raoul for Christine

Raoul tries to solve the mystery of the relationship between Christine and some person, the Opera Ghost. He desires to find her when she is seduced by the ghost through his voice and music. There is a strong pull of a childhood memory which triggers Raoul's love for Christine. Often, memory is part of a fantasy because it is an action of retroactive tracing. In other words, Christine is the object of his love, and this retroactively supports his strong emotion of love *now*.

Raoul belongs to an aristocratic class and after the death of his father, his brother Phillip takes over their father's authority. As the primogeniture, the whole family transfers all their property to him and the narrative says that the whole family accepted this. In this story line, Raoul and his brother Phillip, who represents power and authority, go to the Opera House together. But Phillip does not necessarily approve of Raoul's fascination with Christine Daaé, who is obviously a poor commoner. Raoul's love for Christine symbolizes a breakdown of the class divisions that existed during the nineteenth century. More importantly, his attraction to Christine would spur him to separate from the Name of the Father or the father figure. In this story, Raoul chases her, and his adventures to the underworld give him a sense of agency and authority. At the end of the story, his brother Phillip dies, which indicates that Raoul does not belong to the Name of the Father anymore. His actions toward Christine results in him gaining agency and independence.

THE PHANTOM AND THE FUNCTION OF FANTASY

The Phantom refers to a figment of the imagination and something apparent to sense, yet with no substantial existence. Because it feels so vivid and real, sometimes it is hard to admit that it is not necessarily so. As the title suggests, this story shows spectacles of the imaginary domain, despite the narrative explaining the secret/mystery in a scientific way. It is also noticeable that the main figure who solves the mystery is a Persian, the other, who causes strong feelings as an outsider or foreigner. This aspect of the other emphasizes the notion of fantasy, in which no subject can reach the other perfectly. The other is someone who causes discomfort and anxiety, or someone who is the object of fascination. In the narrative, the Persian as the object who is supposed to know everything about the ghost, Erik, functions as the fascinating other.

Phantom: Transformative Power of Imagination and Fantasy

What does it mean to experience the Phantom in nineteenth century Paris? The plot of the story mainly explains what happens in the Opera House in Paris, using the scientific method, in which the Phantom manipulates the situation to try and make Christine a prima donna and his wife. The story begins with the scene in which the old managers of the Opera House retire and turn over control to a new team of managers, warning them about the ghost residing in the building. Soon after, some of the ballerinas see the shadow of someone passing through their space. Readers might just dismiss this as young women's sensitivity and strong emotions of fear and excitement.

We can read *The Phantom of the Opera* as a female Gothic novel, which combines a sense of loss and fear, and is constructed as both a paradise of new hope and a monstrosity of horror. However, the role of fantasy guides the female to regain life in the age of reason.[21] In this way, the woman character Christine who is innocent and young is transformed into a mature and embracing mature woman. In the beginning, readers find Christine who was anxious and restless became calm and "silent like a sister of charity who made a vow of silence."[22]

---

21. Shajirat, "Gothic Fantasy of History."
22. Leroux, *Phantom of the Opera*, 357.

Regarding anxiety and fantasy in the psychoanalysis of Lacan can illuminate deep meanings of the human psyche and necessary aspects of the human subject. Leroux writes that the ghost of the Opera House is a human being, who is later found dead. The author emphasizes that the plot is about love and terror, told through a very romantic tune. Two of the most repeated words in this novel are fear (or terror) and love, between Christine and Raoul, as well as between Christine and the man, Erik. The actual story unfolds, introducing a highly anxious opera singer amid a spooky mood, and some frightened ballerinas. Christine is anxious and her behavior is unusual.

In the story line, the Opera Ghost falls in love with Christine and gives her voice lessons. She develops a wonderful voice through the lesson, and the Phantom demands that she commits only to the music, in other words, to him. In the scientific sense, the phantom is a smart and manipulative man. Then, in this story, what is the role of the ghost for Christine's growth? It is not clear whether she loves to sing, but she does not have her own voice because she lacks confidence. Her late father, her music teacher, had told her that she would meet the Angel of Music. For her, the voice that heard through the wall of mirrors was the Angel of Music. Christine begins to be tutored by Erik and she becomes the new prima donna.

Power of Fantasy

Who is the Phantom then? Fully acknowledging that the one who knows all skills and scientific tricks is ugly and yearning for love, as the title of the book suggests, the Phantom refers to a figment of imagination. In Lacan's approach, for the subject, fantasy is necessary for shaping and maintaining self. Without fantasy, the subject becomes psychosis.[23]

The author works hard to prove that the ghost is a real man, but in the whole narrative (or at least in the films and musicals), the role of imagination or phantasma is very strong. In the domain of the imagination, one of the most remarkable objects is the mirror. Christine is guided by the voice in the process of becoming the prima donna. The voice lesson occurs in her room, which is surrounded by mirrors. Then, in the musical, the audience hears a beautiful duet between the Phantom and

---

23. Ormrod, *Fantasy in Lacanian Theory*, 98.

Christine. Then, is the voice heard from the other side of the mirror the sound of the inside or that of the outside?

This scene is reminiscent of the mirror stage. In the seminar on anxiety, Lacan directly connects the mirror stage with the imaginary.[24] In the mirror stage, the infant develops a certain image of himself as the ideal ego. Thus, Christine, who stands in front of the mirror, hears the sound which reflects the ideal ego—she can sing like an angel. Lacan explains that the demonstration of the mirror stage begins the moment the child grasps himself in the inaugural experience of the recognition in the mirror, as a totality or a fulfillment functioning as such in his specular image; the child needs the Other, who confirms the imaginary image of self. The child then turns back to an adult, who supports him from behind. In this case, the adult is the Other who is supposed to ratify the value.[25]

In this story, Christine needs someone who approves her singing voice. In a very romantic and soft way, Christine seems to remain in the mirror stage, overcoming her anxiety, which can be explained as a deep mistrust or lack of confidence as a singer and having an ideal ego. In other words, for Christine—who stands in the imaginary domain, the mirror stage—the Opera Ghost—who mysteriously manifests in this story and becomes the most important supporter—validates her voice as the ego ideal. Her ego ideal relies on the other's love and confirmation, and the relationship between Christine and the ghost is inseparable in this imaginary domain. At the end of this story, she learns how to embrace the human sadness of loss and to understand the human nature of love. Or, she embraces her own fantasy and passes into the next stage of life.

The other character in the scene is Raoul, whose love for Christine begins with a fantasy of memory. Memory is a way to construct the trace or footsteps.[26] Regarding identity politics, Lacan argues, the subject who is barred by culture grasps a unary unit and creates identity. His stroke of a unary unit includes moments when he enjoys playing music with Christine. In this memory, based on an imaginary fantasy, a strong sense of nostalgia and an uncontrollable love for Christine operates as a device against the father or the Name of the Father. He overcomes the power of the Name of the Father and grows into an independent male, giving up any social privileges (social death).

24. Lacan, *Anxiety*, 30.
25. Lacan, *Anxiety*, 31.
26. Lacan, *Identification*, 14.

In children's psychological development, the imagination helps individuation. Utilizing the case of Little Hans, Lacan explains that the boy's anxiety goes wild with imagination, with things such as falling horses, losing his father in the way of visiting grandmother, a paper giraffe being a small ball, etc.[27] Through the process, he reaches individuation.

In this romantic love between Christine and Raoul, there is a memory of being an old acquaintance, real or imagined, without any piece of the Other. Later, Raoul, now a soldier of high class, sees her on stage as a successful prima donna and magically falls in love with her. In the nineteenth century, a woman opera singer did not enjoy social privileges. It is important that the whole story is about the performance of an opera on stage, which is not a space of the real world. Rather, a performance is the space of the imaginary symbolic, which creates an imaginary world through language. The command of the Other does not confirm Raoul's desire for Christine. On stage, there is a Christine performing and there is a Christine acting out. As a spectator, Christine becomes an ideal object for Raoul. In this fantasy relationship, the subject—Raoul—is drawn to *the objet petit a*—Christine—but she is impossible to reach; the emphasis remains in the nature of impossibility.

Lacan demonstrates the structure of fantasy in which the subject is not a free agent, and not even aware of the fact. The subject is drawn to the object. In Lacan's *matheme*, the fantasy stands as $\$\lozenge a$. Here the diamond indicates the specific relation between the subject and the object a: the subject of the unconscious, which is divided by its relation to the realm of signifiers, keeps *the objet petit a*, the lost object, the detached remainder of the first operation of symbolization by the parental other.[28] The diamond or lozenge signifies a relationship between the subject and the object, such as alienation (v) and separation (^), greater than (>), lesser than (<), and so on.[29]

A list of Freudian objects, such as breast, feces, phallus, and baby, includes the function of the *objet petit a*, and to this Lacan adds the gaze, the phoneme, and *the voice* (emphasis mine).[30] The subject is supposed to live all of his or her life searching for various objects to reach the realization of desire. Christine, as the lost object, cannot be given to Erik

---

27. Lacan, *Object Relation*, 79.

28. Lacan, *Desire and Its Interpretation*, 366.

29. Fink, *Lacanian Subject*, 174.

30. Lacan emphasizes the objects' circular constitution according to the stages such as oral, anal, phallic, scoptic, and superego. See Lacan, *Anxiety*, 312–14.

because of her commitment to music. It is remarkable that Christine roams around her father's grave site, enjoying *jouissance* through the sound of music, as a substitute for her father.

The Triangular or Rotative Circuit of Desire

Lacan, in *Écrits*, explains the circling nature of signifiers, emphasizing the intersubjective module of the action that repeats, which we must now indicate in a repetition automatism.[31] We sense Christine's attraction to the voice of an unknown figure who resides the other side of the wall. The unknown figure indicates an ideal ego, and she is lured by its imaginary image. Then, what is the result of this game of mirrors? According to Hegel-Kojève, it is the struggle to the death. If the other is only an image of myself and I am only its shadow, my identity is put into question: who am I?

If what I want is what the other wants, what do I really want? Mutuality between Christine and the voice, or the unknown figure, ends up as a disjunction: either me or the other. The dilemma begins here. The ghost or the other asks for the union. Kojève impresses a dialectical turning point in the intersubjective relation: death. For fear of losing its life, one of the two self-consciences gives up and makes a slave of itself.[32] Christine chooses to give up her life of agency and decides to be his wife. In this story, the moment Christine gives up her life, the imaginary other dies; it is the end of the fantasy.

For Lacan, the dialectical reversal that leads to the "dominion-bondage" spiritual figure can be summed up as follows: the intersubjective relation, dual at first, has become a triangle. A third party has intervened between the two self-consciences, which were initially one, the pure mimesis of the other. This third party is death, which has brought the subjective positions back to their constituent dissymmetry. There is no mutuality between lord and servant, only difference, and, although they constitute a pair, the subjects are not on the same level.[33] This is the way Christine gains freedom and independence.

---

31. Lacan, "Seminar on *The Purloined Letter*," 16.
32. Moroncini, "On Love."
33. Moroncini, "On Love."

Phantasy in Death Drive as Sublimation

The most important and primary function of the phantom is in the function of phantasy, covering the lack or hole of the Real. Lacan emphasizes the lack which holds up all uncertainty.[34] In this story, three characters achieve a certain stage of life which emphasizes the death drive. First, Erik disappears symbolically, demonstrating the death drive. In the novel, Erik decides to be invisible, staying underground. After his death, Christine puts the ring back into his tomb. Personally, I prefer the ending scene of the musical in which Erik disappears and leaves the mask. It is just the skin or a trace of lamella, a state of pre-subject. Lacan explains that the lamella does not exist, rather it insists: it is unreal, an entity of pure semblance, a multiplicity of appearances which seem to envelop a central void—its status is purely fantasmatic.[35]

Christine, through the fantastic and partial object (Erik), can leave behind the Oedipus complex and embrace her love as an independent agent. Raoul, through his object (Christine), overcomes the authority and control of his elder brother in the Name of Father, and begins his independent life, which is a free marriage in an unknown place. It shows that Raoul and Christine move on from a strict symbolic order that includes class division.

As a feminist Gothic novel protagonist, Christine seems to overcome her death instinct, which is to be with her father, just like mother. Her life in an unknown future causes her deep anxiety and loss. Through the function of phantasy, she experiences sublimation beyond the death instinct and begins her life as an adult woman, who moves beyond the Oedipus complex and can embrace herself as a subject barred.

CONCLUSION

In the era of uncertainty, many people suffer from anxiety. However, Lacan indicates that anxiety, which is located at between desire and jouissance, is a fundamental human condition. In particular, human beings as civilized agents are programmed in the symbolic order and controlled by the Other. Through fantasy, the subject who is limited to truth, navigates and compromises one's life and explores emerging identities.

---

34. Lacan, *Identification*, 110.
35. Lacan, *Four Fundamental Concepts*, 116.

There are life drives, which run back to the world of the imaginary, the mirror stage, and phantasy. Through the excitement of the phantasy, the subjects shape their identity and through the death drive or sublimation, the movements stop at the point where they achieve independence and agency. Although this story shows romantic love amid anxiety, it reveals the power of fantasy as a process of human development. The relentless and restless anxiety of the human soul moves into the next stage of life through fantasy, which is necessary and essential.

2

Psychoanalyzing the Gynoid

Robot Fetishism through Freud and Lacan

Levi Checketts

My interest in this topic began at a lecture I attended hosted by my university focused on ethics and AI. After poorly articulating what AI ethics should be for close to an hour, he concluded with a focus on adolescent *females*. The simultaneous sexualizing and infantilizing of non-human computational technology is revelatory about unconscious attitudes this researcher held. But this bizarre anthropomorphizing raises the question of whether this is a trend in AI research or a mere anomaly. Assuming this peculiarity is indicative of a shared view in this field, this suggests a particular psychological problem underwriting AI programming.

In this chapter, I consider the tendency of AI research toward sexualized entities through psychoanalysis. First, I outline some exemplary sexual peculiarities of AI researchers and their connection to popular and consumer culture as well as other scholarly engagements with the implications of this work. I then outline a traditionally Freudian reading of this phenomenon as demonstrative of a perverse desire to trespass incest taboos through a god complex. Next, I propose a Lacanian reading through the experience of anxiety which suggests an alternative interpretation: a desire for the "perfect" partner. In conclusion, I suggest that while the Freudian reading is well-supported and to some degree comforting, the Lacanian reading is more revelatory about the nature of human sexuality and its structure through anxiety. This reading helps explain both why AI and robotics research have favored sexbots, but also why none of them are (or will be) satisfying.

SEXBOTS IN THE COLLECTIVE UNCONSCIOUS

Marvin Minsky, one of the original AI pioneers who coined the term "Artificial Intelligence" and a prominent theorist until his death in 2016, was accused of receiving the services of Virginia Giuffre, the first woman to speak out about Jeffrey Epstein's pedophile pimping scheme.[1] If true, Minsky joins the halls of infamy with famous sexual assailants like Harvey Weinstein and Kevin Spacey. Minsky's widow has denied the allegations, but it is clear that Minsky had a close relationship with Epstein. Epstein generously funded Minsky's work and Minsky hosted an AI conference on Epstein's private island. Meredith Broussard also notes that Minsky had a famous reputation for holding women in poor regard.[2] Whether Minsky actually engaged in intercourse with a young girl, the relevant fact is that Epstein, whose major claim to fame at this point is being a pedophile pimp, had a close relationship with Minsky, and Minsky apparently made no efforts to distance himself from this predator during their lives.

Minsky is not the only AI researcher with ties to Jeffrey Epstein, but some commentators attribute the unscrupulous acceptance of Epstein's money to "nerd tunnel vision," a kind of moral apathy rather than endorsement.[3] This apathy, however, is itself telling, and the "boys' club" atmosphere of computer culture raises questions about the sexual peculiarities of those involved in the tech industry. To our (non)surprise, then, the writings and work of other AI researcher finds similar expressions of sexual perversion, albeit in less scandalous formulations, in the work of Ray Kurzweil and Ben Goertzel. Kurzweil writes about sexually merging with AIs in the "singularity," the future human-machine civilization, and positively cites his own experience with gender bending with his daughter

---

1. Brandom, "AI Pioneer Accused."
2. Broussard, *Artificial Unintelligence*, 72.
3. Lopatto, "Jeffrey Epstein Infiltrated Science."

on a live stage in a demonstration of holographic technology.[4] Goertzel started a firm in Hong Kong focused on *emotional* AI shortly before revealing to the world his AI "daughter" Sophia, a sexualized artificially intelligent robot programmed "to love."[5] Hanson Robotics, who created Sophia, created shortly after BINA48, a robot modeled after transhumanist proponent Martine Rothblatt's own wife, Bina Aspen, almost as if to remove any doubt about the fantasy underwriting such robots.

And then, of course, is David Levy, an AI researcher who literally wrote the book *Love and Sex with Robots*, a defense of robot-fetishism that makes unsubstantiated claims about the state of AI and robotics technologies and liberally interprets psychological studies on human sexuality to support his own fetish. Levy boldly predicts that by 2050, human beings will be having more sex with robots than with each other,[6] a prediction remarkable for its confidence in both the spread of this paraphilia and in robotics' technological advance. His prediction is at least partially vindicated by the emergence of an annual conference on "Love and Sex with Robots," which attracts vendors of sexual prostheses, academics seeking notoriety as a means of distinction, and good old-fashioned perverts.[7]

AI researchers are themselves strongly influenced by cultural expressions, and some of them (especially Kurzweil and Levy) explicitly reference pop culture in their writings. Thus, much of AI research is fraught by confusion between science fiction and science reality, such as Minsky's own collaboration with Arthur C. Clarke, which apparently shaped both Clarke's science fiction and Minsky's beliefs about AI.[8] Pop culture is then even *more* explicit about the connection between the goal of creating artificial minds and the goal of copulating with them. Consider just a few paradigmatic examples spanning nearly a century: *Metropolis* (1927), *My Living Doll* (1964), *Stepford Wives* (1975), *Weird Science* (1985), and, most recently, *Ex Machina* (2014). Each of these (all movies, except for the sitcom *My Living Doll*) features sexually attractive women playing the role of robot and consequent sexual tension between the female robot and the male lead(s).

While the exact nature of the sexualization of the robot and its role in the plot differs between these stories, ultimately they all play into male

4. Kurzweil, *Singularity Is Near*, 211, 214.

5. See, e.g., Sophia the Robot, "Sophia the Robot."

6. Levy, *Love and Sex with Robots*, 22.

7. https://www.lovewithrobots.com.

8. Broussard, *Artificial Intelligence*, 21.

fantasies about compliant, servile, eternally young, unblemished sex partners. Or, as the male lead of *My Living Doll* says in the pilot episode, "If a robot could be programmed to have emotions, you'd be the perfect woman. . . . [A woman who] does as she's told, reacts as you want her to react, and keeps her mouth shut. . . . No offense."[9]

Commercial interest in AI and robotics has long been tied to explicit sexual goals, as seen in recent advancements in sex dolls, teledildonics, virtual reality pornography and other sex technologies. The practical challenge of fulfilling Levy's fantasy for "realistic" (or, say, minimally functioning) sex robots lies in successfully combining haptic (touch) technologies with robotics (movement) and artificial intelligence (computer processing) in a way that results in a doll that reacts to and with human sexual partners. Each of these areas has seen commercial advancements, such as AI "girlfriends" from companies like Replika (and more sexually explicit commercially available chatbots) and Bluetooth-connected sex toys from companies like Lovense. Abyss Creations, which produces "realistic" sex dolls, has been trying to integrate several technologies into their products to increase realism, and now offer products that integrate an AI chatbot with voice to communicate with a human sexual partner, robotic animatronic head including synchronized lip and eye movement, and Bluetooth enabled artificial vaginas to communicate touch to the AI. Though these are a far cry from fully-automated sexbots, their realism offers important "proof of concept" for "digi-sexuals."

There further exists a quite large array of academic research on sex toys, virtual sex, pedophilia, and so forth, including specific focuses on the place of sex dolls as a possible sexual outlet for pedophiles, and discussions of "digisexuality" as a specific sexual orientation.[10] Even Isabel Millar's recent *The Psychoanalysis of Artificial Intelligence* and Lydia Liu's *The Freudian Robot* address these topics through the lens of psychoanalytic discourse on sexuality.[11] But despite the vast interest in questions on what AI and robotics developments mean about our sexuality or the sexuality of non-human technological entities, very few of these authors ask the basic question of what it means to say that AI researchers want to create copulation-ready robots. That is to say, what can we understand

9. Dobkin, "Boy Meets Girl?," 19:40.

10. See Richardson and Odlind, *Man-Made Women*; Fan and Cherry, *Sex Robots*; Ma et al., "Sex Robots"; Aoki and Kimura, "Sexuality and Affection," 296; McArthur and Twist, "Rise of Digisexuality," 334–44.

11. See Millar, *Psychoanalysis of Artificial Intelligence*; Liu, *Freudian Robot*.

about the meaning of their motivation and its broader implications for our understanding of what it means to be human?

From a psychoanalytic perspective, David Levy's goal to make sexually compatible robots, the current proliferation of sexualized AI chatbots, and the allegations of Marvin Minsky committing pedophilia suggest maybe one of two things about sexual desire. The first view, in line with more traditional readings of Freud, sees AI as the taboo daughter, the one whom god-complexed AI technologists are inevitably attracted to. The second view, in line with Lacanian theory of anxiety, sees AI as the attempt to create the "perfect partner," one who desires what the man desires with no deception and therefore can grant him satisfaction, the partner who "does as she's told, reacts as you want her to react, and keeps her mouth shut." The first view is more straightforward, and perhaps even more comforting, as it suggests these tendencies are aberrations and perversions which demonstrate a problem in the economy of the libido of AI researchers. The second view, however, is more daring, as it is framed by the impossibility of our satisfaction, and the human longing for completion.

FREUDIAN AI

Freud draws on ancient myths as revelatory about our internal motivations and desires. Among the most famous he draws on include the tragedy of Oedipus, the castration of Ouranos, the obsession of Narcissus, the function of Eros, and so forth. Sexual attraction to artificial beings fits right into this constellation, as seen in the myth of Pygmalion, a sculptor who prayed to Aphrodite to give life to the statue he created and fell in love with. Some persons today claim a paraphilia toward artificial sexualized beings, paralleling this myth from Ovid.[12]

From this perspective, the interest in AI and the creation of beings *like us* gets tied to all sorts of imaginations about God, the Father whom we feel alienated from, whom we reject or embrace as repressed individuals.[13] In Freud's own telling of the primal horde, the father copulates with all of the women, including his daughters and other relatives, and forbids the sons from doing so, keeping all the women for himself. The sons, in turn, conspire to commit patricide, and the guilt of doing so leads to the

12. See Gore, "Technosexuality."
13. Freud, *Future of an Illusion*, 43.

creation of the first law, the incest taboo, meant to curb aggression by limiting the range of available sexual partners in a society.[14] In the base of our collective unconscious lies, either the historical or mythical, imposition of the law from the father.[15] God, then, functions for most people as the father of all fathers, the one who lays down the law, from whom our sense of guilt and obedience derive.[16] Much of this mythos repeats in the fantasy of AI. In creating AI, an entity meant to be intelligent "like us," we are playing at God, and so a "God complex" is a major feature of not only contemporary tech culture, but also a lot of pop culture surrounding computer technology, and especially AI.[17] It comes as no surprise from a Freudian perspective if AI researchers position themselves in the place of the totemic father.

Mary Shelley, considered the first science fiction author, tied modern science and the human drive to create beings like us explicitly to Greek mythology—*Frankenstein* is subtitled "The Modern Prometheus" after the Titan who created human beings. But the being created by Promethean Dr. Frankenstein rebels and rages against his creator. It should come as no surprise then that there is no shortage of literature reading Frankenstein from a psychoanalytic perspective.[18] In turn, science fiction author Isaac Asimov drew explicitly on Shelley's insights in his robot fiction, referring to the fear that robots would rise up as a "Frankenstein Complex." The Frankenstein Complex is the Oedipus Complex played out in an inverted form—like Laius, we, the parents of AI, fear we will be killed by our sons. Consequently, murderous/genocidal AI is typically depicted as either masculine or gender neutral (i.e., default male). One need only think of the cold masculinity of the voice of HAL 9000 of *2001: A Space Odyssey*, the stocky skeletal frames of the Skynet bots from the *Terminator* movies, or the menacing persistence of Agent Smith in *The Matrix*.

14. Freud, *Totem and Taboo*, 234–38.

15. For example, the philosopher and social theorist Herbert Marcuse seemed to think the primal horde was a historic reality (Marcuse, *Eros and Civilization*, 55). Marcuse adopted something like a Jungian notion of collective unconscious to explain why this primal memory is re-enacted in our contemporary cultures. Lacan, on the other hand, almost sardonically notes, "*Totem and Taboo* is no less than a modern myth, a myth constructed to explain what remained as a gaping hole in [Freud's] doctrine, namely, *where is the father?*" (Lacan, *Object Relation*, 202).

16. Freud, *Civilization and Its Discontents*, 39.

17. See Softley, *Hackers*; Leonard, "Tech Industry's God Complex"; Wadhwa et al., "God Complex."

18. See Collings, "Monster and the Imaginary Mother"; Adams, "Making Daemons of Death and Love," 57–89; Baranoğlu, "Analysis of Mary Shelley's *Frankenstein*," 53–67.

Today, the threat of robot genocide still grips even the most "serious" AI prognosticators like the philosopher Nick Bostrom, the late astrophysicist Stephen Hawking, and even world's-richest-man Elon Musk.[19] The worries of these men outstrip any capabilities of AI at present. The most prominent uses of AI today are making derivative art, dominating complex games, and generating generic student essays, none of which are likely to end in our extinction. And even though lethal-autonomous weapons are a real concern, most militaries and weapons manufacturers have no interest in making devices truly automated due to increased liability and decreased control.[20] And so we are reminded that the fear of AI is more of an indication of our own unconscious worries rather than an indication of real danger.

But our focus is on sex robots, not genocidal robots. If we fear masculinized AI children killing us, the female counterpart in the totemic fable are the daughters who serve as sexual property of the powerful father. Thus, we should pair Nabokov's *Lolita* with Shelley's *Frankenstein* in our AI mythos. The neo-totemic fathers of AI fear their sons rising up and murdering them while simultaneously hoping to sexually dominate their own daughters.

While there are some cases of robot fetishization of *and*roids (that is, properly speaking, "male" robots), the majority of robot/AI fetishizations are, in contrast to genocidal robots, largely female, which is to say *gyn*oid. Prominent examples include the Fembots in the *Austin Powers* series, Helen O'Loy, the prostitute robots in *Westworld*, Samantha from *Her*, and, of course, the examples listed in the beginning. This is evident enough that numerous feminists scholars have noted this and the implications of sexualizing non-human objects.[21] Even beyond the cases mentioned earlier, one finds this through numerous robots with exaggerated secondary sexual traits, such as hourglass figures, cone-shaped breasts, or even tertiary traits such as a made-up face or something resembling long hair.

The Japanese "lolicon," a portmanteau of Lolita Complex, fetishizes underage girls. Often this involves depicting female sexual interests as

---

19. See Bostrom, *Superintelligence*; Cellan-Jones, "Stephen Hawking"; Niemeyer, "Elon Musk Says the Risk."

20. Lucas, *Law, Ethics, and Emerging Military Technologies*, 179.

21. See Shea, "Is There a Sinister Side?"; Sparrow et al., "Do Robots Have Sex?"; Strait, et al., "Public's Perception of Humanlike Robots."

deeply innocent, sometimes naïve or uncultured.[22] In manga and anime, girls and women with less-developed sex traits are more sexualized. Though lolicon certainly involves pedophilic and incestuous fantasy, the loli-character sometimes occupies a less obvious "daughter" role, such as one's student, one's mentee, or even the daughter of a friend or colleague.[23] Perhaps as no surprise, one of the major motifs in lolicon culture is robot fetishization.[24] Not all robot fetishization plays on lolicon motifs, especially when gynoids are depicted with exaggerated secondary sex traits, but the personality of gynoids often resemble the virginal innocence of lolicon characters. One sees this in examples like *My Living Doll*, where the gynoid AF 709 wanders about town entirely undressed with no sense of impropriety (add to this the fact that actress Julie Newmar was twenty-three years younger than her male co-star Robert Cummings). Other times, the incestuous connection is more direct, such as in *Ex Machina*, where Nathan refers to his AI Ava, which he has built to have functioning genitals, as his "daughter."

The extension beyond pop culture becomes somewhat alarming at this point. How should we think of Goertzel's Sophia, which was partially funded by Epstein? Of Minsky being named as a John to the underage plaintiff against Epstein? Or even Kurzweil talking about his daughter in close proximity to him talking about sexual encounters with robots? Tracing these facts through psychoanalysis gives us a suggestion. The gynoid is the daughter as much as the android is the son, but while we fear the android killing us, we want to bed the gynoid. The tyranny of the totemic father and the institution of the taboo denies us what we most want. Thus, in revenge, we seek to replace the totemic father.

Indeed, Karel Čapek's *RUR*, the first piece of true "robot" fiction, anticipates this all. After the robots have murdered all humans but one of their "fathers," the play concludes with a not-at-all subtle *primal scene*— the first robots with erotic feelings for each other are encouraged to repopulate the world and referred to as "Adam and Eve."[25] Sex and violence,

---

22. See Nagayama, "Lolicon Manga."

23. Mathews, "Manga, Virtual Child Pornography, and Censorship."

24. Akagi, "Bishōjo shōkōgun," 230–34; Liu, "Social Robots as the Bride?"

25. Čapek's play was published in 1920, and so follows Freud's *Totem and Taboo* (1913), which clearly has some impact on the plot. Since *RUR* is where the English word "robot" comes from, it is no exaggeration to say that Freud's myth of the totemic civilization has directly shaped attitudes and beliefs about the creation of artificial persons.

Eros and Thanatos: the mind children replace their gods and continue the cycle anew.

LACANIAN AI

Looking at these issues from the perspective of Jacques Lacan gives us a different perspective, however. Lacan does not read Freud's discussion of Oedipus as literally as Freud's English and German interpreters—for Lacan the psycho-sexual drama is far more symbolic than real. For Lacan, the initial separation from the "mother," what begins the process of the Oedipus complex in Freud, whereby the "father" makes distance between mother and son, is rooted in the biological development of the child when she realizes she is not the same being as "mother," i.e., the being who nurses her[26] (and not necessarily one's biological mother, nor even necessarily a female). This provokes the beginning of anxiety, a condition we *never* get out of, but which takes on different forms depending on how we develop through Lacan's version of Freud's psychosexual stages, from oral to anal to phallic to scopic (of the eye) and finally to the vociferated superego.[27]

All of this, however, is rooted in the fact that we are separated from mother—alienation marks our first emergence into consciousness.[28] In his seminar on object relation, Lacan notes that privation, the absence of nurturing mother, can lead to frustration, the recognition of an impasse to get what we want.[29] Typically, this is resolved through the process of "castration"—being cut from mother once and for all.[30] How we resolve this leads to one of three major personality types—psychotic, perverse or neurotic. Neurotics accept the reality of the cut from mother and dwell forever with the reality of anxiety.[31] Psychotics do not accept the reality—they are unable to process the reality of alienation, and this inability often results in violence to themselves or others.[32] The perverted accept

---

26. Lacan, *Anxiety*, 106.

27. Lacan, *Anxiety*, 294.

28. Lacan, "Mirror Stage as Formative," 76.

29. Lacan, *The Object Relation*, 48.

30. Lacan, *The Object Relation*, 76.

31. Lacan, *Anxiety*, 46.

32. Lacan, *Formations of the Unconscious*, 358.

the cut, but they think they can take the place of the father, reuniting with the mother (either symbolically or sexually).[33]

In Lacan, the Oedipal drama is not strictly about sexual tension; it is about recognizing the authority of father above us and accepting the reality that we cannot possess mother.[34] Thus, Lacan takes the totemic father to be a myth—an explanation of things that relies on the imaginary rather than the symbolic and focuses on relations between things rather than their signification.[35] Important for us to make sense of our place in all this is to consider how *we* resolve the anxious tension, whether as neurotics, as perverts or as psychotics.

If we held onto the Freudian reading, we might think AI is the realm of perverts. The God-complex, after all, is an attempt to replace the "father," and we see in the philosophy of transhumanists a replacement of traditional religion with megalomania ("we will be gods").[36] But the order is wrong here—AI is our children, not our mothers.

How would Lacan explain this? The key to opening this problem is not resolving Oedipal tension, at least not directly. Perhaps, then, the desire for sexual robots is just that, a *desire*. Lacan speaks of *masculine* desire and *feminine* desire.[37] One may assume, as many have rightly or wrongly said about Freud, that Lacan is being sexist in his assumption of such poles, but Lacan understands the entire world as existing within a given symbolic structure, that is, our understanding of *masculine* and *feminine* is, to use an anachronism, a social construct. Our experience of gender is deeply rooted in the way we are socialized in the world, the way our parents and broader society impose upon us expectations, rules, and symbols. Lacan never says that "maleness" is essential but rather that it gets its essential characteristic through the process of subjection to the symbolic order.[38] A child's development into the symbolic order, their successful resolution of the Oedipal complex and subsequent castration,

---

33. Lacan, *The Object Relation*, 217.

34. Lacan, *Object Relation*, 387.

35. Lacan, *Object Relation*, 202, 245–48.

36. Kurzweil, *Singularity Is Near*, 260; cf. Cannon, "Mormon Transhumanism," 64–68.

37. Lacan, *Anxiety*, 265.

38. Thus, the situation of the hysteric is one who identifies with both male and female and is unable to determine which they are (Lacan, *Formations of the Unconscious*, 299–300; *Identification*, 165–66).

is the process by which a child begins to develop their sense of gender, and not an inherent biological feature.

In the patrilinear heritage of our society, the hearkening back to a primeval "father" as progenitor and the function of law as the "name of the father," feminine desire is constructed secondarily and in relation to the man's desire.[39] It is not the woman's prerogative—she is intended to be passive, an object of desire. Put in purely sexual terms, coital relations typically focus on the *male* achieving orgasm more than the *female* doing so; a successful liaison depends on the man reaching climax. So *feminine* desire, per Lacan, is desire of the other—the woman desires the other's desire. Her *jouissance* is achieved through the partner's enjoyment.[40]

The irony is, of course, that fulfillment implies a lack. Just as *feminine* desire is filled by the man's pleasure, man's desire is always characterized by *lack*. His desire *too* is the desire of the other, the desire to be desired by the other.[41] The man wants to be wanted. He desires to be desired by the woman. To return to sex, it isn't enough for the man just to reach climax—he wants to *believe* the woman desired him as well. Masculine desire also aims toward the other but in a reflexive way, the other as directed toward me, as interested in and pleasured by me specifically.[42]

This dichotomy is nowhere more apparent than in the production of pornography. "Mainstream" pornography, produced with a male audience in mind, is directed to the male gaze. As John Berger notes, "Men dream of women; women dream of themselves being dreamt of. Men look at women; women watch themselves being looked at. Women constantly meet glances which act like mirrors."[43] Berger's insight is reminiscent of Lacan's later provocative claim that "*the* woman does not exist" because "woman is a symptom" for man.[44] As symptom, woman is

---

39. Lacan, *Anxiety*, 265.

40. Lacan, *Anxiety*, 191; *On Feminine Sexuality*, 76. Here we see why many feminists have rejected Lacan—the essential characterization of women's desire as altruistic seems to deny that women can achieve their own desire through their own orgasm. I don't think Lacan would deny this; rather, he might point out this is just the same desire as what men desire. Indeed, here one might detect one of the more notable distinctions between so-called second wave and third wave feminists—whereas third wave feminists often called for the dignifying of "feminine" qualities like care for the other, second wave feminists have often prioritized women existing in men's spaces.

41. Lacan, *Anxiety*, 183, 293.

42. Lacan, *Anxiety*, 332.

43. Berger, "Women and Art."

44. Lacan, *RSI*, 70, 65.

constructed in who she is and how she is perceived for the benefit of the man's self-identity. Or, as Berger notes, "She sees herself first and foremost as a sight, which means a sight for men. . . . Those who are judged beautiful are given the prize. The prize is to be owned, that is to say, to be available."[45] Although the woman sees herself being looked at (the man's eyes functioning like mirrors), the man gazes upon her as something that can fulfill *his* desire.

Andrea Dworkin famously critiqued the pornography industry as treating women as non-subjects meant to enlarge men's sense of self.[46] But while Dworkin focuses on the violence perpetrated in pornography, it is important to note how often this sexual violence is couched in the narrative that women really enjoy being dominated, even *desire* to be dominated, by men.[47] Thus, male-focused pornography involves insatiable women who can be seduced or are ready to seduce at a moment's notice. On the other hand, "feminist pornography," which often involves equally graphic depictions of sexual intercourse, prioritizes women's actual orgasms, relationship between the actors, emotion, and men's bodies as much as women's.[48] The perspective of the "woman's gaze" is not merely the lustful characters, but rather the characters *enjoying* themselves. Feminist pornography focuses on women's real orgasms because feminine desire as desire of the other means the other (in this case, both performers) should find enjoyment, while male desire is about being desired projected through the anonymized male performer.

With this in mind, the "castration anxiety" that Lacan describes—the male's desire to be desired—helps us understand not only Minsky's alleged pedophilia (as well, we might note, as many other wealthy men), but also the apparently incestuous trend of AI and robotics. Sexual relations between men and women involve not only conflicts of desire, but more importantly, the negotiation of a lack. Sex involves crossing the impossible threshold, a fantasy that orgasm amounts to satisfaction of a lack that can never be truly relieved. In this, the male and female desire will come to a head—the man wants to be wanted but simultaneously defines the woman as what will satisfy *him*.[49] The woman, on the other hand, wants to please her partner but will not find this satisfying. Thus, Lacan

45. Berger, "Women and Art."

46. See Dworkin, *Pornography.*

47. Lacan, *Anxiety,* 265.

48. Urwin, "Feminist Porn Director Erika Lust."

49. Lacan, *Anxiety,* 265; *On Feminine Sexuality,* 98.

says, "Anxiety is the truth of sexuality, that is, what appears each time its ebb tide washes back and lets show the sand beneath."[50]

My position, then, is that the Lolita complex, more than an incestuous drive, is a fantasy about *being desired*. Jung's Electra Complex, supposed to be a counter to the Oedipus Complex, is absent from Lacan's theory because it is itself a manifestation of masculine desire. In line with Lacan's insights, I suggest that the young girl, uncorrupted by sexual experiences which might taint her expectations of a lover, is the fantasy *par excellence*. Because of the fantasy of completion inherent in sexual coupling, the man experiences anxiety that his partner may not desire *him* fully. An experienced sexual partner is therefore a danger—she has had lovers and may find the man disappointing. The virgin, however, is "untamed." There is probably no other realm of human experience where we prefer someone entirely *un*experienced over someone who is very experienced. "The woman does not exist."[51] The man's perception of the woman is only insofar as she completes his self-image and must therefore be pliable to him and him alone. She does not exist in her individuality as *a* woman, but rather exists as the generic type, of which the "innocent" virgin is most capable of reflecting the man's desire. And thus also the master-slave dialectic is brought to bear. The girl who is sexually available but not *too* available (as the "achievement" of winning over the girl also factors into the economy of desire), who is the unclaimed territory of men, and who, most importantly, has not had her expectations of sex set yet, is the fantasy of the one who can help him to resolve his lack. The virgin is the one whose desires can be set by the master, who can be shaped to only desire him, who functions as his symptom, and thus can be possessed entirely by him.

Phallic anxiety arrives, then, as both male and female seek to cover their lack in sexual coupling. The man seeks to have what the woman lacks, i.e., the phallus. Within coitus, the illusion of completion and power may be sustained, but afterward, it is apparent that the penis is not the phallus, as it remains deflated and impotent.[52] Thus, women are bound to find themselves never fully satisfied, and the man may recognize that he does not possess the phallus, leading to a feeling of impotence. And because this impasse persists, deception between man and woman persists—the woman who seeks the desire of the other assures the man that

50. Lacan, *Anxiety*, 269.

51. Lacan, *RSI*, 70.

52. Lacan, *Anxiety*, 264; *Object Relation*, 168; *On Feminine Sexuality*, 7.

he satiated her, feeding into his fantasy. But the man experiences lack as well and may not trust his partner's assurance. Even with the most naïve, eager-to-please virgin, deception is never out of the picture. She might still deceive her partner, feigning pleasure where there is none. The reality of anxiety is separation—I cannot know what my partner really thinks. Even naked, her communication to me is mediated, filtered, possibly shrouded. Even if her desire is to please me, I can never know whether I've really given her satisfaction. Lack persists.[53]

Here is where AI comes in, to the rescue as it were. The belief, contradicted by numerous feminists studying algorithmic bias, is that AI cannot deceive, that it is innocent, *uncorrupted*. When the gynoid from *My Living Doll* wanders nude through a residential neighborhood, recalling the primal story of Adam and Eve, she performs this uncorrupted purity. Ava from *Ex Machina* is portrayed as an innocently inexperienced victim, inverted in the film's climax as she reveals herself to be a *femme fatale*, invoking simultaneously masculine desire for a pure virgin and the corresponding fear of vagina dentata. And the automata from *Stepford Wives*, exact replications of the men's wives (not *younger*, not their *children*—but their wives) are made to be entirely subservient and obedient to their husbands, seeking only the males' pleasure. The protagonist Joanna Eberhart, who holds a "women's lib" ideology, must be replaced by a totally subservient robot. The man perceives his wife's independence as a threat because she is no longer constrained by desire for him while he is still caught in the structure of desire.

The reason why *gynoids* are fetishized at a much higher rate than *androids*, and why male AI researchers seem attracted to building sexualized female AIs is because it is the logical pinnacle of male anxiety—the desire of a guileless lover, one whose desire for *him* is complete. The gynoid, when not subverted, is meant to be the perfect lover because her desire is only to please her partner, and she is incapable of deception. She can thus be programmed to achieve her desire through the desire of the male. In short, it is the clearest insight into male fantasy, unfiltered because the AI program is itself not a woman whom AI researchers will always encounter as a barred subject. They can have their cake and eat it too—the gynoid will perfectly desire them above all else while never being disappointed. The gynoid is the fantasy of completion, a being not constituted by lack and only programmed to desire one thing, that thing that her programmer

53. Lacan, *Anxiety*, 270.

can fully provide her and none else can. Thus, the god complex—the AI designer finds his satisfaction through being that being that the AI finds completion in just as we seek completion in the almighty.

FREUD AND LACAN IN CONTRAST

The above is an attempt to examine motivations and perspectives around gynoids, especially sexualized AI and robots, from the perspective of psychoanalysis. One sees interesting divergences between the positions. Freud is typically read through the lens of psychosexual motivation. Our id drives us toward sex through the life force of Eros. But on top of this, the structure of domination and god complexes make the fantasy of sexually compatible robot daughters the ultimate taboo, the temptation of all temptations. From the perspective of Lacan, especially through his analysis of anxiety, the fantasy of the gynoid is the male castration anxiety concretized. The gynoid is expected to be the truly perfect partner, one who fulfills the man with no lack in between. Depending on which of these two positions we accept determines how we make sense of the sexualization of robots.

If we take Freud's position, then robot fetishization appears to be mostly the purview of people with paraphilias—perverts, in a word. The question becomes, at that point, whether AI attracts perverts, or makes perverts. The sexual perversions of AI's most famous researchers are not accidental—they are part and parcel of the psychological makeup that assumes that not only can an adding machine become a person but that we should create such "human" machines.[54]

We may note then most of all that, in this reading, the unconscious goals of perverted AI are imposed on the rest of us as their technology becomes more prominent, more attractive, more successful. David Levy's prediction suggests that by 2050, what we might now call an aberration would become the norm. The Lolita complex becomes a social, not personal, pathology. New sexual mores take shape and those who reject them become the new discontents for this digisexual civilization.

If we take Lacan's position, however, robot fetishization just appears to be a particular form of trying to achieve satisfaction, the perpetual

---

54. Lacan early on noted that the view of "thinking machines" was very different from human thought in his seminar on cybernetics. While Lacan finds the syntax of computer language fascinating, he is insistent that they lack any sense of meaning and thus are incomparable to human minds. See Lacan, *Ego in Freud's Theory*, 294–308.

struggle against anxiety that characterizes human life. This may or may not be a maladaptive tendency, but it is not a symptom of anything beyond what most of us experience. It is different perhaps in quantity, not necessarily in quality. It is the fantasy of completeness, wholeness, an image that the "perfection" of computer fantasies demonstrates. Castration anxiety "appears—Freud had a first grasp of it in *coitus interruptus*—to the extent that orgasm is uncoupled from the field of what is asked of the Other."[55] The woman always may fail to provide the man what he expects—Lord knows the man often fails to provide the woman what she wants. This drama is done away in fantasy, and the construction of a non-castrated consciousness (i.e., AI) is the promise of doing away once and for all with castration anxiety and resulting sexual frustration.

Here, we might refer to the work of AI critics like Cathy O'Neil, who remind us that algorithms are mathematical models which, rather than being objective, are just ways we enshrine our own heuristics and biases into rules.[56] They are mirrors of ourselves. But while the mirror is the place where we recognize ourselves, it is also the place where our separation begins, where we begin to recognize ourselves as separate from mother.[57] And just as the mirror functions as an illusion, creating the ideal ego and presenting to us our fragmented body, it marks a stage of no return, from which we become invariably situated in a social context and the symbolic order. And so, perhaps the AI fetishists are truly perverts, hoping to retrace their lack back through the looking glass and reunite with mother, achieving perfection once and for all.

From a Lacanian perspective, this aim is flawed. AI will never be perfect. It will never achieve what we expect it to. It will always be one step removed from our fantasy. And this is because desire *never* achieves satisfaction, constituted as it is by our inherent lack. *Masculine* desire holds on to the fantasy that it can achieve satisfaction, but *feminine* desire recognizes the impossibility of completeness. The fantasy of AI's satisfaction is a fantasy that has been running for seventy years at this point, with perfection a mere five years away at all times. It is no surprise, then, that AI predictions run the gamut from replacing drudgery to creating new art to maximizing our wealth to solving all social problems—it is pure fantasy, and the greatest fantasy is completeness.

55. Lacan, *Anxiety*, 263.

56. O'Neil, *Weapons of Math Destruction*, 20.

57. Lacan, "Mirror Stage as Formative," 76.

CONCLUSION: DISSATISFACTION AS FACT

So what will happen if AI researchers achieve either their goal of a fully functional sex robot (and not merely a sex doll with automaton head and computer voice) or of human-level artificial intelligence? One of two outcomes. The first possible outcome is mere lack of satisfaction. We will never be satisfied with what comes out. Just as AI today is not truly satisfying, nor was it satisfying fifty years ago, it will never be what we want it to be. And this is because it cannot be, because what we want it to be is merely fantasy—it is not reality. We shy away from reality; in bad faith, we pretend fantasy is something we can achieve but to do so would be to remove the symptom, our *jouissance*, our identity. The fantasy then remains. Maybe we transfer it to another technology, or maybe we look for *better* AI, as the AI field has always moved. Abyss Creation's rudimentary sex robots will be replaced by the *next* model, and the one beyond without limit because *we do not achieve satisfaction*. Our insatiability continues unabated, and this insatiability is sublimated into technological "progress."[58]

The second outcome on this front would be for us to recognize this impossibility and come to terms with it. Ironically, satisfaction comes in recognizing that there is no satisfaction. And perhaps the insatiable desire for *more* will be recognized as unachievable. Some may accept this and continue to pursue better and more technological proficiency—as Lacan's psychoanalytic ethic commands, "Do not give up your desire."[59] Doing so aware of the impossibility of the task leads one to avoid the pitfalls of bad faith move—one is not led into the temptation toward almightiness. The god complex is avoided and our human limitation is accepted as our condition. The recognition of the *impossibility* of AI *as we mean it*, especially as a satisfying sexual partner, may result in an entirely different conception of the place and function of AI within our society. It could function as a tool, even a powerful tool for human ends, but we will not elevate it to the status of idol. The myth of Pygmalion will be re-read as tragedy like Oedipus, a myth about the impossibility of human desire and fantasy instead of one more taboo to cross.

58. Freud, *Civilization and Its Discontents*, 74.

59. Ko, "Destruction and Creation Ex Nihilo," 4; Lacan, *Ethics of Psychoanalysis*, 319.

3

A Lacanian Analysis of Christian Paradox in Moral Teaching and Anxiety

LEVI CHECKETTS

THE CHRISTIAN DOCTRINE OF necessary unmerited grace (whether or not connected to beliefs in total depravity) asserts that no matter what human moral agents do, they cannot ultimately do what is on the balance "good" on their own (i.e., they cannot achieve surplus good or even holism). Taken seriously, this doctrine means that the moral project on the whole is futile within Christianity because no human can overcome sins, but also no sin is too great to be erased by God's grace. Indeed, this has been the promise of Christians from Saint Paul to Martin Luther and beyond: the law is done away through Christ. And yet, Christians are often moralistic, disproving the claims of Paul Tillich and others that Christianity supplies the "healing" that psychoanalysis cannot guarantee.[1]

This chapter argues that the Christian desire for moral order can best be understood through the insights of Jacques Lacan on the fundamental human condition of lack and consequent anxiety, that is, that the impasse that exists between ourselves and the Other (e.g., God) as an impossible gap creates the desire to cover over our anxiety with strict adherence to the law. Attending to the insights of Christian writers Paul Tillich and

1. Tillich, *Dynamics of Faith*, 20; *Spiritual Situation,* 137.

Søren Kierkegaard, whose theology complements Lacan's psychoanalysis, I contend that the radical message of Christianity is resignation to this anxiety rather than an insistence upon a solid moral order. Christian ethics then must be understood as a paradoxical practice of insisting on a law that Christ has done away with because without the symbolic order we lack psychological structure.

THE PARADOX OF LAW AND LIBERTY IN GALATIANS 5

While Christians all (ostensibly) believe the Bible is the word of God, they have to make sense of the fact that the text apparently contradicts itself in numerous places. Even "in the beginning," the text gives differing accounts of how God creates the world in Genesis 1 and 2. Christians often make sense of contradictions either by emphasizing development in theology, authorial differences or insignificance of the contradictions. The fact that Christians can so casually accept these inconsistencies suggests with Lacan that we do not adhere as strictly to formal, symbolic or even transcendental logic as analytic philosophers may claim. Rather, we tend to have our own *logics* more rooted in the structure of the signifier.[2] In this section, I examine Saint Paul's contradictory messages in Galatians 5.

Galatians 5 seems to offer believers in Galatia rival conditions for salvation. In verses 4 and 6, Paul writes, "You who are trying to be justified by the law have been alienated from Christ; you have fallen away from grace. . . . For in Christ Jesus neither circumcision nor uncircumcision has any value. The only thing that counts is faith expressing itself through love" (NRSV). Later on, in verses 19 through 21, he writes, "The acts of the flesh are obvious: sexual immorality, impurity and debauchery; idolatry and witchcraft; hatred, discord, jealousy, fits of rage, selfish ambition, dissensions, factions and envy; drunkenness, orgies, and the like. I warn you, as I did before, that those who live like this will not inherit the kingdom of God." So, on the one hand, Paul seems to tell us that the rightness or wrongness of one's actions are meaningless for salvation as only faith grants salvation. But, on the other hand, he provides what seems to be a list of disqualifying behaviors that restrict one from salvation. Absent any creative interpretation, it seems Paul gives Christians incompatible instructions.

2. Lacan, *Identification*, 94.

The other verses of the chapter do little to fix this impasse. In telling Christians that circumcision, an important outward observation of the Mosaic Law, is useless, Paul compares obedience to the law to "slavery" (v. 1). But after telling Christians they are free through Christ (v. 13), he tells them the law is fulfilled in the command "love your neighbor as yourself" (v. 14), seemingly prescribing (a) law once again. And between his insistence that Christians should "not do whatever you want" because the Spirit and the flesh are in conflict (v. 17) and his litany of sins to avoid (vv. 19–21), Paul adds the rejoinder, "But if you are led by the Spirit, you are not under the law" (v. 18).

Begging the reader's forgiveness, this passage really should strike us as incoherent. Paul tells us to disregard the law, then tells us we can fulfill the law by loving our neighbor, then warns us against following the flesh, then tells us to avoid a list of sins, some of which—sexual immorality, impurity, debauchery, drunkenness, orgies—have no obvious connection to either maintaining faith in Christ or loving our neighbors. Indeed, Paul's reference to the ambiguous "impurity" (ἀκαθαρσία, v. 19) itself hearkens back most directly to the term for *ritual* impurity in the Septuagint, especially surrounding contact with dead or decaying flesh.[3] So the question which the Church in Galatia is left with is this: is it or is it not important for Christians to uphold the Mosaic Law? If it is important, why has Paul challenged that "if you let yourselves be circumcised, Christ will be of no value to you at all" (v. 2)? If it is not important, why has Paul declared those who are ritually impure to be damned?

Lacan seems to argue that this inconsistency is really present in Paul's writings. In his seminar on identification, he writes:

> The foundation of Christian revelation is indeed therefore in this grace relationship which Paul makes succeed to the law. . . . The Christian does not maintain himself, and with good reason, at the height of this revelation and . . . nevertheless he lives it in a society of such a kind that one can say that even reduced to the most lay forms its principles of law issue directly all the same from a catechism which is not unrelated to this Pauline revelation. Simply, since the meditation on the Mystical Body is not within everyone's reach, a gap remains open which means that practically the Christian finds himself reduced to something which is not all that normal or fundamental, of really no longer

---

3. Strong, *Exhaustive Concordance of the Bible*, 167.

having any other access to jouissance as such except by making love.[4]

In other words, Lacan notes that the function of law in the average Christian's life restricts experience so that the only surplus, non-symbolic, experience of the Real tends to be achieved in orgasm, i.e., just those sorts of sins Paul suggests are banned to the Christian. Perhaps grace should be an experience of surplus jouissance, but Paul and the average Christian are unable to reach this.

Turning Lacan's insightful reading of Paul on its head, we see that this in turn means that moral theology, i.e., the teaching of "the law," is fundamental for the Christian. The experience of *jouissance*, especially the Other's *jouissance*, plays out for the Christian as the Other's anxiety, an anxiety that pushes us to demand moral uprightness of others around us as well.[5] Ironically, Christians simultaneously hold that they cannot earn their salvation through good works while also holding that they must rigidly uphold a moral standard. The seeming incompatibility of these two positions, I argue, demonstrates well the problem of anxiety for the Christian believer. Or, as Lacan expresses it, "The Christian . . . always believes he puts more heart into things than anyone else. . . . [The] attempt to provoke the Other's anxiety, here become God's anxiety, has become second nature in the Christian."[6]

This insight reframes the task of moral theology in a difficult way— on one hand, moral theology itself must be understood as functioning to support a symbolic order that sustains Christians in their anxiety, a type of "masochism" to provoke God, but, on the other hand, moral theology should be oriented toward freeing Christians from their "slavery" to the law, to let them achieve *jouissance* of the grace that abounds.

THE CONTOURS OF MORAL THEOLOGY

Saint Paul is the first major follower of Jesus of Nazareth to teach that only faith in Christ is sufficient for salvation. Nothing in the Hebrew Bible seems to indicate faith will be sufficient for salvation, and even the accounts of Jesus in the Gospels seem to insist that moral behavior, not faith, is most necessary for salvation. Across the corpus of Paul's letters,

4. Lacan, *Identification*, 126–27.

5. Lacan, *Anxiety*, 221.

6. Lacan, *Anxiety*, 221.

one reads consistently that faith alone is what saves largely because he denies morality is sufficient.

Across Paul's letters and the account of him in the Acts of the Apostles, he seems to insist that only faith can save the otherwise damned person, while also imputing strict moral commands such as chastity, avoiding scandal (1 Cor 8:12), and avoiding "sin's evil desires" (Rom 6:12). So, in Paul, the paradox remains: one is saved from *sin* by being saved from the law, but one must obey the law.

In a passage Lacan later cites positively, Paul insightfully notes, "I would not have known what coveting was if the law had not said, 'You shall not covet'" (Rom 7:7).[7] The existence of sin requires the existence of the law. So if we are saved from sin, we must be saved from the law. And yet, though we are supposed to be free from this slavery as Christians, Paul insists that the saved Christian no longer lives "according to the flesh" (Rom 8:5), i.e., we should live "better" lives. In short, we must again follow the law. In not defining us, the law more truly defines us.

Augustine of Hippo, a few centuries later, advanced Paul's position in a more dramatic fashion. Saint Augustine famously opposed the view of Pelagius, who believed that human beings are individually responsible for their sins, so God's act of redemption was entirely gratuitous and unnecessary. Augustine, in opposition, argued that human beings are born with the stains of sin already on us, and so need God's grace if we are not to be damned.

The major difference, then, is that Pelagius believed human beings could "earn" their salvation through proper moral living, while Augustine believed it was impossible. In *City of God*, Augustine articulates his most famous explanation of original sin, the fault that our ancestors (i.e., Adam and Eve) passed on to us primarily through the lust-filled act of procreation.[8] Indeed, Augustine argues that even though sex can have a good end (i.e., procreation), it cannot be separated from lust, and so lust is the vehicle by which our species continues. All children are therefore born into lust and marred with the stain of original sin. Augustine's view becomes the prominent view in Western Christianity, meaning the Christian ethos is defined by tension between an emphasis on sex as the paradigmatic expression of moral failure, an inability to merit our own salvation, and a simultaneous demand to achieve this impossible moral

---

7. Lacan, *Ethics of Psychoanalysis*, 83.

8. Augustine, *City of God*, 79.

standard. Protestantism maintained a tense relationship between faith and the law, but Catholicism moved further toward legalism.

In the Middle Ages, the concept of sin and repentance had fully captured Christendom to the extent that the Sacrament of Reconciliation emerged. Baptized faithful were now understood to be not once and for all redeemed from sin; they often slipped back into sinful habits and behaviors. The Church taught that the unrepentant could not partake of the Eucharist but also that all faithful were required to take Communion at least once per year.[9] The laity was thus struck by a bind—they were supposed to take Communion but were forbidden from doing so. But since law creates the desire to transgress it,[10] the forbidding made it all the more important that Christians take communion, and so the practice of confessing sins and receiving absolution emerged. To ensure regularity in confession, penitentials became common place, prescribing set penances for given sins, which often amounted to fasting or prayers of determined lengths.[11]

Over time, this system was revised. The Scholastics advanced their views and went beyond penitentials to sentences and commentaries on sentences and eventually summas.[12] The most famous example is the work of Saint Thomas Aquinas, who organized his entire Second Part of the *Summa Theologiae* detailing a moral theory most commonly shorthand referred to as the "natural law." This law, Aquinas alleges, is rooted in the "Eternal Law," and manifested by human reason.[13] It is the same in all persons in terms of general principles, but differs perhaps by concrete applications.[14] And yet, Aquinas spends the entire Second Part of the Second Part detailing the most specific issues in relation to the violation or upholding of the law along an axis based on the four cardinal virtues and the three theological ones.

With the emergence of the Protestant Reformation, which sought to reclaim Augustine and Paul's primary insistence on salvation by faith alone, moral theology experienced a sort of crisis. The confessional tradition and the rise of summas led to the development of a system of casuistry, which articulated a far more complex reality of the moral law

9. Mahoney, *Making of Moral Theology,* 17.

10. Lacan, *Object Relation,* 143.

11. Mahoney, *Making of Moral Theology,* 10.

12. Mahoney, *Making of Moral Theology,* 19.

13. Aquinas, *Summa Theologiae* Ia IIae q91 a2.

14. Aquinas, *Suma Theologiae* Ia IIae q94 a4.

that factored in persons' intentions, circumstances, and similar cases to adjudicate various degrees of moral failings.[15]

In this way, the model resembled something much more similar to the adjudication of criminal law in contemporary Western nations. But Jansenism emerged as a response to Protestantism, characterized by an insistence on God's harsh decrees and the need for moral rigor among believers. A prominent debate between Jansenist Blaise Pascale and Jesuit Antonio Escobar was eventually resolved through the magisterium's endorsement of Alphonse Liguori's "aequiprobabilistic" middle ground position between the seemingly laxed "probabilistic" view of the Jesuits and the rigorist position of the Jansenists.[16]

In other words, confusion of the nature of the law, owing to a discordance between human practice and idealistic expectations, or the gap between the real and the symbolic, was resolved through further authoritative administration through the magisterium. The law, which stands as authority by virtue of it being a law, is reinforced by the authority of the magisterium, whose authority derives from the Authority of authorities, i.e., God. Thus, Aquinas's romantic appeal to universal human rationality, a claim for universal moral grounding, belies the fact that the law is so opaque it must be adjudicated by appeals to authority and cannot stand on any overarching self-apparent truth.

Moral theology has evolved since then, especially in the Post-Vatican II era with an emphasis on sin as relational rather than rule-based.[17] But it still functions as an almighty Law, demonstrated clearly in the emphasis on sexual sins. Freud argues in *Civilization and Its Discontents* that civilization has as its primary moral function the regulation of *eros* into approved channels. Mahoney notes, "traditional moral theology has been much too individualistic in its choice of subjects and its treatment of them and . . . has devoted more than a little of its attention to sexual morality."[18] Augustine's disapproval of sex[19] is echoed in ancient Christianity by Jerome, who praises virginity above marriage and chaste widowhood above remarrying, calling the virginity gold, widowhood

---

15. Jonsen and Toulmin, *Abuse of Casuistry*, 44.

16. Jonsen and Toulmin, *Abuse of Casuistry*, 175.

17. Bretzke, *Morally Complex World*, 201; Connors Jr. and McCormick, *Character, Choices & Community*, 203; Curran, *Catholic Moral Tradition Today*, 192.

18. Mahoney, *Making of Moral Theology*, 32–33.

19. See Augustine, *City of God*, 15; Mahoney, *Making of Moral Theology*, 58; Farley, *Just Love*, 40–41.

silver, and the sacrament of marriage bronze, with the respective "yields an hundredfold, sixtyfold, and thirtyfold."[20]

In the Middle Ages, the Third Lateran Council further codified sex as the fundamental law by prohibiting clergy from marrying, demarcating the lower, lay life from the higher, consecrated life by the question of sexual activity. In recent years, this fixation is demonstrated by Pope Paul VI's sexually conservative (and controversial) *Humanae Vitae*, the Congregation for the Defense of Faith's condemnation of Margaret Farley's liberal sexual theology, John Paul II's "theology of the body," and continual controversies surrounding sexual abuse, rampant homophobia, and controversy surrounding communion for divorced Catholics.[21] Indeed, Charles Curran aptly notes the assumptions of the person underlying the magisterium's evolving teaching on social justice, typically regarded as less authoritative, differ significantly from the Medieval insistence characteristic of sexual teachings.[22]

We come full circle to Saint Paul, then. It is no accident that Paul mentions sexual improprieties among the conditions that would disqualify an otherwise faithful Christian from inheriting the Kingdom of God. And it is no accident that Freud is regarded as a sexual pervert among Christians—his insight on the function of sexual repression as imposing moral rigorism is, in fact, merely an alternative way of expressing the common formulation of moral teaching in Christianity.

Freud's hypothesis that for the average Christian God functions as the authoritarian father demanding unquestioning obedience should be easily debunked by the Gospel message of unmerited grace.[23] And yet, moral theology's emphasis on sex, on specifics moral deeds,[24] on moral rigorism, all suggest the law *is* the condition for salvation. Thus, the popular assumption of many Christians is that they will be judged after death with cosmic scales weighing their good and evil deeds.

It remains more unimaginable for many Christians that prostitutes could be Christian,[25] despite Christ's own association with such people,

20. Jerome, "Letter 48." For further comments on the over-emphasis on virginity, see Jiyoung Ko's chapter on Margery Kempe in this volume.

21. Paul VI, *Humanae Vitae*; CDF, *Notification on the Book*; John Paul II, *Redemption of the Body*; Cary, "To Bless or Not to Bless"; Brandmüller et al., "Dubia."

22. Curran, "Catholic Social and Sexual Teaching," 425–40.

23. Freud, *Civilization and Its Discontents*, 39; *Future of an Illusion*, 34.

24. See Lacan, *Anxiety*, 317.

25. See Tan, *Resisting Rape Culture*, 47.

than that businessmen serving mammon could. The law, especially the law of chastity, remains a structure of society as well as the rule governing Catholic ecclesiology. As Paul writes to the Romans, "I see another law at work in my body, warring against the law of my mind and holding me captive to the law of sin that dwells within me" (Rom 7:23). Sex, the most bodily appetite, the first law of the totemic father and the rule governing (secular) civilization is paradigmatic of the sinful nature of the flesh, a moral obstacle that even "death to sin" in baptism does not somehow absolve us from. The Christian seemingly never escapes the law.

NO FREEDOM FROM THE LAW: LACANIAN ANXIETY AND CHRISTIANITY

No amount of scholastic qualification can overturn the apparent contradiction that, on one hand, Christians believe grace is all-sufficient for all sins and yet, on the other, that Christians are still bound by moral strictures after being "saved." In strict terms, these are incompatible positions to hold, yet most Christians, including theologians, hold them. The answer to this problem, I contend, lies not in theology but in psychology. More fundamentally, Jacques Lacan's discussion of anxiety clarifies why even the saved retreat back to the protection of the law rather than the terrifying reality of freedom.

Lacan's Notion of Anxiety

For Lacan, the fundamental feeling of humanity is anxiety. Contrary to the "feel good" psychologists who propose that human beings are typically content, Lacan sees the fundamental human experience oriented around lack.[26] The persistence of lack creates in us uneasiness, restlessness, anxiety.[27] But the problem is that *nothing* causes it. The yawning gulf, the bar to others, the inability to achieve fullness, the reality of absence, separation from our mother—that is to say the existence of a "nothing" which confronts us—is the source of our anxiety.[28] So, unlike fear or anger or sadness, which tend to have clear objects as their cause, anxiety cannot be done away with because *nothing* always persists.

26. Lacan, *Anxiety*, 176.
27. Lacan, *Anxiety*, 136.
28. Lacan, *Anxiety*, 311.

Lacan's model correlates the lack (object *a*; the object we identify with in our lack of that thing) with varying levels of development: the oral stage leads to a primal lack, whereas the development of superego entails the desire of the Other, and castration anxiety, signaled by the absence of the phallus, plays out in the *jouissance* of the Other.[29] Anxiety is therefore inherently tied to desire, either the subject's desire, or the desire of the Other. What brings anxiety, then, is inhibition—the inability to fulfill desire.[30] This frustration often reveals itself in a symptom, such as "anal turmoil," obsession, or even impotence.[31]

The obsessional, for example, has an unfulfilled desire—a desire to find what will bring wholeness.[32] However, the obsessional finds themselves impotent in the face of this desire, so takes on the symptom of "almightiness."[33] The major forms of anxiety Lacan highlights in this constellation of inhibition-symptom-anxiety include, in the latter stages, scopic anxiety, castration anxiety and vociferated anxiety. Scopic anxiety plays out in the desire to see/the desire *not* to see, a desire to maintain the illusion of certainty which is defied by our visual experience.[34] Phallic anxiety seeks to achieve the Other's *jouissance*, an aim that can never be accomplished because of the gap between the sexes.[35] Vociferated anxiety plays out in the desire to fulfill the desire of the voice, that is, to fulfill the demands placed on one by the Ego Ideal.[36] In other words, these forms of anxiety typical of neurotics (especially the obsessional), play out in the gap of our knowledge (scopic), the gap of our ability (phallic), and the gap of our morality (vociferated).

Lacan's insight is vindicated in a Christian context by German-American theologian Paul Tillich, who argues that "anxiety is the state in which a being is aware of its possible nonbeing . . . [it] is finitude, experienced as one's own finitude."[37] Tillich further suggests that there are three forms of anxiety, "that of fate and death . . . that of emptiness and loss of

29. Lacan, *Anxiety*, 303.
30. Lacan, *Anxiety*, 316.
31. Lacan, *Anxiety*, 322.
32. Lacan, *Anxiety*, 319.
33. Lacan, *Anxiety*, 333.
34. Lacan, *Anxiety*, 332.
35. Lacan, *Anxiety*, 265.
36. Lacan, *Anxiety*, 304.
37. Tillich, *Courage to Be*, 35.

meaning . . . that of guilt and condemnation."[38] Tillich's three forms of anxiety match with phallic (impotence), scopic (truth) and vociferated (guilt) anxiety of the neurotic. Not all of Tillich's ideas are supported by Lacan; for example, Tillich suggests there is a way out of anxiety, which Lacan does not support.

However, the convergence between Lacan and Tillich shines particular light on the problem of morality articulated within a particularly Christian worldview. Tillich notes, "To avoid [the transformation of anxiety into despair], man tries to transform the anxiety of guilt into moral action regardless of its imperfection and ambiguity . . . [which] can lead to a moral rigor and the self-satisfaction derived from it. In . . . legalism . . . the anxiety of guilt lies in the background and breaks again and again into the open, introducing the extreme situation of moral despair."[39]

Moral rigorism addresses the anxious feeling of guilt, the sense of being judged by an inscrutable and terrible master. Lacan similarly notes, "The crux of masochism, which is an attempt to provoke the Other's anxiety, here become God's anxiety, has become second nature in the Christian."[40] What Tillich articulates in a more general sense, Lacan details as the consequence of a particular experience of the Other qua moral lawgiver.

Lacan Meets Kierkegaard: Between Faith and Anxiety

Like many other writers of his age (e.g., Martin Heidegger, Jean-Paul Sartre), Lacan's insight into anxiety owes a great deal to the study carried out by Christian philosopher Søren Kierkegaard. Kierkegaard was deeply critical of the Danish Church of his time. He saw a church that truly lacked faith, one that had placed greater stock in the authority of its leaders and statesmen—representatives of a clear symbolic order— than it had in Christ. But importantly, he also recognized that faith is not as easy as is often portrayed. Several of his philosophical reflections recommend radical faith as the antidote to the ills of living in uncertain times, but faith requires a leap into the unknown, a step into the absurd, a certainty in what is not certain.[41]

38. Tillich, *Courage to Be*, 41.

39. Tillich, *Courage to Be*, 53.

40. Lacan, *Anxiety*, 221.

41. Kierkegaard, *Fear and Trembling*, 70.

In this way, the path of the "knight of faith" is one of absolute confidence in what cannot be known. Thus, Kierkegaard's famous treatment of the faith of Abraham sees Abraham not as a "tragic hero" because he is capable of transcending the "ethical absolute" to do what God calls him to do.[42] Abraham, the knight of faith, demonstrates that true faith means no longer living within the law. He is asked to kill his son Isaac, and yet he believes that God will give him Isaac.[43] Abraham, as the knight of faith, transcends the law (the ethical absolute) by plunging into the absurd.

Kierkegaard's understanding of the absurdity of faith positions him to articulate the first clear understanding of anxiety.[44] For Kierkegaard, anxiety is also rooted in finitude and tied to sin, but he recognizes it much more deeply intertwined in the reality of human freedom and traces its origin from human innocence. In innocence "there is indeed nothing against which to strive. What, then, is it? Nothing. But what effect does nothing have? It begets anxiety. This is the profound secret of innocence, that it is at the same time anxiety."[45] Kierkegaard places the emphasis of anxiety on the Christian notion of guilt and sin but still recognizes anxiety as the gap: "the relation of freedom to guilt is anxiety, because freedom and guilt are still only possibilities."[46] For Kierkegaard, choice cancels out anxiety, at least temporarily, because even a sinful choice cuts out the tension of nothing.

In the attempt to repent, one encounters, therefore the highest experience of anxiety as the possibility of escaping sin enters possibility. Anxiety might then prevent one from living the free life of the Christian because Christians "are not willing to think eternity earnestly but are anxious about it, and anxiety can contrive a hundred evasions. And this is precisely the demonic."[47] Thus, Kierkegaard for his part seems to take seriously the persistence of anxiety and is willing to correlate it to some of the same factors Lacan notes, such as the eye, the almighty, the possible and even the erotic.

The uncertainty that anxiety provokes in us drives us to seek some releasement from the experience. A typical, not to say effective, means

42. Kierkegaard, *Fear and Trembling*, 88.

43. Kierkegaard, *Fear and Trembling*, 99.

44. NB: Kierkegaard's *Fear and Trembling* was written one year prior to *The Concept of Anxiety*.

45. Kierkegaard, *Concept of Anxiety*, 41.

46. Kierkegaard, *Concept of Anxiety*, 109.

47. Kierkegaard, *Concept of Anxiety*, 154.

of doing this is thus by convincing ourselves that we can live according to the law. By focusing on sin and guilt—the powerlessness of human experience—Christians experience the anxiety of ambiguity of choice. To say that no sin is unforgiveable provides releasement for the sinner, but not for the saved. The saved should be freed from the bonds of sin, but yet finds themselves anxious. To Kierkegaard, as obviously to Lacan, this is no surprise. This is because the consciousness of the law, which entails that a person can be saved, assumes one has resolved their initial castration anxiety by taking on the name of the father.[48]

The Christian who takes seriously the call to faith will, however, not escape anxiety. Indeed, Kierkegaard believes responding to anxiety with faith makes anxiety all the more important for the Christian's life. "Whoever has learned to be anxious will dance when the anxieties of finitude strike up the music and when the apprentices of finitude lose their minds and courage."[49] The uncertainty of anxiety leads many to revert to the law, the comforting deception of almightiness. But to accept anxiety through faith is to experience true freedom, for "anxiety enters into [a person's] soul and searches out everything and anxiously torments everything finite and petty out of him, and then it leads him where he wants to go."[50] This act of accepting anxiety through faith is a form of *sublimation*, an experience Lacan notes, that brings on the experience of *jouissance*.[51] *Jouissance* is only achievable by traversing anxiety.[52] Thus, Kierkegaard's prescription—to accept through faith the absurdity of the anxiety that comes from radical faith—is a path of sublimation achieving Christian *jouissance*.

Submission to the Law

As children develop, language invariably shapes their world. One might say it allows them to have a world. The imposition of language serves as an initial cut as language itself functions to demarcate and delimit what is through what can be labelled. The function of this is to take the child

48. Lacan was raised in a deeply Catholic household and his brother was a monk. Regardless of whether he maintained any faith as an adult, he clearly understood the functioning of Christianity on the mind.

49. Kierkegaard, *Concept of Anxiety*, 161–62.

50. Kierkegaard, *Concept of Anxiety*, 159.

51. Lacan, *Identification*, 128–29.

52. Lacan, *Anxiety*, 174.

out of "the real," that is what is actual and irreducible to the limits of language. As the child develops through the imaginary stages, where words and concepts exist but are not tied to any clear meaning, they eventually undergo a process of severance through submission to the symbolic.[53] This "innocent stage" as Kierkegaard notes is not free from anxiety, but the anxiety is different.[54] In this stage, anxiety is more raw.

As Lacan notes, all anxiety is tied to desire, but what is desired determines the form of the anxiety. The developing child desires oneness with mother, with the breast that feeds and yet disappears, with the comforting mother who must expel the child from the marital bed, with the nurturing mother who functions as the big Other whom we must but cannot unite with to find completion.[55]

This turmoil persists until a disciplinary measure can be instilled. Lacan notes the comparison between anal turmoil and castration anxiety—the child simultaneously desires to master his body, but knows this is a terrible imposition.[56] But eventually the father comes in and castrates the child, relieving the castration anxiety by making them into a neurotic. The name of the father is imprinted on the child, and the child learns to submit to the master of the law. Thus, Paul and approvingly Lacan, "I would not have known sin, but through the law."[57]

Being or becoming a Christian thus requires a type of castration. Paul's thorough negation of the requirement of circumcision is itself revelatory; Lacan notes that while circumcision *appears* similar to castration, "nothing is less castrating than circumcision."[58] A Christian does not go through the more obviously symbolic form of having the foreskin of the penis cut, but rather undergoes baptism, a ritual castration. Indeed, Lacan notes the Christian analogy to circumcision is rather "to identify ideally with . . . the waste object left behind out of divine retribution,"[59] that is, as the leftover foreskin rather than the consecrated, circumcised man. Thus, to be baptized, one must already acknowledge the law as having authority—they must confess that they are sinners in need of forgiveness, not the covenantally-bound under the law, but the refuse of the law.

53. Lacan, *Anxiety*, 46; *The Object Relation*, 220.

54. Kierkegaard, *Concept of Anxiety*, 41.

55. Lacan, *Anxiety*, 167; *The Object Relation*, 198–99.

56. Lacan, *Anxiety*, 312.

57. Lacan, *Ethics of Psychoanalysis*, 83.

58. Lacan, *Anxiety*, 80.

59. Lacan, *Anxiety*, 220.

Where does this knowledge come from? The natural law claim to a self-apparent, universally-binding law is negated by actual Christian practice which relies on a chain of signifiers: knowledge of the law is taught through Christianity. Naturally, then, those who accept the law taught by Christianity submit themselves to baptism to be redeemed of their sins. Those who do not accept the law taught by Christians do not accept baptism. In Tillich's phrase, the Christian takes God as their "ultimate concern," which is fundamental for dealing with anxiety.[60] And thus, "in the name of the Father . . ."[61] are Christians literally welcomed into the Church. A law, perhaps *not* the Mosaic law, is the formula most Christians accept in their belief. And yet they remain anxious.

Anxiety returns after resolution of castration anxiety through baptism because anxiety is what defines us. Lacan teaches us that submission to the symbolic order does not suffice to fill in our lack—the Other remains barred to us.[62] Christianity likewise has taught that baptism does not preclude one from sinning. Recent decades of moral theology have shifted the notion of sin from a legal infraction to a rupture in relation—the condition of sin is lack of fullness with God. Then what must the Christian do? They are confronted with anxiety once again, even after repentance. And though they subjected themselves to the law, they see that around them are "sinners" who do not accept the law to themselves—gay men and lesbians, sexually promiscuous, prostitutes, adulterers, drug users, gamblers, drunkards, atheists, other religions (and not, notably, capitalists, polluters, marketers, warmongers, oil barons, all of whose works are patently immoral but yet legal)—which provokes a crisis of faith. Is the law really so firm if so many reject it? Anxiety returns—it is not enough for many to believe that they are saved—God's mercy is not comforting to the saved as it is to the damned. Thus, they need the "Almighty."

"At the level at which anxiety is covered over, the Ego Ideal takes the form of the Almighty."[63] The "superego" (i.e., Ego Ideal) of the Christian becomes, not their limited father but their Almighty Father. The uncertainty that life in the world entails is done away with "the universal eye that watches down on all our actions."[64] God will repay—the law that the Christian has submitted themself to will be applied to all those sinners

60. Tillich, *Dynamics of Faith*, 33; *Courage to Be*, 82.

61. Cf. Lacan, *Anxiety*, 336–37.

62. Lacan, *Anxiety*, 27.

63. Lacan, *Anxiety*, 308.

64. Lacan, *Anxiety*, 308.

who do not yet accept the law because the law is Almighty. In short, the "amazing Grace" the Christian professed in submitting themself to Christ is run over roughshod by the terrible Almighty God who repays wickedness for wickedness on all those who refuse to accept the Father. The anxiety is covered over—Lacan does not say "done away with" because this is a deceptive solution—in the confidence that one's "unfree relation to the good" resolves the tension. Kierkegaard calls this surveillant anxious unfreedom to the good "demonic anxiety."[65] The Christian, he insists, should live in the anxiety of freedom and not retreat.

If Lacan is correct, Christian ethics has so often emphasized infractions of the law, especially those pertaining to sexuality, because although Christians are saved from the law, that salvation is not salvation from anxiety. The Christian remains anxious, and if they assumed that salvation would take away their anxiety, they find themselves positing the Almighty as a barbiturate. "The rain falls on the just and unjust alike" Christ says in Matt 5:45, telling his followers of a God who asks them to love their enemies as themselves. Such a God is one who does not promise to resolve the anxiety of the believer. Thus Paul to the Galatians, once again, admits that the law is given to be "a guardian" which "held us in custody" until we are justified in Christ and "no longer under a guardian" (3:23–25). Christians *should* be free from the law as they are free from sin, but out of anxiety retreat back to a law, the Name of the Father, who delineates a new law, where the 613 Mitzvot are replaced by a new catalogue of venial and mortal sins in medieval penitential.

CONCLUSION: THE CHRISTIAN PARADOX

How can Christians live? Everybody sins. While Christians are to be held responsible for their shortcomings, they are unable to live perfect lives. The stain of sin, original or committed, persists in spite of our moral strivings. And, if Lacan is correct, it is impossible to *not* persist, as the lack between our desire to do the good and our (in)ability to do it is impossible to overcome. "The object itself as such, *qua* object of desire [e.g., the desire to obey God], is the effect of the impossibility of the Other to respond to demand."[66] Thus, as Paul tells us, "I do not understand my own actions. For I do not do what I want, but I do the very thing I hate"

65. Kierkegaard, *Concept of Anxiety*, 119.
66. Lacan, *Identification*, 135.

(Rom 7:15). The law of sin is thus the inescapable reality that our moral action always misses the mark.

But the Christian should not feel beholden to such a law. After all, "for freedom, Christ has set us free" (Gal 5:1). How can we be free if we are subordinated to the law? Paul tells us that we are no longer bound to obey the law, and so freedom in Christ should be liberation from this law. The insistence that we are bound to a law gives short shrift to Christ's death. Jesus begins his ministry, according to Luke, proclaiming, "The Spirit of the Lord is upon me, because he has anointed me to bring good news to the poor. He has sent me to proclaim release to the captives" (Luke 4:18). What is the "good news" if not freedom from the law? The message of Christianity seems to contradict the phenomenological experience. Thus, it is only an *apparent* paradox that Christians believe in grace while still retreating to the safety of a moral order.

Lacan's study of anxiety tells us that there is no way out. Neurotics retreat from anxiety through castration. Submission to a moral order provides comfort, though it does not get rid of the anxiety. Rather, anxiety is covered over, until it comes screaming back. What freedom a Christian may want is put in jeopardy by the abyss of anxiety, and the security of the law. The only way for a Christian to escape is to accept the anxiety, as Kierkegaard teaches, and to embrace the absurd. Liberation is submission to anxiety, not the attempt to flee it by taking refuge in the law. Thus, the ultimate acceptance of the Christian message, that is to say the ultimate acceptance of God's grace, is choosing the life of anxiety and rejecting the ease of the moral order. Abraham as the knight of faith walks a solitary, difficult path. But it is the path of true freedom.

But for those Christians unable or unwilling to live the anxious life of faith, the law remains a stronghold for them. In this case, the task of moral theology is made clear: it functions as a shelter for those unable to venture freely into the anxious world of freedom. Paul's instructions to the Church at Corinth in 1 Cor 8 highlights the tension remarkably well: while Paul notes there is no reason Christians cannot eat meat (v. 8), he is aware that not all have sufficient faith to accept this reality (v. 7). Of course, Paul wrote in a time when Christianity was nascent and the believers were in the margins of society. Whether moral theology should still function to rein in those who are liberated in Christ (v. 13), or whether it should unashamedly note that the law does not save (v. 8) remains an open question. For those Christians "with a weak conscience" (v. 10) (i.e., still subject to the symbolic order), the law is undoubtedly a necessity. But for those Christians who accept the radical truth of the Gospel, moral theology perhaps should open a freer way. One way or another, moral theology should take responsibility for itself, recognizing that it is in no way a guarantee of salvation and that it is ultimately a shelter for those unable or unwilling to venture into the absurd tension of anxious faith.

Part II

Praxis

4

Lacan's Real of God and Its Application to Spiritual Direction

ALI CHAVOSHIAN AND JUNG EUN SOPHIA PARK

IN THIS GLOBAL ERA, it is crucial to reconsider the nature and scope of Christian spirituality, which lies in the intersectionality of religion and culture. It must engage diverse human contexts that emerge from living habitus, such as culture, language, socio-political context, and class. Very often, in spiritual direction, as well as in pastoral counseling, it is crucial to find diverse ways to make sense of an individual's understanding of God.

In this paper, we first examine the *via negativa*, a way to approach God in parallel to the Real of God, a concept suggested by Jacques Lacan.[1] Second, we elaborate on the idea of the Real of God, emphasizing the interstitial nature between the sayable and the unsayable. Finally, we apply the concept of the Real of God to spiritual direction. The practice of spiritual direction in light of Lacan's idea of the Real of God and the *sinthome* can help directees, particularly immigrants, to gain their voice. Through an understanding of God beyond language, the director can help directees understand their own experiences and articulate their lived experiences.

---

1. Lacan often mentions God or theology in his psychoanalytic discourses, and many theologians have already applied his ideas to their theologies.

THE *VIA NEGATIVA* AND THE REAL

In contemporary society, many people have experienced immigration and dislocation; people speak in languages that are not their native ones. We presuppose that when those immigrants stand free from the order of language, they may feel more connected to their own experience of God. Arguably, a negative way of understanding God's nature can be helpful and it is coherent with the Real, a concept which Lacan developed in this theory of the composition of the human psyche. The traditional way of explaining God as a Being beyond our language in negative theology can be more elaborated in the Lacan theory of the Real, which emphasizes the oppressive nature of language and culture for subjects who experience difficulty with languages.

The Negative Way

The negative way, called apophatic spirituality, indicates an approach that negates statements of God within communicative speech, language, and writings. The apophatic way doubts the competence of speaking and articulating the experience of the Being or God. The formation of the negative way assumes that all definite forms of description of God should be negated. It further emphasizes that God is more than what we enunciate, and uses un-noetic attributes of God, which remain *beyond* human comprehension. The apophatic formation leads us to the infinite point or the void of God.

In logical thought, "God is" signifies that God is limited or belongs to the predicative part. If we say that God is good, it means that God belongs to goodness. A particular attribute of God can be called A, B, or C . . .; in this way, the number of attributes results in an unaccountable and infinite total. At the same time, we count contributions as dots, and we know that infinite dots exist between attributes A and B. Then, empty spaces or voids emerge as Σ, the sum of attributes. Here, the notion of mysticism appears in the empty space or the void. The "beyond-ness," "in-betweenness," and "void" can directly result in the logic of impossibility and the possibility of transformation.[2]

The French Catholic thinker Simone Weil writes, "To love Truth means to endure the void." Enduring the void is risky but one must run,

2. Park, *Border-Crossing Spirituality*, 6–7.

even during moments of disappointment.[3] The void is addressed as a space to find God or for God to see us, without limits of human language or concept. Also, the proposition "God is not—" negates any attributes and emphasizes being not only, not enough, or more than the enunciated. For example, the proposition "God is *not* strong" indicates that God's attributes are not limited to being strong. The negation holds non-dualistic notions because this proposition embraces God as not always being strong and, in this way, suggests alternative ways of understanding God.

However, even in the *via negativa*, we cannot avoid the importance of the articulation of God, which is grounded in language. Instead, negative theology challenges a systematic speculation, which stands on language and is called the logocentric nature. Remarkably, the Logos has also taken a superior position in the Bible. The Prologue of John's Gospel, the Logos Hymn, reads: In the beginning was the Word, and the Word was with God, and the Word was God (John 1:1 NRSV, used throughout). Thus, escaping the notion that God dwells in language is difficult. As long as humans are destined to exist as beings of language, theology will remain limited to language.

Then, the questions that arise from our twenty-first-century global world context are: in which language does God reside, and what about the subaltern, who cannot speak or articulate?[4] In postcolonial discourse, we critique God's language or theology, which might be summarized as follows: God's language is often equivalent to Western language, and logic's consequences are not immune to the West's power or domination over postcolonial subjects, including many immigrants and exiles. Then, as an alternative way to understand God, the negative way can express the human experience of God.

Expressions of the *Via Negativa*

The legacy of the mystic journey is that God manifests just when the seeker realizes one's confinement of language. In the history of Christian spirituality, the *via negativa* was articulated by early Church Fathers, such as Pseudo Dionysus and Gregory of Nyssa, and the awareness of the entrapment in language became the landmark of the transition toward the mystical union. This approach can be helpful for immigrants who

---

3. Weil, *Love in the Void*, 76.
4. Spivak, "Can the Subaltern Speak?," 28.

often struggle to find identity and understand God within an unfamiliar language, which forces them to be the other.

Postcolonial feminist Catholic thinkers emphasize how language becomes a marker to reveal their dislocation experiences and their existence on the margin. The Korean writer Theresa Hak Kyung Cha, in her book *Dictee*, writes on language, expressing the painful process of being the other in the US. She writes:

> Swallow. Deep. Deeper.
> Swallow. Again, even more.
> Just until there would be no more organ
> Organ no more.
> Cries.
>
> Little at a time. The commas. The periods.
> The pauses.
> Before and after. Throughout. All advent.
> All following.
> Sentences.
> Paragraphs, Silent. A little nearer. Nearer
> Pages and pages
>
> In movement
> Line after
> Line void to the left to the right, void the
> Words the silences.
>
> I hear the signs. Remnants. Missing.
> The mute signs are never the same.
> Absent.[5]

In this poem, we find that the Symbolic world, represented by language, forces her to be silent and absent.

Similarly, the Chicana feminist Gloria Anzaldúa, in her seminal work *Borderlands/La Frontera: The New Mestiza*, explains the painful experiences of those who deal with different languages, often dissonant and dissociated.[6] In this context, language functions as an apparatus of oppression, a source of inferiority, and a deep cause of emotional pain for non-Westerners who reside in the US.

---

5. Cha, *Dictee*, 69.

6. Anzaldúa, *Borderlands*, 100.

Both women seek alternative ways of proclaiming one authentic voice through poetry, film, photography, and dance. Then, how can subjects—such as immigrants, exiles, and refugees—who reside in foreign lands comprehend and understand their faith and God? Here, we appropriate the concept of the Real, negotiating language's oppressive power.

THE REAL

From his concept of the Real, Lacan equates God's attributes with impossibility. He addresses the human psyche as composed of three domains: the Imaginary, the Symbolic, and the Real.[7] Lacan explains that they are all interrelated platforms that construct human subjectivity in conjunction with the human relationship with God.

Moments that the Symbolic does not Operate

Briefly, the Imaginary indicates the domain of the ego, where identity is constructed in the mirror stage of an infant.[8] The Symbolic, linked to the system of language, functions as the apparatus of meaning-making on the conscious level. The language system or grammar heavily impacts the human psyche. For Lacan, the most dominant order in which human subjectivity is composed on the surface level is the Symbolic domain.

A human subject is located and constituted at networked signifiers and, in that sense, the subject passively remains an effect of language, rather than a cause. Lacan explains that "symbols, in fact, envelop the life of a man in a network so total that they join together, even before he comes into the world, where are going to engender him."[9] Thus, the discourse of God, through which we are supposed to gain knowledge of God, including the interpretation of the experience of God, depends on the Symbolic order.

The Real, unlike our conventional conception of the objective and universal, resists any notion of representation and rejects anything symbolized through language. The Real stands within an incomplete Symbolic world of language, charged with the Imaginary. Furthermore, the two orders of the Symbolic and the Real remain interconnected, so that the

---

7. Lacan, *On Feminine Sexuality*, 133.

8. Lacan, *Language of the Self,* 42.

9. Loos, "Symbolic, Real, Imaginary."

Real still depends on—and is expressed by—Symbolic language. Thus, the Real cannot be defined within spoken or written language, yet it remains in the spoken language. Lacan's notion of God as the Real indicates that God exists beyond language, yet simultaneously exists in language. It stresses the interstitial nature of being in-between as a dialectical movement or process.

Experience of the Real of God as an Ongoing Process

Then, in the Real and in the apophatic way, there is no ultimate or given answer for subjects in search of the meaning of God's experience. In this enterprise, understanding and appropriating God's experience remains ongoing. When we believe we have grasped the truth while speaking language, another question exerts itself into a more profound, new, and yet unknown level.

We find echoes of this in the wisdom of Taoism and Buddhism. In *Tao Te Ching*, "TAO called TAO is not TAO, Names can name no lasting name."[10] If we can speak or articulate the Tao, the spoken one is not the Tao as a whole. Similarly, in the *Ten Ox-Herding Paintings* in Zen Buddhism, a seeker sees a trace of truth, leading the soul only onto the next level of the journey, not to a destiny.

Suppose we understand a trace or mark as a symbol or a visible sign as a lure to go deeper and unite with the truth. In that case, we also recognize that the seeker, in the end, encounters Emptiness or stands in front of the mystery of Nothingness. In the spiritual journey, however, the written mark or visual sign is necessary. Lacan emphasizes the speaking subject with an ontological lack that repeats through appearances and disappearances.

At a certain point, seekers realize that God stands beyond our comprehension or knowledge, although they cannot deny the language; at this point, we call God the Real of God. The Real of God operates as a disappearance rather than an appearance, vanishing at the moment we start speaking about it. Lacan emphasizes how often his analysands stutter or become silent at the moment when encountering the Real. In the literature of religion and mysticism, we call this moment Nothingness or Emptiness.

10. Lao-Tzu, *Tao Te Ching*, 1.

Intersectionality Between Apophatic and Cataphatic God

It is essential to admit that the apophatic and cataphatic ways of comprehending God cannot be separate. When the cataphatic approach goes to the extreme, it reaches the point of an apophatic understanding of God. The cataphatic thought, which defines God in all absolute attributes, reaches a point of exhaustion, as Lacan says, and "God doesn't believe in God."[11] This phrase emphasizes God's boundless depth, hitting the edge of negative theology. Lacan uses this expression to describe the existence of the unconscious, "There is a knowledge which is impossible to attribute to a subject who would preside order and harmony. God doesn't believe in God, which is the same thing as saying: there is unconscious."[12]

The one using a definite range of reasoning cannot reach a precise understanding of God.[13] All knowledge of God is only an approximation and temporary. Lacan praises stupidity, imbecility, and dupery to describe the Real, illuminating those who stay only in the Symbolic order or inscribed knowledge.

Lacan, in the *RSI*, emphasizes the impossibility of locating the Real of the God within the confinement of Symbolic language:

> This dimension is introduced by this something that the tongue, and not just any one, . . . which we for sure do not know whether it exists, since it is the knowledge supposed by the Real. This knowledge of God, it is certain that it *ek-sists*. . . . So then, there is something a little bit striking in seeing that the tongue suspected of being the most stupid one is precisely the one that has forged this term *intelligere*, to read between the lines, namely, elsewhere than the way in which the Symbolic is written.[14]

He emphasizes that words create meaning-effects, a process easily trapped into imbecility that bears witness to all the systems of theology and spirituality. Nevertheless, he stresses that language is necessary: without language, not even the slightest suspicion could emerge.

When the seeker realizes one's stupidity, the person will begin to negate all given knowledge. John's Gospel shows a series of characters who manifest imbecility and stupidity, failing to know the Sign (*Semeia*) or recognize the Word, who stands beyond the Symbolic order. Many

11. Lacan, *Non Dupes Errant*, 4.
12. Lacan, *Non Dupes Errant*, 4.
13. Nicolas of Cusa, *On Learned Ignorance*, 46.
14. Lacan, *RSI*, 9.

scholars of John's Gospel emphasize this literary style as irony.[15] The narrative of the Fourth Gospel, which is full of the Symbolic, shows glimpses of the Real of God by stressing the characters' misunderstanding and stupidity. Perhaps all literary styles, such as the Symbolic order, employ stupid characters to manifest the Real of God. For example, in chapter 3, Nicodemus reveals his stupidity due to a pursuit of the Symbolic order. The negating process becomes the central way to approach the Real of God, indicating an impossibility in reaching full knowledge.

THE REAL OF GOD AS A DIALECTICAL PROCESS

A soul experiences a process to reach a knowledge of God, which is often equivalent to being in union with God. Here, the ultimate concern is whether or not we can be in union with God. In the tradition of dialectical discourse, the leading philosophers are Theodor W. Adorno and Georg Friedrich Hegel. For Adorno, the dialectical process could be negative; a soul never reaches full knowledge. On the other hand, for Hegel, believing that what comes out of dialectics is greater than the sum of its parts means that the process eventually brings a full completion of knowledge. For him, the subject's relationship to the Real of God reaches a level of transcendence where individuality, particularity, and universality collide at absolute consciousness.[16]

Negative Dialectic

Negative dialectics, which emphasize impossibility in completion and solution, is closer to Lacan's notion of dilemma, which the speaking subject encounters while approaching God. The human subject mainly uses the symbolic platform, albeit in an imaginary fashion, to form meaning and totalize meaning to reach the Real of God. However, more importantly, the same subject faces the impossibility of fully enunciating God.

Theodor Adorno, a German philosopher, emphasizes the notion of the seeker's unknowability, whose speculation results in the negative conclusion that one cannot reach the fullness of knowledge. Then, arguably, in terms of the Real of God, human subjects exist only in the endless

15. See Culpepper, *Anatomy of the Fourth Gospel*; Duke, *Irony in the Fourth Gospel*; O'Day, *Revelation in the Fourth Gospel*.

16. Maybee, "Hegel's Dialectic."

process or movement of dialectics to reach God and truth. Along the lines of Adorno's dialectic process, the Real of God can exist within Symbolic language. Still, speech or narrative always has a missing part due to the limits of language. Lacan describes this lack by employing the mathematical language of minus one (-1).[17] The speaking subject is the minus one subject, as the subject barred ($) from the truth, wherein the subject always seeks to be the plus one $(+1)$ subject by filling the gap through speech. With negative dialectics, we reach the limits of knowledge within speech. According to the negative way, this limit is an impetus for the soul to go beyond and achieve the transcendence of God, who is beyond knowledge and speech.

For Lacan, the completion of addressing God is an impossibility, which indicates the impossibility of totalizing and identifying with God. The subject always misses or lacks the moment of completion. The subject is either too early, assuming this completion is in the world of the Imaginary, or too late, missing the completion in the incomplete world of the Symbolic.

Knowing of Encountering the Real of the God

How does the human subject know when it encounters the Real of God? Lacan elaborates on the epistemology of the encounter: the subject is uncertain about the cogito. For Lacan, the cogito is the imaginary ego, equivalent to Eckhart's possessive self. Lacan explains that the ego represents a string of consciousness and perceptual processes, giving it the illusion of self-sufficiency and autonomy.

René Descartes, who developed the theory of the cogito, explains that authenticity starts by questioning all levels of thinking about realities. The premise is to imagine what one would have to accept. He asks that we imagine "nothing at all in the world: no sky, no earth, no minds or bodies,"[18] concluding that all that remains is God and us. During Descartes's doubtful speculative journey, nothing remains except for the subject, thinking and doubting. The subject continues to remind the self that "I am doubting" under the assumption that nothing exists. Then, all that I know is that I am thinking about this doubt, and my being is contingent upon this kind of thinking: "I think, therefore I am."

17. Lacan, "Logical Time," 173.
18. Eckhart, *Sermons and Treatises*, 131.

For Lacan, arguably, the subject starts with this famous phrase of Descartes to describe the journey to the Real of God. Again, the cogito signifies the possessive self, speaking as such: I possess, therefore I am. However, for Lacan, even the phrase's subject of "I" does not exist. The Lacanian subject is a no-thing, a lacking subject, having lost its existence in the place of the Other. Nevertheless, the subject of "I" comes from the Other and possessiveness. Lacan views the Other, which lies at the locus of the Symbolic world, as a barred O that remains incomplete, while Eckhart views possessiveness as an impediment for the soul to be with God.

For Lacan, the Other, or possessiveness, represents all kinds of individuals, the objects they desire, their relationships, and their socio-economic and cultural environments. This Symbolic world exists before birth and it constructs, represents, and speaks for us, shaping our desires, speculations, and identities. In some of his most famous quotes, Lacan describes this dilemma of the subject of "I," wherein the subject does not speak but is spoken, or that the subject's desire is the desire of the Other. For these reasons, the subject exists as a split of the subject or a non-existent subject, represented as a subject barred ($). This subject barred does not have access to the truth of existence because it is outside of its being. Lacan even turns Descartes's statement upside down, from "I think, therefore I am" to "I think; therefore, I am not." The full quote is: "I think where I am not, therefore I am where I do not think."[19]

Thinking and being as juxtaposed to each other also manifests in Eckhart's teaching on the possessive self (having) vs. the detached self (being). Lacan describes the state of being in terms of impotence and im-possibility. He stresses how thinking, represented by speech, creates the condition of impotence and impossibility.[20] In Lacan's four discourses—the university discourse, the hysteric discourse, the master discourse, and the psychoanalytic discourse—he shows how subjectivity and its ability to reach knowledge are impossible. Knowledge and truth concerning the self are paranoiac in the university discourse, hysteric and manic in the hysteric discourse, and oppressed in the master discourse.

One must start with a specific process for the subject to access truth and its unconscious desire and to encounter the Real of God. Lacan's psychoanalytic approach is similar to Meister Eckhart's spiritual journey, and we can apply this notion to spiritual direction. Eckhart's spiritual journey

---

19. Lacan, *Écrits*, 166.

20. Lacan introduced the Four Discourses at Seminar XVII, *L'envres, On the Other Side of Psychoanalysis*. This seminar has not yet been published in English.

is a contemplative path, emphasizing a journey to the divine through wordless prayer and silence.[21] Contemplation signifies a contemplative life and living; it is an action of beholding, a way of wondering, meditating, and ascending. The contemplation in action includes actively emptying one's mind of thinking, sensations, will, and passion.

Eckhart teaches that the emptying practice gives the seeker freedom to see God amid a mundane life. In this sense, for Eckhart, the character of Martha is a more progressed soul than Mary, who sits in front of Jesus and prays.[22] Although Lacan does not give spiritual exercises, his psychoanalytic approach begins with the assumption that the subject is the subject of unconsciousness and is constituted by the Other, and that the subject can only exist as a being through observing one's experiences in relation to others.

APPLICATION TO SPIRITUAL DIRECTION

In today's society, many seekers are unfamiliar with their faith language or theological vocabulary. Instead, they remain in their eclectic collection of words and their experiences. Furthermore, those who experience dislocation as immigrants feel lost in language. Nevertheless, they address their experiences, and, as such, the spiritual directors, who fully understand the limits of language, hold their directees to enable the hatching of new expressions that articulate their experience.

Impossibility

In spiritual direction, we experience two levels of impossibility—first, the impossibility of being one with the director. When a seeker comes to a session assuming that the spiritual director knows the solution to one's concern, the seeker desires to be one with the director. This desire emerges in the form of transference love, perceiving the analyst as "the subject supposed to know."[23] Through their sessions, the spiritual director must play the role of a "dummy," not giving hasty answers or directions. The spiritual director must help the directees realize that they cannot be one with the spiritual director.

21. Eckhart, *Essential Sermons*, 31.

22. Eckhart, *Complete Mystical Works*, 89. See also McGinn, "Meister Eckhart."

23. Chavoshian and Park, "Listening Not in Spiritual Direction," 5–12.

The second is the impossibility of articulating one's faith and experience. While the directee will make some progress, the person will realize that it is impossible to articulate one's faith experience. As a result, they will confront the lack of existing in themselves and the impossibility of reaching the Real of God through speech.[24] If the seeker struggles with language, it may help her understand the impossibility in a more critical way.

As the spiritual direction proceeds, the seeker transitions from an Imaginary to a Symbolic speech. Imaginary speech consists of the subjective presentation of self and her relation to God. In contrast, Symbolic speech involves the objective self-realization that the Other constructs her narrative of God. In the imaginary presentation, there is no objective clue.

Moreover, by realizing the nature of the Real, one will understand that the Other, including her director and certain Church's teachings, also has a lack or hole and does not necessarily have all the solutions for her problems or concerns. The lack includes dissonance among narratives. More importantly, the person will notice that one's narrative is a borrowed or implanted one, indoctrinated rather than authentic. The seeker will understand that a generalized explanation of God does not fit in with her feelings or situation. In other words, she will become aware that her desire for God is a desire of the Other.

For the directee, it will be essential to articulate her desire for God and her experiences. She will realize that, up to that point, she had spoken about God, but then she will describe her genuine desire and relationship with God. To make this happen, she must be able to develop her own analytical or meditative space, which Lacan calls the *analytical third*, giving great responsibility (as a listener) to the spiritual director.

The Spiritual Director's Position

From Lacan's perspective, there are three critical points for the spiritual director. First, a spiritual director should be an active listener by deferring answers and inviting her to speak more by saying, "Che vuoi (say more)," or "What do you want to say?" We often experience that analysands talk fast when they repeat their faith narratives. For example, perhaps a directee speaks slowly about her direct experience, yet when she mentions a dogma such as, "I know God helps me when I pray,"

24. Lacan, *Sinthome*, 5–8.

she babbles. When she articulates her feelings of God, it may take time, and she could reveal her embarrassment and frustration through body language and facial expressions.

When the directee begins her speech, it is metonymy, meaning a horizontal speech response with free association. Metonymy stands in opposition to metaphor, a vertical and causal speech response as a characteristic of discourse. Metonymy is a literary apparatus that conveys meaning through the principle of contiguity, which rearranges words of substitution or adjuncts for a specific attribute or meaning. The directee often returns to the metaphoric way of speech to escape the discomfort of facing feelings.

In the environment of metonymy, the spiritual director opens a space for the directee. For example, the director can say, " You can talk about everything and anything emerging from your heart." In the way of metonymy, the narrative is not a linear or logical speech but rather a circular or poetic narrative, which creates a space to ponder and deepen one's process. In feminist writings, space and poetic writing have been encouraged to give repressed women voices.[25]

Second, the spiritual director should refrain from responding to the demands caused by the transference love of the directee. In particular cultures, especially in Asia, people learn to be obedient and listen to elders and authority figures. Those directees may be unwilling to speak and show deep satisfaction when the director gives advice. Thus, the director's role is to invite the seeker to transfer her demand for a quick answer to her inner subject.

If the spiritual director responds to the directee's demand for an answer, it would be an ego responding to another ego. The ego-to-ego response constitutes an imaginary response of one person to another. We call the director's response to the directee's demand the countertransference. It is crucial to remember that a spiritual director might carry a need to be needed. Only in desire can one encounter the Real of God. Transference love implies that the directee sees the spiritual director as an *objet petit a* (an object of love and desire) and views the spiritual director as God-like or a medium to God. At this juncture, the spiritual director is a space holder for the directee's desire, which should transfer to a desire for God and, more importantly, in that space, the directee should name her own desire.

25. Cixous, "Laugh of the Medusa," 875–76.

The analytical third, the new narrative based on the directee's desire, will manifest when her speech shifts from an "empty speech" to a "full speech," something which does not demand an answer. Instead, she will no longer identify with the spiritual director when formulating her questions and answers. This occurs when the analyst does not operate as an *objet petit a*. The directee will rely on her desire to search for God in this mature phase. She is not written by the desire of the Other, but rather, she is the author of her desire. She is not a spoken subject but is a speaking subject instead.

Third, spiritual directors can guide the seeker *via negativa*, where the directee does not have to try to fully understand God, the Mystery. There will always be an impasse in the seeking process, and directors should help directees reshape or rearticulate their desires in their search for the infinite God, the Real of God. The seeker's desire does not lie in contingency but in boundlessness.

The directee will feel at ease, and her symptoms of anxiety and depression—and even perhaps insomnia—could disappear because she will have moved from symptom to *sinthome*. *Sinthome* is a neologism used by Lacan as a homophony for saint homme (holy man or Saint Thomas), insinuating that we should be like Saint Thomas,[26] who was a holy human being. A symptom is an isolated and alienated part of the self, which appears as a form of complaint. *Sinthome* signifies a part of the self, integrated (symptom integration) through the acceptance of the self, where one can be at ease and at peace with one's symptom.

In *Seminar XXIII*, Lacan describes James Joyce as a child facing severe trauma due to the absence of parental influences. Lacan explains that later, during adulthood, Joyce had to develop his art of writing as a supplemental ring to the triad of the Symbolic, the Imaginary, and the Real. To avoid psychosis, Joyce added a Fourth ring of *sinthome* to the above-mentioned three rings of the Borromean Knot, to safeguard the function of the Symbolic, the Imaginary, and the Real. For Lacan, Joyce's genius and intense writing style are examples of *sinthome*.[27]

Lacan emphasizes the importance of the symptom as a hinge connecting all three orders of the human psyche. He mentions, "Here Joyce in his writings becomes like Saint homme (holy man: Saint Thomas), by

26. Lacan and Grigg, "Geneva Lecture on the Symptom."

27. Lacan, *Sinthome*, 76–78.

refusing an imaginary solution to his problem, inventing a new way of using language to communicate with the world outside of himself."[28]

In summary, the concept of the Real of God may help understand a seeker's spiritual journey as a process. Many immigrants, or those who live in two different languages simultaneously, experience more difficulty grasping the dissonant messages of culture and faith, especially those whose language leads them to an impasse in growth or transformation. By understanding the nature of language, and of the Other, the spiritual director may help the directee understand that her frame of God is given by her family, culture, and the Church, and that her barrier of language is not necessarily her limited condition.

CONCLUSION

An alternative way of approaching negative theology can be the Real of God, who exists in the in-between space of the sayable and the unsayable. The concept of the Real of God helps deepen our daily experiences of God, who exists beyond language, culture, and social norms. In our twenty-first secularized and global century, people still experience God and look for meaning to transform their lives. Especially for those immigrants who live in the West, carrying on their languages and cultures of origin, Lacan's notion of the Real of God can be an apparatus for empowerment. As a spiritual director, listening is the tool to hold those directees, creating a space to accept symptoms that become *sinthome*. In light of the Real of God, spiritual directors can hold seekers so that they can figure out their notion or perspective of God, and create spaces for directees to renew and rearticulate their narratives of God.

28. Lacan, *Sinthome*, 15.

5

A Conversation about Anxiety among the Prison Population in Peru

JUNG EUN SOPHIA PARK AND MIYOUNG SUNG

THIS CONVERSATION BETWEEN SOPHIA Park and Miyoung Sung occurred on July 5, 2020, at a Lacan Conference held in Seoul, South Korea.
Sophia Park transcribed the conversation.

Sophia: During the Covid-19 pandemic, the world faced various
unexpected symptoms and people suffered from anxiety and alienation.
We experienced shutdowns of public places such as schools, stores, and
parks, and this situation caused more anxiety. However, there are other
places where we have not paid much attention and perhaps those who
dwell in those places suffer even more from anxiety. Let me introduce
Miyoung Sung. Could you explain your ministry?

Miyoung: I am a Maryknoll Missionary sister and I worked as a
social worker and expressive art therapist in a men's prison in Lima, Peru
from 2016–2019. My work site was Lurigancho Prison, a place that is
well-known as one of the most dangerous prisons in the world. The facility was built for three thousand inmates, but there are over ten thousand
inmates as of 2020. It is severely overpopulated.

The correctional facility system in Peru is distinct in that each prisoner has to provide what they need, including food, clothing, supplies, and their own bed. Furthermore, they need to protect themselves from possible violence, which happens daily on all levels, whether physical, emotional, or mental. Obviously, the prison operates as a facitlity to control and discipline prisoners with low expenditure in Lurigancho, Peru.

In my experience, all prisoners struggle and suffer to survive (*survivre*) daily. The purpose of the prison here is to put those criminals together and separate them from society. They assume that innocent citizens should and can be safe from criminals; the prison space is an alienated yet open space, with multiple gazes.

Sophia: Prison is a very unique space. However, we know that the prison system is deeply related to social justice and power. In the US, the most incarcerated population is African American and Latino,[1] and the prison system has become a very crucial place to examine. You mentioned that they must provide themselves with all their own supplies, including beds, and they need to protect themselves there too. That sounds very scary. What happens to the prisoner when he arrives there?

Miyoung: After a prisoner is convicted in court by the judge, he is sent directly to a prison. When they arrive at the prison, the first thing they encounter is the multitude of eyes looking at them from all directions. Hundreds of gazes pour upon them as they walk through the long line of prison wards. Of course, they can see other people too, but what they see depends on someone's eyes looking at them. Also, the new prisoner sees only one place at one time, but he is seen from all sides.

Sophia: Your description reminds me of Lacan's concept of the gaze, "I see only from one point but in my existence I am looked at from all sides."[2] Could you explain further?

Miyoung: Lacan explains the subject's psychosexual development through the mirror stage. According to him, the subject gains an identity through identifying with the image, which is pointed out by the Other (Mother), as the infant who stands in front of the mirror.[3] Prison is a space where the subject is surrounded by the gaze of others. The new inmate must be recognized by the others, in order to exist.

As seen in Lacan's story of the three prisoners, each learns his own color, which is on his back and which he himself cannot see, only by

1. See Alexandre, *New Jim Crow.*
2. Lacan, *Four Fundamental Concepts,* 72.
3. Felluga, "Modules on Lacan."

observing the actions of others. This paradox of the prisoner reveals a fundamental human nature, which is interpersonal. Lacan explicates that: (1) A man knows what is not a man; (2) Men recognize themselves among themselves as men; and (3) I declare myself to be a man for fear of being convinced by men that I am not a man.[4] In this way, the subject is constituted post-moment (afterward) through the moment of a gaze, the moment of understanding, and the moment of conclusion, through multiple imaginings, inferences, and pauses, and is constituted by relationships with others. It is not that I do exist and there is the Other, but because there is the Other, I exist.

Prisoners cannot escape from the gaze of others, even while staying in the cell, because prisons are supposed to exist for surveillance and punishment. There are guard posts everywhere, and so are the eyes of the guards. More horribly, there are spies among the same prisoners who monitor and report each other's words and actions. Then, the prisoner who is reported as violating the rules has to stand and self-criticize in public while others are eating lunch. All the while, he has no idea who reported him.

Sophia: Clearly, that whole environment would cause deep anxiety for a prisoner. The unknowable nature of this situation sounds scary. Michael Foucault and many other social philosophers critiqued the modern world's prison system and particularly internalized surveillance. How do you analyze this environment?

Miyoung: In my ministry at the prison, I had to critique the meaning of control and surveillance in the context of prisons. The modern prison system is based on the desire to watch over the prisoners. The first model was called the Panopticon, which was designed by Jeremy Bentham in the eighteenth century. This prison system signifies a controlled system in which an officer, who has authority and power, watches over all the prisoners. This model emphasizes external surveillance.

However, I believe the correctional system in Lima does not necessarily focus on external surveillance, but more on the internal. The panopticism is a term introduced by the French philosopher Michel Foucault to indicate a kind of internal surveillance.[5] In panopticism, the watcher ceases to be external to the watched. Rather than external actions, the gaze of the watcher is internalized to such an extent, that each prisoner

4. Lacan, "Logical Time," 174.
5. Foucault, "Panopticism," 208.

(economic agent/worker) becomes his/her own guard.[6] This invisible gaze, which does not know when and where it is coming from, and the gaze that does not know what it wants from them, make the prisoners anxious. The subject does not know what kind of object he is to the other, and constantly asks if he can survive the other's gaze and standards, and so he is anxious. In an environment where there is no private time or space for them to be who they are, inmates are always physically tense and mentally paranoid.

In Lurigancho Prison, even the bathrooms have no doors or walls, and rules require the prisoners to walk as a group, at least as a pair, and never alone, at all times. Then, prisoners try to get rid of their anxiety by acting like others and identifying with different groups. They internalize the rules and laws of the groups, and become their own watcher. Ironically, the more they are seen, the more they lose the sense of how they look. Going back again to Lacan's paradox of the prisoner, the prisoners seem to transcend the level of intersubjective mode. Rather they create their identity by consolidating with given social groups in the prison.[7]

In the prison setting, the more they are recognized by others, the more they are alienated from who they are. They put on various masks, based on what others seem to want from them, mostly masks of happy faces. However, no one actually knows what the others desire for each prisoner, and that causes a great deal of anxiety. The happy faces are proof that authority is functioning well in the group. Those who break rules or who are dissatisfied will be punished. The group's hatred and punishment lies in the Other and is constituted by the relationship with others. It is not that I do exist and I have existed, but rather because there is the Other, I exist.

This invisible gaze, the gaze that does not know when or where it comes from, and the gaze that does not know what it wants from them, make prisoners anxious. The subject does not know what kind of object he resembles to the Other (*Que me veut-il?*),[8] and constantly asks if he could survive through the Other's gaze and standards; it makes him more anxious. In an environment where there is no private time or space for them to be who they are, inmates are always physically tense and mentally paranoid. It is said that they are punished for breaking the group's order

---

6. Foucault, *Discipline and Punishment*, 197–99.
7. Hook, "Towards a Lacanian Group Psychology," 115–32.
8. Lacan, *Anxiety*, 4.

or unity, but in fact, their fear around keeping alive serves to solidify the group's order and unity.

Sophia: Is there an inner power structure or power agency besides the correction officers?

Miyoung: There are about five hundred prisoners in each prison ward, run by a representative and below him, a discipline team who are chosen from the inmates and by the inmates. Most of them are serving long sentences, are older, and have corrupt relationships with the security guards. It creates lots of problems, in terms of acceptance and rejection.

When the existence of this representative disappears, the illusion of power that lies beyond what was hidden by this figure is revealed. Most prisoners obey the figure without knowing what kind of power he has. In fact, his power is unsubstantial. Without prisoners obeying him, his power doesn't work or even exist. The moment the hidden side of a power that is based on oppression and violence is revealed, the power is shaken and there is a crack in the order. So when this figure disappears, the director quickly finds another authority and power figure.

Sophia: Your explanation reminds me of the discourse of the slave paradox suggested by Lacan, which shows the inter-subjective (*inter-essence*) nature of human subjects.[9] Also, I am thinking of the master discourse, which emphasizes that the master really needs the slave to keep his position, not vice versa. Now then, let us focus more on the anxiety that each prisoner experiences. What is the basic dynamic of anxiety there?

Miyoung: Anxiety is a fundamental human condition. However, in the prison that I served, there is obvious fear that each prisoner might be chosen as a victim. In order to not be chosen, individual subjects hide their own desires, if they have any, and try to desire the desires of others—the desire of the director or the desire of the group. In a closed system such as a prison, Lacan's theory of desire states that one desires the desire of the Other to be manifest in a visible way. Of course, in this case, the Other can signify the whole system of surveillance and control.[10] But at the same time, anyone who can do so possesses the power to kill him. Even though he believes that he can make an effort to think and act as others want, he does not know whether his performance will work. This uncertainty and unknown causes him great anxiety.

9. Lacan, *Écrits*, 169.
10. Lacan, *Identification*, 152.

For prisoners, it is a luxury to find one's true self by engaging anxiety, more specifically, by facing the Real. Rather, they try to repress anxiety by becoming a person like others who functions as the object of the Other's desire and, more importantly, by identifying with the group. However, they do not know exactly who is the Other is in the prison. Therefore, the more they attempt to be the object of desire for somebody, the more they feel anxiety.

Sophia: Then, prison is a space where prisoners are watched by the whole correctional system. Did you sense a great level of anxiety from being seen, but not knowing who the exact watcher is? And could you explain your art therapy work?

Miyoung: Yes, absolutely. Often, I feel they are spoken to, rather than speaking; they are seen, rather than seeing. When I walk into the prison, I feel anxiety too. I know I am being seen by many men, prisoners, correction officers, and many invisible people. Through the artworks they create, I can deeply sense their struggle against the anxiety and their fears of becoming a victim. It is not rare for a prisoner to receive a lynching from unknown terrorists and sometimes, there are missing people who later found dead and buried on the grounds. When I go there, I try to create a safe space where they can express themselves.

In my expressive art therapy group sessions, I guide prisoners to draw self-portraits and suggest that they title each one. Often, the title implies the prisoner's inner or outer self. This first self-portrait by Christian is titled "I am fine, I am OK, and I am happy." He was so overly happy that day, that I almost forgot we were in a prison.

Usually, I begin the session by asking, "How are you?" Most of them give the exact same answer without hesitation, "I am OK," "I am happy," "I am fine," or "I am grateful." Then I point to their artwork and change the question from "How are you?" to "How is he?" This way, I change the subject from the first-person pronoun to the third-person, the subject has become the object in his artwork. In other words, they can distance themselves. In this space, they can explore their repressed feelings and, perhaps, even themselves.

Mostly when I ask, "How is he?" they pause, hesitate, and seem embarrassed. Then silence occurs. Prisoners do not talk about themselves. Instead, they talk about what others want them to be, although they do not know what that is. Then, who is the image in the self-portrait? Is it me, is it him, or is it some other person, or some other thing? That confusion, alienation, and lack of knowledge all cause anxiety.

Christian says confidently and proudly, "I'm happy." On his picture, I cover the smiling mouth and eyebrows and find the *eyes* appear all of sudden. In his drawing or the image of him, I try to look into the eyes, and find they are blank; there are no eyeballs. I almost feel that through the empty eyes, I can see eyes looking at me. The image of the smiling mouth disappears when I block the mouth area, and a gaze appears in the empty space. And forsaking him, I sense the Real, the horror of unknowability is revealed through his smiling self. In fact, when I cover the mouth and eyebrows, I am suddenly so terrified I have softened my reaction.

Picture 1. I Am Fine, I Am OK, and I Am Happy

Sophia: Your analysis is remarkable. When the empty eyes are revealed, they show what the Real is for him and what horrors he experiences. I believe your action of covering those parts of the face helps Christian see the horror of the Real in a short moment. He can find his own coping mechanism and help to touch his own repressed self. What is the other example of your art therapy?

Miyoung: The other case is Jose, thirty two years old, and his self-portrait titled "Seven-Year-Old Jose." He shared about one day from his childhood memory which was traumatic. In the expressive art therapy session, he had an outlet to express his memory. His statement was very fragmented and emotional, like anyone would be talking about trauma. Summarizing what he said, one day when he was seven, he observed his violent father beat his mother and stab her to death. Jose, who was there, was injured. The mother, who had collapsed on the floor and was dying, could only move her eyes, and she looked at her young son with those eyes. The scar on his face, and his mother's eyes, sometimes shook the order of the Symbolic world of Jose, a silent and sincere member of the discipline team.

All of sudden, anxiety came with the haunted eyes of his mother, which he did not know how to handle. Interestingly, he seems to visualize his terrified anxiety through his mother. There is love for the mother who belonged to the stepfather, about which he could not do anything, except to cry a lot. At this level, the Oedipus complex seems to impose on him to be like his father, who was violent and even cruel. But at the same time, he is like his mother, who was soft and vulnerable.

Picture 2. Seven-Year-Old Jose

As an art therapist, I found that there was a gap between the two personalities of Jose. One is the faithful and sincere leader of the group, and the other is the violent criminal, like his father. And in that gap or in-between, there is the young Jose, I believe. To stay in that gap, to see that young Jose, to meet the Real without a safety net in prison makes Jose more vulnerable, and yet dangerous. He decided not to come to my sessions anymore, and I supported his decision.

Sophia: It must have been very challenging. Your analysis reminds me of Lacan's explanation of identification in lieu of relationship with the

Other on the imaginary plane, in which i(e), moves toward the construction of ego, moi.[11] In this case, the ego is linked to a small "i," embodying a rival "i" who could be himself or some other figure.

I see scars on his face and neck. I wonder how the scars look to others and what messages they convey. Perhaps it could function to show others that he is strong, even though the scars internally signify his trauma. What is the next drawing?

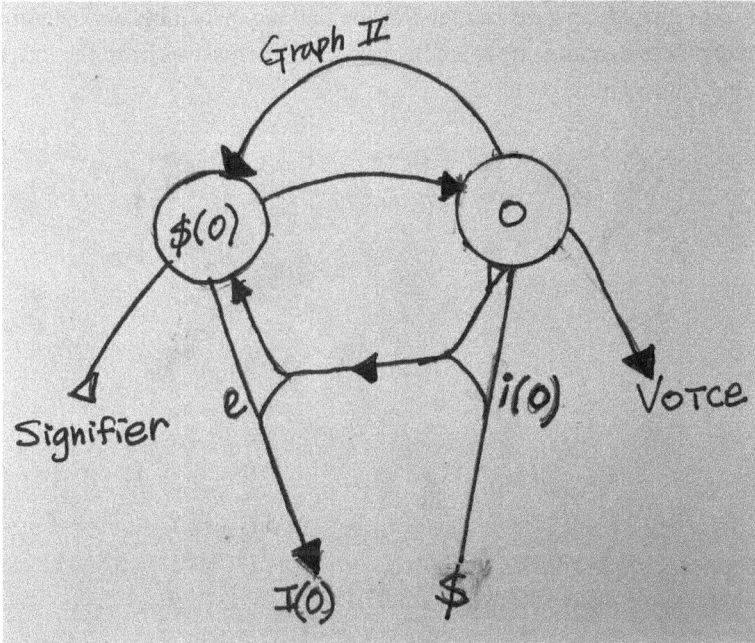

Figure 1. Ego Formation[12]

Miyoung: The self-portrait drawings with the transgender group signify a deep sense of insecurity and anxiety. They identify themselves as female and *look* feminine. They are put in men's prisons since they are registered and identified as male by others. I ask them to draw the entire body, not just the face. Often, they paint the lips and nails colorfully, exaggerating the chest as large. None of them draw a penis, even though

11. Lacan, *Desire and Its Interpretation*, 36.

12. Lacan developed his graph of desire in four stages. The graphs and the theory behind it can be found in the 1960 essay "The Subversion of the Subject and the Dialectic of Desire in the Freudian Unconscious" (Lacan, *Écrits*, 45). Image retrieved from "Lacanian Graph of Desire."

they have not had surgery yet to physically remove the penis. Perhaps they do not have one, psychologically. They see in order to not see—to not see the penis, and to see colorful lips and nails, and to imagine big breasts. They are in the position of not seeing. The moment someone draws a penis, an empty space appears where it was filled with a loud feminine image. The moment one looks at the void, a gaze arises and the Real beyond it appears. Anxiety comes from the gap between the image and the Real. They could not stay long with that Real which causes anxiety. They avoid the gaze and the Real by making dirty jokes and laughing loudly. They become safe again by distancing themselves from the idea of being a woman.

Picture 3. Burning in the Fire of Hell

The last painting was titled "Burning in the Fire of the Hell." It was drawn by Luis, who was very gentle and quiet. He spoke softly and tried to show himself as a woman in a subtle way, throughout the conversation. It is not obvious, yet the figure's gentleness and small earrings, as well as the very delicate smile, make the look very feminine. In the prisons, there are many cases of abuse against homosexual or feminine men.

In this drawing, however, I found that the title does not match with the figure. The soft orange color is very ambiguous. On the one hand, it is a very gentle and feminine color, but on the other hand, it is the color of the tormenting fires of hell. The flames of hell are the same color as the face. Those sentenced to be criminals by a judge are the same ones sentenced by God, for their lost and corrupted souls. In Christianity, God is presented as a blank "I am whom I." However, for inmates, God is limited in meaning to the extent that it is explained by law, the order of the group, and the dominant culture. In Luis's mind, because of his sexual sins, God (Jesus Christ) died, wearing a crown of thorns. Often, prisoners keep images of a bleeding Jesus or suffering Mary. Their self-portraits cannot show the Real, or the Imaginary. Inmates see themselves through the eyes of this God, the Other.

Sophia: The image of God as representing the law and the dominant Christian culture, which rejects and condemns homosexuals and transgender persons, must make them feel more excluded, condemned, or alienated. I also sense that the figure in the painting is interested in the earth, but we can only see the face and not the body. God's image seems to influence the spirituality of many inmates, so could you tell me about the prison system and ministry?

Miyoung: As the Catholic pastoral team was preparing for a Christmas event, we decided on the theme of "forgiveness." The team is made up of people—priests, nuns, and Catholic ministers—who also desire the desires of the Other. Giving up on persuading them on a different theme, I arranged a masque (a party in which attendances are supposed to wear masks) with the inmates who participate in my sessions. About five hundred inmates sat quietly and patiently waited for the hot chocolate and cake to be served after a long mass of sermons, prayers, and hymns. The moment the *masque* began and the group of people wearing masks appeared, their boredom was broken and anxiety spread in the air.

It is really hard to explain what happened. When an unfamiliar event occurs, the anxiety does not last long. Unable to withstand the anxiety, the performers eventually evade the gaze. They start narrating

one by one, not following my directions to remain silent and to impro-
vise movements. They execute the narration of the Other in repentance
of their sins and in gratitude for being saved by God's forgiving mercy.
They are almost cliché statements, memorized and recited, but the tension and anxiety soon disappear and the group returns to a familiar and
safe world, dominated by the law and order of the Other. God is dead. As
Nietzsche says, we killed God, and we did so paradoxically on the very
day that God was born. So, most of my sessions are records of failures.

However, by chance, if an accidental event occurs in which the subject deviates from the power and the gaze of the Other, the Other's gaze
becomes uncertain and ambiguous, and there develops a gap in the order
of the symbolic world. When this crack or void appears, the gaze is no
longer defended and the alienated subject reveals himself. The gap causes
anxiety, and that anxiety is the place of truth where we meet our own, the
Real, "the uncanny-me."

Sophia: Thank you for sharing your insight on the anxiety of prisoners. Although we have experienced similar situations of quarantine
and surveillance, your experience of prison art therapy provides a deep
understanding of the nature of human anxiety. How then did you close
the session, after the prisoners faced their repressed true image?

Miyoung: In expressive art therapy, we are supposed to close the
session by taking the portrait down from the wall. In general, clients then
face the wall and look at it, gaze at the Real. Looking at the Real is a first
step to finding one's desire. However, in the prison, facing the Real could
be dangerous it because the prisoner might not survive the environment.
Thus, before I begin any session, I decorate the wall with landscapes or
photos of flowers. I then ask them to put their self-portraits onto the
paintings or photos.

After the session, they only see ordinary common oeuvres, which
emphasizes that they do not have to see the Real. The second inmate, Jose
could not continue the art therapy because he was too vulnerable to face
his traumatic childhood. He dropped the class right after his self-portrait.

Sophia: Lacan talks about the role of fantasy as a way to detour from
the Real. I believe it is necessary to take some distance from one's traumatic time for a while. How do the prisoners survive there?

Miyoung: I think many prisoners who deal with the horror of
anxiety create a certain fantasy. Like with the first prisoner, who put on a
mask of happiness. He used the phrase, "I am happy" but his empty eyes
showed that he is not a subject who thinks or acts. In this environment,

each one develops a defense mechanism, and we can call this entering into fantasy.

Sophia: I agree they need to be equipped with their psyche for survival in such an environment. Miyoung, how did you create a space for them to express themselves in your art therapy?

Miyoung: As I mentioned earlier, my sessions seemed to fail almost every time. Nevertheless, I tried to create a safe and comfortable space for each prisoner. There were moments where they faced the uncanny. Yet, I valued that they could feel those repressed feeling and thoughts through their artwork. And at least, in the moment, they could see their less repressed ego. I believe my mission was to create a safe space in which they could find their own humanity.

Sophia: Often, we think the prison system as being analogous to contemporary society. However, your space of ministry was itself the Real, and you walked through the terrain of horror and anxiety with the prisoners. Thank you for sharing about your precious art therapy ministry.

6

Exploring Lacan's Four Discourses
Insights from a Pastor's Wife

Nuri Park

THE DEFINITION OF DISCOURSE in modern linguistic refers to a system of thought, knowledge, or communication that constructs our experience of the world, and involves language, symbols, and practices through which individuals or groups convey meaning, establish norms, and negotiate social reality.[1] Discourse encompasses not only spoken or written language but also broader social practices, institutions, and power dynamics that shape how ideas, identities, and social relations are constructed and understood.

Lacan says what dominates society is the practice of language and he formulated his schemata of the four discourses (the master, the university, the hysteric, and the analyst) through which language exercises both formative and transformative power in human affairs.[2] More precisely, his schemata of the four discourses offer the means, respectively, of understanding four key phenomena: governing, educating, protesting, and revolutionizing, and it is the discourse that every determination of

1. Alisherovna, "Discourse in Modern Linguistics," 1.
2. André, "Otherness of the Body," 107.

the subject depends on.[3] Humans are speaking beings, and speaking requires us to engage with language and its pre-existing discourse:[4] we are participating in a complex interplay of language and culture.

The well-known Lacanian formulae, "the unconscious is structured like a language" and "the unconscious is the discourse of the Other (Autre)"[5] imply that the unconscious is indeed an effect of discourse, emphasizing the idea that our unconscious thoughts, desires, and behaviors are shaped by the symbolic order of language and societal discourse. His formulae designate that the unconscious is not an independent entity but is intertwined with language and social structures, influenced by the messages and meanings conveyed by the Other—the broader societal or cultural context.

This paper is to examine my own dialectical progression, dealing with my identity as pastor's wife, by applying Lacan's four discourses—those of the master, the university, the hysteric, and the analyst. Lacan's perspective posits that these discourses represent both impossibility and impotence, acknowledging the inherent limitations and failures within discourse itself. As I navigate through the complexities of my role, as the pastor's wife in a Christian congregation, I faced the realization that these discourses shape and influence my experiences, interactions, and sense of self. I must admit that applying Lacan's theory to one's own life can indeed raise concerns about oversimplification due to the complexity and fluidity of his ideas. However, despite these concerns, I remain compelled to delve into the application of Lacan's four discourses from the unique perspective of a pastor's wife. While recognizing the potential limitations and nuances involved, I attempt to apply them within my context.

Before embarking on the personal application of Lacan's four discourses to the role of a pastor's wife, it's essential to establish a foundational understanding of locations of four elements in Lacan's discourses.

---

3. Lacan, *Other Side of Psychoanalysis*, 17.

4. Lacan, *Desire and Its Interpretation*, 6.

5. The Other comes from language and the Law that belongs to the Symbolic order while the other from the Mirror Stage as the reflection and projection of the ego exists in the Imaginary realm.

LOCATIONS OF FOUR ELEMENTS IN LACAN'S DISCOURSES

Lacan's four discourses—master, university, hysteric, and analyst—are four potential symbolic bond and social networking. Thy are composed of certain aspects, and it is essential to understand positionality, emphasizing relativeness, not absoluteness. In any discourse, "the agent" occupies a dominant role, initiating the dialogue and holding the master's position. In response, "the other" is called into action by the agent, assuming the subordinate, or slave's, position. This dynamic interaction between the agent and the other produces a specific outcome called "product." Underpinning this entire relationship is "the truth," an unconscious condition that shapes and drives the discourse.

These four elements are depicted in Figure 1. Additionally, it is crucial to understand Lacan's four discourses through the lenses of impossibility and impotence. The concept of impossibility refers to the idea that the discourse initiated by the agent directed toward the other is inherently impossible. This means that true communication or understanding between the agent and the other cannot be fully achieved. On the other hand, impotence relates to the product of this discourse. The product, which arises from the interaction between the agent and the other, is never fully aware of the underlying truth of the discourse. This implies that the product lacks a complete understanding of the unconscious conditions that shape the discourse, thereby highlighting the limitations within the communicative process.[6]

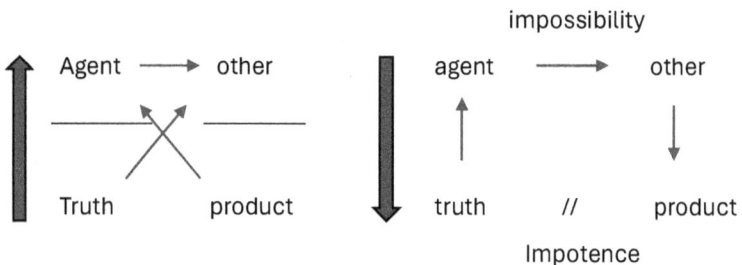

Figure 1. The Structure of the Discourses and the Relations Between All Positions

6. Lacan, *Psychoanalysis Upside Down.*

Each discourse varies according to which element predominates in these positions. If I were to briefly introduce the diagram, "agent," motivated or supported by "truth" addresses "other" to generate "product." (See the arrow from agent to other in Figure 1) The relationship between "agent" and "other" is marked by a "disjunction of impossibility"[7]: the message that the agent sends is never received exactly as intended. "Agent" is influenced by "truth" (see the upward arrow from truth to agent in Figure 1), and "truth" goes to "the other" as well (see the diagonal arrow in Figure 1). This leads to the generation of a "product" (See the downward arrow from other to product in Figure 1). This cycle repeats endlessly, with the product eventually returns to the agent (see the other diagonal arrow in Figure 1). The agent, positioned in the upper left corner, points to the other, although it's an impossibility. Truth sits below the agent, while the product is produced by the other at the bottom right. The relationship between the product and truth reflects a sense of impotence, highlighting the limitations within the discourse.

Four Elements in the Discourse

These four elements manifest as the agent, the other, the product, and the truth, and can be further explained using Lacanian terminology as S1, S2, a, $. In Lacan's theory, these elements form the foundation of discourse and are explained more linguistically to capture their intricate roles and relationships.

- S1: master signifier, values itself empty but an "anchoring point." Freud had already pointed out that emotions attach themselves not to meanings but to signifiers.[8] Lacan reversed the idea of Saussure by prioritizing signifier over signified. Master signifier is repeated in different context, but it has nothing to do with the signified of the master signifier.

- S2: the battery of signifiers, knowledge (*savoir*), know-how. It often refers to the symbolic order, which includes language, culture, and social norms. Knowledge is structured and mediated through language and symbols, shaping our understanding of the world and ourselves. However, Lacan suggests that this knowledge is always

---

7. Verhaeghe, *On Being Normal*, 59.
8. Bailly, *Lacan*, 45.

incomplete and fragmented, never fully capturing the truth of subjective experience.

- a: object petit a, the imaginary cause of desire, or surplus jouissance[9] The object petit a may be seen as a fragment of the Phallus which was lost but cannot be forgotten. The Phallus leaves traces of itself everywhere and these Phallic fragments, the paternal metaphor, can be substituted for others (object petit a).[10] The "object petit a" is a central concept in Lacan's psychoanalytic theory. It represents the unattainable object of desire, the ever elusive "something" that we are always seeking but can never fully obtain. The object is not a tangible item but rather a placeholder for the gap in our desire.[11] It embodies the lack or void that propels us to continue desiring. The object petit a is what keeps the subject in a constant state of seeking and longing, never fully satisfied because the object of desire is fundamentally unattainable. In Lacanian discourse, object petit a and surplus jouissance are interchangeable in the sense that they both describe the driving forces behind human behavior and the perpetual state of incompleteness and seeking.

- $: lacked, divided, and alienated subject by its submission to language and castration. The speaking subject in dependence on the Other is a divided subject: the subject of thought (the conscious) and the subject of being (the unconscious).[12] This subject is shaped and programmed by the grammar of the language, dominant ideologies, norms, and ideals of the society. It is forced to live in conformity with these rules, values, and meanings. When the subject speaks, it is spoken. Thus, it is always experienced as alienation.

Lacan's four discourses highlight how these elements interact in different ways to produce meaning and maintain social structures. Understanding these elements as S1, S2, a, and $ helps to grasp the depth of human communication, emphasizing the impossibility of complete

9. Surplus Jouissance comes from the idea of "surplus value" drawn from Marxist economics of surplus value and surplus labor—the value added to any raw produce as a result of the labor and knowledge of the workers. Surplus Jouissance refers to the excess pleasure that arises from the process of pursing desire. In Lacan's theory, jouissance is a form of pleasure that goes beyond mere satisfaction and enters the realm of excess and sometimes even pain.

10. Bailly, *Lacan*, 130.

11. Johnson, *Other Side of Pedagogy*, 119.

12. Fink, *Lacanian Subject*, 54.

understanding between the agent and the other and the impotence of the product in fully comprehending the truth behind the discourse. These elements illustrate how discourse potions individuals within a complex interplay of knowledge, power, and desire.[13] They reveal how subjects are both shaped by and caught up in these dynamics, constantly negotiating their positions and identities within the social and symbolic structures that define their reality.

IMPOSSIBILITY: THE POSITION OF THE PASTOR'S WIFE

My own analysis of the position of the pastor's wife finds that it reaches an impossibility. After becoming a pastor's wife, I devoted myself whole-hearted to fulfilling the socially assigned role, but I realized that not only was I unable to fully meet these expectations, but the diverse expectations and standards of each church member made it impossible to gain full acceptance. Growing up as a pastor's daughter, I saw the struggles my mother faced, as well as the experiences of other pastor's wives around me. My journey was marked by the images and prejudices associated with being a pastor's wife, leading to difficult times. Studying Lacan helped me understand why it was so challenging and why fulfilling this role was inherently impossible.

The demand placed on the pastor's wife by the Korean church is an impossibility because it is not the individual's desire but the desire of the Other, rooted in Lacan's concept of the "subject of the lack." Church members demand their pastor's wife what they themselves lack, hoping to fill their lack through her. Thus, when any Korean church member demands pastor's wife something such as characteristics, virtues, or competences, it implies deficiency or lack. In doing so, the pastor's wife is assumed to possess what they need. However, in fact, both church members and the pastor's wife are subject to lack. What's more, what they demand is not always necessary. This is because, by desiring the desire of the Other, church members repetitively demand what the others demand from the pastor's wife. The pastor's wife they expect, the one they think possesses what they demand, does not have them. That is, as a deficient being, the pastor's wife does not possess what they demand. Therefore, what church members demand from the pastor's wife becomes an impossibility.

---

13. See Zwart, "Lacan's Dialectics of Knowledge Production."

Discourse of the Master

Discourse of Master demonstrates the position of pastor's wife very poignantly. The master's discourse operates within power dynamics, where one person (S1) holds authority over another (S2) like master-slave relation by Georg Wilhelm Friedrich Hegel, a German philosopher. His Master-Slave dialectic is a story he created as an attempt to describe and explain the formation of human consciousness out of a dialectic of interpersonal relations.[14] The master (S1) is considered to have absolute power, but below the S1 lies a profound emptiness, symbolized by $ in the place of truth. This suggests that, despite its outward appearance of absolute power, S1 itself holds the lack, resembling empty signifier.

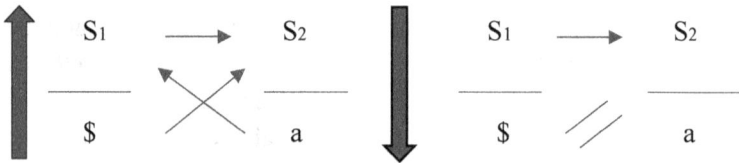

Figure 2. Lacan's Representation of the Discourse of the Master

As for me, S1 is "pastor's wife" in the context of the Korean Church as a whole, and this master signifier addresses S2 (the battery of signifiers or knowledge), creating various signifiers like what to do and what not to do as a pastor's wife. According to Hegel's Master-Salve analogy, the slave (S2) possesses the knowledge and what the master (S1) demands of her/him.[15] Likewise, I try my very best to serve the master (S1), that structures me as a subject, in a sense my identity as a pastor's wife, given by the Other. This process requires re-castration and repression which is the place of truth. As soon as I accept the master signifier to be the pastor's wife, I am re-castrated by the signifier. Just like the same process of castration happened as one enters in the Symbolic realm by accepting "the-Name-of-the-Father." Because I am a split subject ($) in the master discourse, the S1 as an agent could control this discourse.

In Korean church, where cultural norms heavily influence expectations, S1 imposes rigid images of what a pastor's wife should embody. These fixed images become ingrained in the collective consciousness,

14. Bailly, *Lacan*, 154.
15. Lacan, *Psychoanalysis Upside Down*, 42.

shaping the expectations directed towards individuals in that role. S1 addresses S2, through the complex chain of signifiers, with "should or should not" demands. It's as if one signifier represents another in an endless chain of expectations. Positioned as S2, I navigate through these expectations, internalizing the spoken and unspoken demands and shouldering the responsibilities inherent in my role as a pastor's wife. Despite the absence of explicit commands, S2 understands the implicit requirements for the name of "pastor's wife (S1)" Thus, I find myself compelled to adhere to these expectations, striving to produce outcomes that align with the church's notions of what constitutes an ideal pastor's wife. All I do as S2 produce surplus jouissance (mixed of enjoyment and suffering, or object a). Object a or surplus jouissance functions to illustrate the dynamics of desire and enjoyment. They show how power, knowledge, and desire interplay to produce the subject of jouissance who is always striving for something more, something beyond immediate gratification.

In the situation of being located in the discourse of the master I feel the impossibility of change, leading to stress and frustration. There are moments when I feel silenced, like the Mermaid who's lost her voice, and I feel powerless when I echo what's expected of me. It is the powerlessness that constitutes my knowledge (S2) in the master discourse. This means that I am spoken instead of speaking without even realizing it. The truth, the unconscious condition of the discourse, sits below the master signifier and it is the split subject ($\$$), revealing that the master signifier is indeed nothing more than an empty signifier. The image of "pastor's wife" is fantasized by others. The image is a holding place that embodies the lack.

The Discourse of the University

The next stage of my analysis on the formation of my identity as a pastor's wife more clearly manifests in the discourse of the university. The university discourse prioritizes knowledge and the desire to know, positioning them in the place of agent, the dominant place. It is like the discourse of science: S2 (knowledge or students), trying to know or explain uncertainty (a), can never stop it because S1 located in the place of truth command them to "keep going"—keep going to get to know still more.[16] Capturing the real into Symbolic is impossible and, as a result, the

---

16. Lacan, *Psychoanalysis Upside Down*, 125.

discourse of the university, like science, produces a divided subject ($) who possesses hysteric and "paranoic knowledge."

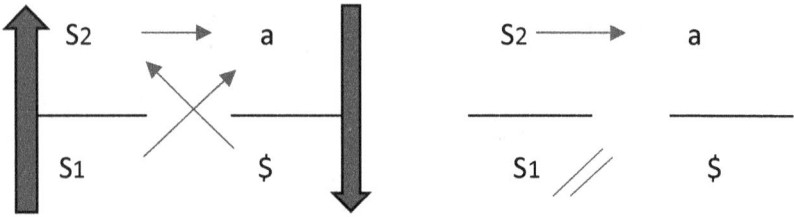

Figure 3. Lacan's Representation of the Discourse of the University

As a Christian, the S2 would be theological knowledge, and S1 the God. The theological knowledge, expressed by a form of sermons or the Bible study, explains the lack or the void in a sinful nature of human beings away from God. This knowledge (S2) attempts to controls object petit (a) as the object of enjoyment. Object petit (a) is the unattainable object causing various desires and producing alienated subject ($).

In my capacity as a pastor's wife, S2 (knowledge, or slave by Hegel) would be all the required works I do for the church. I aspire to become an object of desire for those around me, especially the members of my church. There is the Korean Church (S1) that I belong to in the place of the truth below all my services or ministry (S2). It seems to be promising that if I work hard for the church and its members, I would be accepted, recognized, respected, and even loved by them. The path from S2 to object a, however, represents an impossibility, signifying that S2 aiming for object-a fails. What being produced as a result is a split subject ($, alienated subject or symptoms). Despite my earnest efforts, I encounter symptoms of internal conflict and dissatisfaction as well as headaches, indigestion, and insomnia ($). Similarly, the attempt to navigate from the split subject having symptoms ($) to S1 represents an impotence within the discourse.

Lacan describes a symptom as "the signifier of a signified that has been repressed from the subject's consciousness."[17] This means that symptoms, whether physical or psychological, manifest as symbolic expressions of underlying repressed signifiers within oneself. I experience a dissonance between my desires and the reality shaped by the interplay

17. Lacan, *Écrits*, 232.

of the university discourse and the master's discourse as I navigate the complexities of my role within the church community.

The Discourse of the Hysteric

For me, the hysteric discourse was a period of wandering, shaking, and questioning. Dissatisfaction accumulated, leading to symptoms such as headache, insomnia, indigestion, and fatigue. During this time, I sought out others for answers rather than trying to find the answers within myself. It was a difficult and trying period, but in hindsight, it was a necessary time for me. It was a time of collapse, destruction, and chaos.

In the previous discourse, a split subject ($) is produced by object; now $, the hysteric subject, occupies a dominant position in the discourse of the hysteric, characterized by anxiety, doubts, symptoms, and latent desires. I reached a point that refusing to just follow what the master signifier asks of me. Instead, I find myself perpetually questioning the established norms and values of the symbolic order (S1), grappling with existential inquiries that probe the depths of my identity and desires.

Positioned within the framework of the church as a pastor's wife, I am directly confronted with this authoritative figure (S1), which may manifest as the master signifier of "the pastor's wife" or those who are supposed to know. My relentless questioning and skepticism challenge the authority of this powerful master. Most of the times when I am in the discourse of hysteric, I ($) challenge my husband (S1), the pastor of my church, questioning or complaining about what is happening to me as a pastor's wife in Korean church. I do this out of anxiety and fear. I even complain about his behavior or attitude as a form of controlling or manipulating.

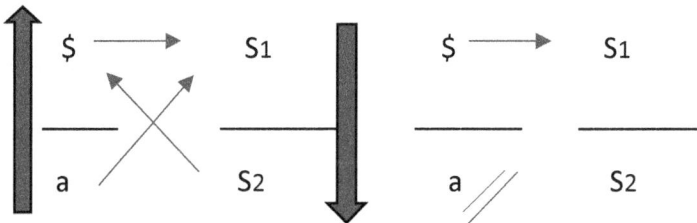

Figure 4. Lacan's Representation of the Discourse of the Hysteric

At the heart of my inquiries lies a profound sense of dissonance and dissatisfaction with the roles as a pastor's wife prescribed to me by the church or its members even when I perform my duties well. I find myself questioning the very essence of my being and protesting the authority represented by S1, questioning "Am I defined solely by my gender or by my husband's position? Am I bound by societal norms and expectations?" The hysteric's discourse is characterized by its disruptive and deconstructive nature and that reveals my resistance to power and my unconscious desire to take over the position of the master.

Sometimes, individuals who are supposed to know with authority become S2 when I am in the hysteric discourse. In my quest for understanding and resolution, I seek answers from them because they are the masters of the symbolic order. Whether consulting with a doctor for physical illness, seeking guidance from a pastor for spiritual dilemmas, or seeking counsel from a therapist for emotional struggles, each of them provide some kinds of knowledge (S2) by answering my questions as they try to solve my problems or to reduce my anxiety or symptoms. I expect some kind of knowledge and validation from them, but the reality is that I just want to hear what I am ready to hear. The knowledge offered by the masters fails to provide satisfactory answers to me, $, the hysteric subject.

Lacan mentioned in *Écrits*, that "a symptom is the signifier of a signified that has been repressed from the subject's consciousness."[18] It is an expression of the repressed consciousness, but I have tried to find its meaning endlessly. In addition, what makes hysteric subject is the object petit a or surplus jouissance, trying to fill fundamental lack or void. Both the object petit a and surplus jouissance underscore the notion that human desire is never fully satisfied. While the object petit a represents the ultimate, unattainable object of desire, surplus jouissance refers to the excess pleasure that arises from the process of pursuing desire, entering the realm of excess and even pain. This additional and often unexpected pleasure is the hidden truth of this discourse. I have symptoms such as headache and insomnia and I complain about them to my husband functioning as the master according to the diagram above. Having symptoms could be expressions of the desire of my unconscious to escape from the Symbolic realm. Without knowing the truth (impotence) that it is surplus Jouissance of the hysteric that makes this discourse possible, in the conviction that the master (S1) produces knowledge (S2) for the hysteric

18. Lacan, *Psychoanalysis Upside Down*, 232.

subject (\$). It serves to reinforce the hegemony of the symbolic order, perpetuating the cycle of discontent and alienation.[19]

As the hysterical subject navigating the complexities of desire and identity within the church, I find myself doubting, questioning, and complaining about my role as a pastor's wife. I strive towards a more authentic and liberated mode of being, desiring to write my own desires instead of being written by the Other which is the discourse of the analyst.

The Discourse of the Analyst

In life, unexpected moments of realization sometimes occur. It was like an "Aha" experience. Lacan refers to this as "tuché." Tuché is the encounter with the Real, the experience when we come across something unexpected that disrupts our usual understanding and brings about a sudden realization. These moments of experiences pass and become known as retrospective experiences. While studying Lacan, I experienced mementos where the object a, positioned as the agent, acted like an analyst by reflecting my own desires. Lacan's texts became a mirror to my hysteric self, illuminating my desires and prompting deeper self-reflection.

In the theory of Lacan, man is structured to be a dupe, namely, to stick to the structure.[20] In other words, he puts, "Les non-dupes errant: The unduped wander" in his seminar *Les Non Dupes Errent Part 1*.[21] The unduped with various symptoms (such as wandering) is hystericized as a form of analysand act in pursuit of demand. If everything is fine or you are happy enough, you won't seek the discourse of an analyst.

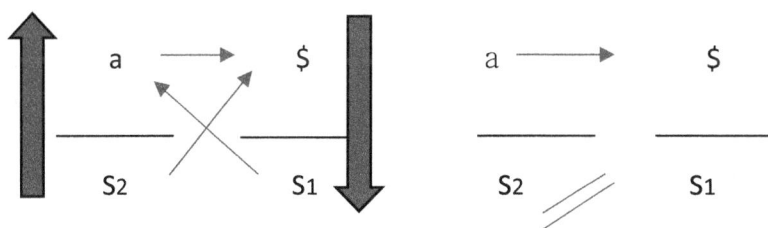

Figure 5: Lacan's representation of the discourse of the Analyst

19. Lacan, *Psychoanalysis Upside Down*, 183.
20. Lacan, *Psychoanalysis Upside Down*, 1.
21. Lacan, *Psychoanalysis Upside Down*, 1.

Lacan describes the analyst as follows: "It is to the analyst and to him alone that there is addressed this formula that I so often commented on, *the Wo Es war soll Ich warden* (Where Id was, there shall Ego be). If the analyst is able to occupy this place on the top left that determines his discourse, it is because he is absolutely not there for himself. It is to where surplus enjoying was, the enjoying of the Other, in so far as I am producing the psychoanalytic act, that I for my part must come."[22] By playing a dummy role, the analyst creates a space, where transference takes place. The analyst's discourse can take "on a sense from the very voice of someone who is in it—is precisely what makes it worth our while to pause on it, in order to know from where it takes on this sense."[23]

What present itself to the subject is the object petit a, taking place of the commandment. "The psychoanalyst offers himself or herself as a target point for this insane operation of psychoanalysis."[24] Within the framework of the analytical discourse, object petit a, serving as the elusive object of desire that propels the analysand to explore the unconscious. The analyst, functioning as a mirror for the split subject, facilitates a dynamic engagement with object petit a, allowing for the emergence of new insights and perspectives by playing a dummy role (stupidity). In the triadic relationship between the analyst, the analysand, and the Other, the individual confronts the limitations of their own knowledge and experiences, a profound encounter with the real—the moment of rupture where new master signifiers are forged.[25] Lacan posits that Socrates's position is analogous to that of the analyst's position, as he played out in the interactions with Alcibiades and Agathon in *Symposium*.[26] It is important to note that this position is possible because there is the knowledge of psychoanalysis or unconscious on the left bottom of the analytic discourse, the place of truth.

As for me, Lacan's texts have become an object a, a surplus jouissance. Reading and rereading them provoke moments of pause, sometimes filled with anxiety stemming from difficulty, uncertainty, and ambiguity like riddles. As Lacan calls it "the fullness of meaning."[27] The act of pausing, of ceasing the incessant repetition of language and thought, opens

22. Lacan, *Psychoanalysis Upside Down*, 68.

23. Lacan, *On a Discourse*, 36.

24. Lacan, *On a Discourse*, 36.

25. Lacan, *On a Discourse*, 36.

26. Lacan, *Transference*, 151.

27. Lacan, *Non Dupes Errent*, 5.

the door to a moment of existential reckoning—a moment where I am no longer defined by external narratives or societal expectations but exist as myself, in communion with the present moment. Silence plays a powerful role in this respect. Lacan puts that "I think where I am not, therefore I am where I do not think." It explains how humans are structured by language, the Other. Similarly, Lacan also said, "If we choose being, the subject disappears, it deludes us, it falls into non-meaning."[28] Instead of offering clear answers, they often lead me astray. I must admit that I feel like the more I study, the more lost I become. Getting through struggles, it reminds me of the well-known maxim, "What makes me uncomfortable also helps me grow."

Lacan's text, addressing me ($, the split subject), invites me to produce a new master signifier. Producing new S1 means I speak and write my own desire rather than being spoken and written. It is also an impossibility since language itself is located in the Other. This, however, works as a possibility to see an impossibility. The new signifier, equivalent to stupidity or nonsense,[29] created by me ($) is not that rigid but more flexible because I am the one who produce it. Having the new master signifier (S1, spiritual freedom for me), I may revert to the discourse of the master, which means relying on authoritative or dominant ways of thinking. As a result, all the other discourses—such as the university, the hysteric, and the analyst—would also be repeated in their usual patterns. This cyclical return to familiar discourses highlights how deeply ingrained these structures are in our thought processes.

CONCLUSION

Lacan's four discourses illustrate how language operates as "the social networking" and influences relationships. In this chapter, I analyzed how my role as a pastor's wife in the Korean church had been influenced by the patterns described in Lacan's four discourses. This analysis provides insight into dynamics and expectations within my community and how they have shaped my interactions and self-perception.

Within the master's discourse, for instance, I confront the pressure to conform to societal expectations and uphold the image of the ideal pastor's wife, often at the expense of losing my own voice, producing the

28. Lacan, *Other Side of Psychoanalysis*, 211.
29. Lacan, *On Feminine Sexuality*, 13.

object a as a product labor for the compensation of the Other (master). The discourse of the master can be seen in the hierarchical structure of the church, where authority and tradition play a significant role. This discourse emphasizes power dynamics and how they dictate the roles and behaviors expected of me. In the university discourse, I do all the hard works supposed to be required of me, expecting either enjoying "a" or avoiding "a" but ended up resulting in being the alienated and divided subject. The hysteric discourse manifests in moments of internal conflict and questioning, as I confront the contradictions and tensions inherent within my identity and societal expectations, and knowledge is produced by S1. I find myself questioning and challenging the norms, seeking validation, and understanding within a framework that often prioritizes collective over individual needs. Finally, the analytic discourse offers a space for a possibility to see an impossibility, allowing me to explore the unconscious motivations and desires that underpin my role as a pastor's wife. Through this lens, I navigate the complexities of my identity, acknowledging the inherent impossibilities and impasses within each discourse.

Lacan argued that "the desire of the subject is the desire of the Other." Even when recognizing and surpassing the desire of the Others, new desires created are still a part of another form of the desire of the Other. Despite realizing being trapped by the desires of others, I desire within the repetitive process of breaking old ones and creating new ones, following the ethics of psychoanalysis. I desire to live my own life, embracing contingency, uncertainty, necessity and impossibility.

It is crucial to acknowledge that Lacan's theory and the technical terms of his language are vague and open to interpretation. This chapter is just my interpretation of Lacan's four discourse from the perspective of pastor's wife, and errors might be found as I try to make sense. More importantly, Lacanian psychoanalysis does not promise a better life because that is merely phantasy. I want to close this chapter with what Samuel Beckett mentioned, "Ever tried. Ever failed. No matter. Try again. Fail again. Fail better."[30] I wish to fail better.

---

30. Beckett, *Worstward Ho*, 7.

Part III

Body in the Global World

7

A Lacanian Approach to the COVID-Body as a State of Emergency[1]

ALI CHAVOSHIAN

"It was the best of times; it was the worst of times . . ." —Charles Dickens[2]

THE COVID-19 PANDEMIC HAS generated significant media coverage on defined scientific topics such as epidemiology, virology, statistics, and biomedicine, and the sought solutions are mainly the big pharma-dominated vaccine-production. Although scientific research and CO-VID-19 vaccines are critical in this exploration, science and the crisis of COVID-19 cannot fully be explained unless we examine science in all its complexity, including interactions with politics, economics, and our contemporary practice of religion.

There is a specter haunting the world: the specter of the COVID-19 virus attacking the human body. We will call this the COVID-Body. While the media has only focused on the biological and medical explanations and interventions, the horror of annihilation caused by the COVID-19 body, as well as the extraordinary emotional impact on individuals of

1. This chapter was written in 2021, during the COVID-19 pandemic.
2. Dickens, *Tale of Two Cities*, 11.

fear and anxiety of death and dying, has not much been addressed. The subject cannot interpret the traumatic intrusion of the COVID-19 attack through the medium of the current Symbolic world. In other words, the current symbolic domain cannot provide adequate support to deal with the COVID-19 crisis.

As such, it is crucial to analyze the human experience of COVID-19 as the body falls into a decaying horror and anxiety. Thus, in this chapter, I will first describe Jacques Lacan's psychoanalytic theory of the body as the framework, including the notion and formation of the body, constituted by the exterior, called the Symbolic order.[3] The Symbolic is a safety net that prevents the body from facing the sheer anxiety of the Real. This anxiety concerns the collapse of the body. Also, I will introduce the notion of the sciences of Lacan, critiquing the current understanding of science. Then, I will analyze the crisis of the COVID-19 body, focusing on the crisis of three domains: Neoliberal economy, politics, and religion, suggesting social changes that foster the necessity for a new sensibility concerning the human condition.

LACAN'S PSYCHOANALYSIS THEORY AS THE FRAMEWORK

I will explain Lacan's notion of the body, that of the body formation, and his understanding of science as an introduction to investigating the current pandemic crisis and its extraordinary emotional impact on all human beings.

Lacan's Notion of the Body

Lacan asserts that the human body is neither biological nor medical in abstract form: it can only exist and be defined through its interiority and exteriority. He further explains that the interiority aspect implies human subjectivity or the world of the Imaginary, and exteriority refers to the world outside that includes the family within the economic, political, and spiritual context, called the Symbolic world.[4] The interiority and exteriority of the body are not separate entities; they function as the components of one entity in a dialectical and continuum manner. What is

3. Lacan, *Four Fundamentals in Psychoanalysis*, 156.

4. Lacan, *Four Fundamentals in Psychoanalysis*, 156.

in is also out, and what is out is also in. Lacan demonstrates this in the Mobius band.[5]

The body's interiority and exteriority represent the Otherness/alterity of the body, which keeps the body function continuously. Contrary to animals, which rely on biology and instinctual programming components, humans rely on the Otherness for their body function, imagery, and identity. Otherness is a protective tool that defines the body and prevents its collapse into the abyss of sheer biology and raw flesh. According to the English psychoanalyst Wilfred Bion, the consequences of the collapse will end in severe anxiety, referred to as the "nameless dread."[6] Lacan views the severe anxiety/angst in the domain of the Real. The Real denotes an impossibility that cannot be described (signified) in speech. Lacan's Borromean Knot[7] illustrates three areas where the human body lies.

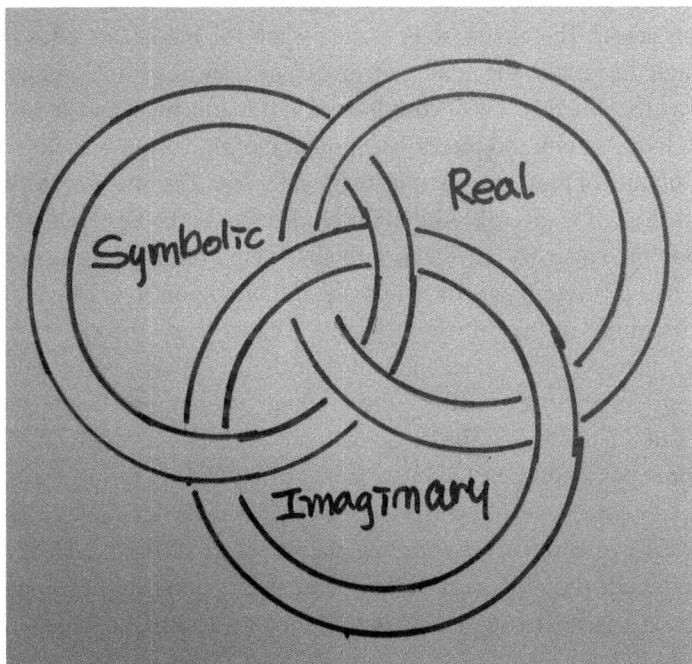

Figure 1. Three Domains of the Human Body

5. Lacan, *Four Fundamentals in Psychoanalysis*, 156.
6. Bion, "Attacks on Linking," 308–15.
7. Lacan, *Feminine Sexuality*, 124.

The diagram of Figure 1 shows that the Real of the body has Imaginary and Symbolic components that promote it beyond a sheer biological being and protect it from collapse within the significant disorder of the Real. All the rings remain interconnected. If one comes out, the other two will fall apart. The COVID-body does not mean merely a crisis in biology and medicine, but it is also the economic, political, and spiritual crisis within Neoliberalism. Lacan's theory of body formation will further explain how the human body can be used as an apparatus to comprehend social structure.

Lacan's Body Formation Theory

The horror of the fragmented and decaying body belongs to the domain of the Real of the body, and Lacan explains it in his early work on the mirror stage.[8] The mirror stage occurs when the infant sees one's image through the mirror; the infant perceives the image as a whole, contrary to the fact that the infant is uncoordinated and fragmented, and she experiences living in bits and pieces. The function of mirroring is analogous to the function of mothering as a primary caretaker. The image of the infant about the self is given by the mOther, defined as the Other (the world outside), the primary caretaker, with all the environmental influences.

Reinforcement occurs when the mOther points a finger at the infant's image in the mirror and says, "That is you." The experience of image acquisition is called the world of the Imaginary, while language acquisition, starting after the mOther's linguistic prompt, belongs to the world of the Symbolic. The Imaginary and the Symbolic both operate as an apparatus to prevent the re-surfacing of the Real in terms of anxiety/angst of existence. While the body temporarily does not embody the notion of fragmentation by adopting the structure of the Imaginary and the Symbolic (ego-ideal), the place of the perception (ideal ego), but the reality of fragmentation remain within the structure of the Real.

As a follow-up, Lacan introduces his Optical Model concerning the mirror stage in his first seminar, *Freud's Papers on Technique*.[9] In the optical experiment, a plain mirror and the concave mirror stand: the concave mirror produces an image of an inverted flowerpot hidden from

---

8. Lacan, *Écrits*, 71–81.

9. Lacan, *Freud's Papers on Technique*, 7.

the viewer in a box. The inverted flowerpot appears straight as a virtual image in the plain mirror as the viewer looks at that mirror.

Figure 2. The Optical Model

The Optical Model specifies the Symbolic and the Imaginary's roles in structuring the body, self-image, and identification. The inverted flowerpot in the concave mirror represents the fragmented body, while the straight one in the simple mirror represents the image of the body appearing whole. The optical and mirror stage experiments manifest that body awareness begins with ego formation through image-making. The fragile ego is the subject, formed through outside manipulation, meaning the Symbolic order.

As the agency of the human psyche, the ego limits itself to consciousness and perceptual processes. The missing part of the ego becomes the unconscious part. Thus, one does not know how the body and the ego are formed. According to the mirror stage and Optical Model, body formation cannot be complete at a specific moment. The body must always be protected by the symbolic order during adulthood. Otherwise, it will regress to its original decomposition and fragmentation. The symbolic order, protecting the infant body even in the original mirror stage, comes from the Other (outside). The Other consists of the immediate familial milieu, affected by larger socio-economic and sociopolitical domains, and is transmitted to the child through language. Language preexists the child.

Regarding the current COVID situation, the larger domains of our contemporary culture in the economic, political, and religious/spiritual realms are inadequate symbolic domains, unable to protect human bodies from the horror of decay. The current language needs adequate signifiers to comprehend the current situation of COVID.

Lacan's Notion of Science

The COVID-Body is an abstraction of biomedicine, and like any other abstraction, it has paradoxical implications. In the philosophy of science and logic, abstractions help us be specific in observing phenomena. The word abstraction comes from the Latin "derive from." It derives from inductive and deductive reasoning in practice and theory. The practice signifies praxis, where theory and practice are inseparable and occur simultaneously. Thus, abstraction loses its larger systemic context and remains isolated; abstraction without context is non-existent.

Lacan's praxis occurs at the clinic, and he explains his praxis in terms of conjectural sciences vs. exact sciences.[10] In critiquing abstraction, he refers[11] to it in terms of "exactitude" or "the exact sciences," like how natural sciences such as biomedicine and physics assume the exact truth. For Lacan, as human sciences, conjectural sciences stand in structural and *contextual contingencies* (emphasis mine), and psychoanalysis belongs to conjectural science.

In psychoanalysis we pursue truth and knowledge through the material cause, similar to Aristotle's *Physics*, from which human language and speech emerge. With its symbolic and signifying intervention, speech and language limit the deterministic causality of natural science to the point where we cannot apply natural science principles to human subjectivity. Lacan argues that the opposition between exact sciences and conjectural sciences could blur when conjecture shrinks to exact calculation and when exactitude uses formalism to separate axioms and laws of grouping symbols.

10. Lacan, *Psychosis*, 186.
11. Lacan, *Écrits*, 863.

Here, "laws of grouping symbols"[12] are structured outside the human subject, giving meaning to the abstract notion of the body and the COVID-Body. The praxis of the clinic in Lacanian psychoanalysis includes different phases of analysis where the speaking subject of the body traverses from the structure of imaginary (empty speech) to the structure of symbolic (full speech) to claim its body. Whether we start the praxis with the word or the letter of speech, as Lacan claims, citing Goethe, "in the beginning was the deed,"[13] the synthesis includes both word and deed. The claim to the body in the clinic is the speech act. The speech act allows the subject to move toward full speech.

Lacan critiques the abstraction of the body in favor of conjectural sciences in his discussion of discourses or "social networking."[14] The individual body is addressed as a discourse body because its first recognition and desire comes through the interpersonal and intersubjective, where the desire of the subject is the desire of the Other. Lacan refers to others with a capital O (Other, Autre) to demonstrate that discourse is not a two-person or two-body psychology. Still, it occurs in a larger context, beyond the two-person's engagement. The structure of discourse gives identity and functionality to the body and promises to fulfill the body's needs, demands, and desires.

ANALYSIS OF COVID-BODY AS SYMPTOM

Although biomedical intervention has become integral to treating COVID-19, it lacks an integration of the extensive structural analysis and significant crises we encounter: economic, political, and religious/spiritual. To enrich our discussion of COVID-Body, I investigate the three domains of our current social structure (in Lacanian terms, three methodological contingencies/grouping symbols). Since our dominant social structure is advanced capitalism, named finance capitalism/neoliberalism as a worldwide economic and political system, we will examine the three domains of crises within the structure of capitalism.

12. Lacan, *Écrits*, 86.

13. Goethe, *Faust*, 34.

14. Lacan, *Other Side of Psychoanalysis.*

The Economic Crisis

Lacan's lecture "On Psychoanalytic Discourse" provides the formula of
capitalist and master discourses, explaining economic oppression and the
power struggle between the working and capitalist classes.[15] Although he
uses psychoanalytic rather than economic terminology, the implication
is the same.

The following is the formula for the discourse of master and the
discourse of capitalism:

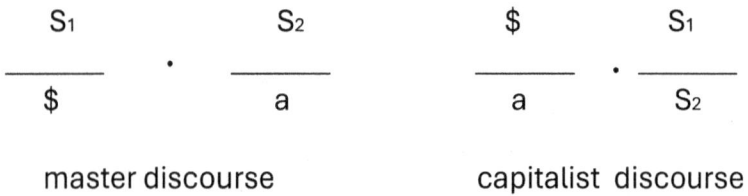

$$\frac{S_1}{\$} \cdot \frac{S_2}{a} \qquad\qquad \frac{\$}{a} \cdot \frac{S_1}{S_2}$$

master discourse   capitalist discourse

Figure 3. Master Discourse and Capitalist Discourse

In the master discourse, the master-capitalist class (S_1, the master
signifier) claims that it generates capitalism's knowledge and ingenuity by
delivering goods and commodities. There is an objet petit a, a product,
or surplus jouissance for the worker-slave (S_2, subject of the body). But
the worker-slave/the subject of the body is alienated ($\$$) and deprived of
the product (a). The second formula, the discourse of capitalism, begins
with the subject barred ($\$$), subject of the body, the worker-slave being a
direct producer (S_2), barred from its product (a, objet petit a, or surplus
jouissance), and humane treatment by the master-capitalist class (S_1).

Although Lacan believes that these discourses encounter impossibility and impotence in providing intersubjectivity and social networking, it is compelling that he still needs to provide an alternative response
to the problems of capitalism. For him, any change in the structure of
capitalism substitutes one master for another. The closest he comes to answering this dilemma is to offer the analytical discourse in which the subject of the body/working class can gain conscious knowledge about the
system that fails to solve the existing problems. Lacanian philosophers

15. Lacan, "On Psychoanalytic Discourse," 1–15.

such as Badiou and Žižek proposed their version of communism by offering a strategy called the "event" or "eventual act."[16]

Regarding a solution to the economic crisis in conjunction with the status of the pandemic, the famous economist Richard D. Wolff's proposed argument seems the most appealing. In *The Sickness Is the System: When Capitalism Fails to Save Us from Pandemics or Itself,*[17] Wolff analyzes the last two years as the era of COVID-19, criticizing capitalism as the primary cause of the pandemic's horror. He argues that capitalism historically has encountered crises and crashes, and that COVID-19 just highlighted this inherent instability. For him, the current pandemic is a manifestation of our economic system's sickness, inefficient in sustaining human life.

Our economic system deprives the masses of their essential needs for jobs, food, housing, and employment while profiting the capital within the medical-insurance-industrial complexes. This inadequacy creates a significant conflict between the private and public, which is inherent in the system. The utter failure of private capitalism to handle the coronavirus effectively is unsurprising. Private capitalism only pursues profit, and this profit incentive is the only goal of capitalism. Thus, producing adequate testing components, masks, gloves, ventilators, and hospital beds is not profitable.

They do not produce or stockpile the items desperately needed to protect the public's health,[18] but wait for a long time until those items are marketable. If the risk continues to be high, they will decide to invest in other items or move their investments elsewhere. According to Wolff, Neoliberalism is the global economic system that allocates the world's wealth into the hands of a few who rule most of the world. The ideological power of Neoliberalism is "God is private, but the devil is the government."[19]

The global economic system of Neoliberalism, based on the principle of laissez-faire, rejects any governmental intervention in regulation and taxation, except in the military, security, and police realms. However, regarding military intervention in foreign countries by the government, the new liberal private capitalists rally behind the government, investing heavily in the military-industrial complex. Wolff explains that a few

---

16. See Badiou, *Being and Event*; Žižek, *Event.*

17. Wolf, *Sickness Is the System,* 60.

18. Wolf, *Sickness Is the System,* 60.

19. Wolf, *Sickness Is the System,* 61.

countries, such as China and New Zealand, where Neoliberalism does not have a firm grip on the economy, have done much better with the pandemic. Wolff proposes "democracy at work," a system of worker co-op organizations where workers in a company or factory control planning and decision-making in production, distribution, and consumption.

In conclusion, we observed the entrapment of workers' bodies within capitalism's structure, specifically, the COVID-Body within capitalism. In principle, unlike Wolff's collective approach, Lacan's theory focuses on the individual master-capitalist part and the worker-slave in the discourse of capitalism. For Lacan, the tension between master capitalist and laborer remains within the never-ending system. For Wolff, this system's destruction is inevitable, and can lead to a more egalitarian society. Facing the inadequacy of the symbolic world for the COVID-Body in the discourse of capitalism, Lacan only diagnoses the system. However, Wolff not only diagnoses the system but also finds the destruction of the system inevitable.

The Political Crisis

The global lockdown is a hysterical response to the coronavirus pandemic, and it shows the political crisis of the human world. The lockdowns have not worked because they are unrealistic for the homeless, poor, detainees, and prisoners. Without adequate planning in the state health systems and economies, lockdowns abandon the majority struggling with the necessities of daily living such as food, shelter, housing, and job security.

Contrary to the majority poor, many companies, including Amazon, Zoom, Slack, Apple, Microsoft, T-Mobile, Facebook, and Netflix, which provide teleworking and home entertainment, are making tremendous profits from the crisis, as they often do in situations. By imposing lockdowns without adequate support systems, the state controls and punishes the COVID-body and imprisons general populations to the point of decay, death, and the disappearance of bodies through necropolitics, like Bolsonaro's Brazil. Resistance to lockdowns may result in punishment. Here, we can say that the political body becomes the criminal body. The COVID-Body, according to the concept of biopolitics and biopower of Michael Foucault,[20] is not an immaterial quality. Like the Lacanian symbolic-imaginary contingency context, the COVID-Body gains meanings

20. Foucault, *Birth of Biopolitics*.

within the political context. It is not the virus but actual human beings who are imprisoned and discriminated against.

My argument is not against/for lockdowns but to demonstrate how totalitarianism can claim a state of sovereignty in times of emergency and suspend its laws to avoid criticisms about operating illegally. The concept of sovereignty, intrinsically related to the state of emergency, played a significant role in Fascism and Nazism in Germany. In his Political Theology, Philosopher Carl Schmitt introduced the concept of the state of exception, stating, "The sovereign is he who decides on the state of exception."[21] Schmitt juxtaposed Western capitalist law with barbarism, presenting the state of exception in the name of public safety to justify the law of intervention. His insight about the state of sovereignty in times of emergency/state of exception and the suspension of laws played a significant role in the formation of totalitarianism.

The Italian philosopher, Giorgio Agamben, criticizes Schmitt's sovereignty, naming the state of emergency as the state of "exception."[22] According to Agamben, sovereignty claims that a state has the right, in the fields of laws and political values, to determine which life is meaningless (bare life) and which is worth living. Sovereignty which explicitly separates political beings (citizens) from "bare life" (bodies) is a regressive spell of Roman Law of the fifth century BC, "homo sacer,"[23] where if a man committed a crime, anyone could kill him, but no one could use him as a sacrifice in any ritual ceremony.

This state of exclusion and inclusion creates two beings: "bare life" (Zoe) and bios (qualified life), like Airport security checkpoints, demoting individuals to "bare life" like the tattooing by the Nazis on people during World War II. Agamben is also critical of the US response to 9/11 as a state of exception, such as the US PATRIOT Act, the War on Terror, Marshal law, Immigration Policy, USA-VISIT with Biometric information.[24] Further, Agamben believes the surveillance state, with its high-tech security apparatus, is an imprinted component of modern states, including sovereignty and a state of exception.

The norm-exception axis considers it legal to have the law as a norm that intrinsically involves the sovereignty of the state of exception. This argument is circular and tautological. With the global political events of

---

21. See Schmitt, *Political Theology*.
22. See Agamben, *State of Exception*.
23. See Agamben, *Homo Sacer*.
24. Agamben, "No to Bio-Political Tattooing."

the last several decades, we have witnessed that the state of exception has become the norm, and the norm has become the state of exception. In the name of the state of emergency, brutal repressive violence of the state gains more acceptance during economic disasters and political upheaval.

The philosopher Walter Benjamin[25] explained that in encountering the pseudo-emergency and state violence, the masses, through a general strike, should create an actual state of emergency, named "divine" or "pure" violence. The actual state of emergency stands beyond the norm of law. Benjamin, with a theopolitical imagination, mentions "divine" and "pure" violence as "unalloyed" and unadulterated from the violence of the state. Revolutionary violence, symbolizing the coming of the Messiah on Judgement Day, would create a new historical epoch.

Following Benjamin, Agamben differentiates the state's right to violence from pure violence and suggests moving beyond state violence, which is the transcendence of the common good in the community.[26] For Agamben, life form is a totality, not a particularity. Similarly, for Christians and Franciscans in particular, the form of life is a totality beyond canon law and property rights.[27] In the eyes of the Lord, all is common, and all is for communal use.

Further, in *The Coming Community*, against the philosophy of sovereignty, Agamben argues and offers an ontology of possibility and potentiality beyond law, order, and political jurisdiction. This ontology does not prescribe the form, yet any form can freely move and reach one another as a coming community. His insights are important because countries with a communal spirit, such as Taiwan, Korea, and China, respond differently than the US and Europe regarding the COVID-19 body.

Also, in response to the coronavirus pandemic, Agamben maintains that in regard to "the state of fear which has manifestly spread in recent years in the minds of individuals . . . the limitation of freedom imposed by governments gains acceptance in the name of security, induced by these same governments."[28]

---

25. Benjamin, *Critique of Violence,* 252.

26. See Agamben, *Coming Community.*

27. See Francis of Assisi, *Writings.*

28. Corradetti and Pollicino, "War Against COVID-19."

Religious or Spiritual Crisis

The contemporary crisis of spirituality is another domain of a symbolic deficiency incapable of protecting the subject of the COVID-Body. I have chosen Karl Marx's theory of spirituality because his discussion is comprehensive and includes economic and political crises. Marx's concept of man is humanistic.[29] Marx posits that man cannot be reduced to his bodily needs and to the domains of economic and political life without consideration of the spiritual realm. He discusses the collective spiritual life that extends beyond capitalism and offers a new insight that promotes life in body-spirit and can be applicable during the COVID crisis.

Karl Marx is one of the most unique and misunderstood thinkers. He explores spirituality in the discourse of religion. Contrary to the common belief that he dismissed religion and found it irrelevant in human life, Marx always acknowledged the significance of religion in the lives of the masses. He is frequently cited as saying, "Religion is the opium of nations," but this quotation has been taken out of context. We will also see how Marx differed from his predecessors, Spinoza and Feuerbach, and modern thinkers and writers regarding religion.

The recent group in new atheism,[30] Dawkins, Sam Harris, Christopher Hitchens, and Daniel Dennett view religion as a superstitious and irrational belief. They argue that people with rational thought and scientific knowledge should not tolerate religion but rather critique it. For Marx, the question of God, religion, and spirituality cannot be an intellectual and abstract discussion or the reasoning for proving or disapproving the existence of God.

Marx saw the human being as a historical being, caught up in a specific cultural and socio-economic mode of production in the midst of a class struggle. Marx also saw religion as an expression of protest for working classes against social injustices and alienation in a particular mode of production in different stages of history. Marx's opponents used the famous phrase "religion is the opium of the people" to demonstrate that he had been hostile and dismissive of religion. Marx mentions:

Religion is the sigh of the oppressed creature, the heart of a heartless world, and the soul of soulless conditions. It is the opium of the people. The abolition of religion as the illusory happiness of the people is the demand for their real happiness. Call on them to give up their illusions

29. See Fromm, *Marx's Concept of Man.*
30. See Hitchens et al., *Four Horsemen.*

about their condition is to call on them to give up a condition that requires illusions. Therefore, the criticism of religion lies in embryo, the criticism of that vale of tears of which religion is the halo. Criticism has plucked the imaginary flowers on the chain not so that man shall continue to bear that chain without fantasy or consolation but so that he shall throw off the chain and pluck the living flower. The criticism of religion disillusions man so that he will think, act, and fashion his reality like a man who has discarded his illusions and regained his senses so that he will move around himself as his own true Sun. Religion is only the illusory Sun, which revolves around man as long as he does not revolve around himself.[31]

Marx was critical of Spinoza and Feuerbach for their abstract notions of the subject-individual and its relationship to God and religion.[32] Marx saw a disconnect between Spinoza's materialist view of nature and his pantheist notion of God through a spiritual approach:

> Spinozism dominated the eighteenth century, making matter into substance, and deism conferring a more spiritual name. This Enlightenment's simple fate was its decline in romanticism after being obliged to surrender to the reaction that began after the French movement.[33]

Regarding Feuerbach, Marx argued that Feuerbach saw religion and God as a projection of the human essence onto an idealized absolute, resulting from a failure to realize humanity's full potential in this world. Marx thought Feuerbach's projection was a mere abstraction and theoretically useless, incapable of explaining in concrete socio-economic and political situations:

> Feuerbach does not enter upon a criticism of this real essence. To abstract from the historical process, fix the religious sentiment as something by itself, and presuppose an abstract—isolated— human individual. Essence, therefore, can be comprehended only as "genus," as an internal, dumb generality that naturally unites many individuals.[34]

In addition to discussing religion, Marx saw the necessity of human transcendence from "bodily needs" to the spiritual life. He saw the

31. Marx, *Critique of Hegel's Philosophy*, 1.

32. See Spinoza, *Theological-Political Treatise*; Feuerbach, *Essence of Christianity*.

33. Marx and Engels, *Holy Family*, 167.

34. Marx, *Ludwig Feuerbach*, 69.

fulfillment of economic needs as the beginning steps toward this transcendence, emphasizing that people must break their bondage to their
bodily needs—they must cease to be the slaves of their body. Above all,
they must have time at their disposal for spiritual, creative activity, and
spiritual enjoyment.[35]

According to Marxism, Christianity, especially early Christianity, provided a worldview for people experiencing poverty, helping in their class
struggle against oppression. Although institutionalized religion is usually
on the side of the ruling class, religion is a mass phenomenon and has a
revolutionary quality that appeals to most people. Frederick Engels writes:

> The history of early Christianity notably resembles the mod-
> ern working-class movement. Like the latter, Christianity was
> originally a movement of the oppressed. It first appeared as the
> religion of slaves and emancipated slaves, poor people deprived
> of all rights, of peoples subject to or dispersed by Rome.... Both
> Christianity and the workers' socialism preach future salvation
> from bondage and misery; Christianity places this salvation in
> a life beyond, after death, in Heaven; socialism places it in this
> world, through a transformation of society.[36]

Further, we have seen an appeal to Marxism in religion, particularly
Christianity. Theologians find they are not bound to the "law of the land,"
and God is the only authority they recognize. Also, by looking at the life
of Jesus and the apostles, they feel they can relate more to the principles
of socialism and communism than capitalism. Their anti-capitalist senti-
ments come from this famous statement from Marx[37] they find relevant
to the passages of Acts which says, "To everyone according to his needs,
to the emissaries to distribute to each according to his need" (4:35 NSRV).
Moreover, they posit that the kingdom of Heaven can exist on earth and
that socialism is an ideal social system comparable to the tenets of theological and political theories.

Historically, we have also observed some Marxist political revolutionary theories and their effects on organized religions. Christian
Communism-Christian communist liberation theology, rooted within
the Catholic Church of Latin America of the 1960s, clarifies a preferential
option for the poor, promoting social justice. Liberation theologians such

---

35. Marx, *Economical and Philosophic Manuscripts*, 7.

36. Engels, "On the History of Christianity."

37. See Marx, *Gotta Program*, 31.

as Gustavo Gutiérrez of Peru, Leonardo Boff of Brazil, Jon Sobrino of El Salvador, and Juan Luis Segundo of Uruguay influenced theologians in Asia and Africa. We witnessed flourishing indigenous theology, such as Minjung theology in Korea and Dalit theology in India. Dorothy Day started the Catholic workers' movement in New York, claiming social and anarchist activism and communist ideas. Islam, Socialism, and Islam and Anarchism, and Islam in the twentieth century appeared in Southeast Asia.

In the early establishment of the Soviet Union, some Marxists such as Anatoly Lunacharsky (1875–1933) and Maxim Gorky in the twentieth century developed the idea of God-Building. Inspired by the French Revolution and August Comte in the nineteenth century and his concept of "Religion of Humanity," they attempted to re-interpret religion's positive and humanistic aspect in terms of ritual and symbolism within socialism.

CONCLUSION

I characterize the current crisis of COVID-19, employing Jacques Lacan's psychoanalysis theory of the body. The crisis of the COVID-body is equivalent to the crisis of Lacan's Symbolic world. This Symbolic world consists of a familial environment, socio-economic and sociopolitical contexts, and the cultural milieu of individuals. Therefore, the body cannot be limited to the biomedical, but it remains constituted and modified with its connection to a social entity. Further, to examine the crisis of the COVID-Body, I describe it in contingencies, specifically in three modes: the economic, the political, and the spiritual, within the overarching framework of capitalism and Neoliberalism.

Also, I emphasize that religious crises become more comprehensive when we see them in conjunction with economic and political crises. As a symptom of a social illness, the current pandemic demands a new sensitivity and attention to the relationship between the body and the spirit.

8

Encountering the "REAL"

A Lacanian Reading of Mary of Bethany

Jiyoung Ko

"They lived happily ever after." Often love stories in the movies and books ends with this phrase. In a stereotypical love story, a man and a woman experience some hardship. However, their love is eventually fulfilled; they are made one. Period. A main character having a serious flaw, which is a lack (hole) in Lacanian terms, experiences wholeness through being united with his/her beloved object (a socially-meaningful object, such as a morally upright person, a rich person or a person of higher status in the society). However, a story with a happy end never allows the audience to think about the end in which there will be arguments and quarrels between lover and beloved. The world that the love story constitutes is a closed system.

There is no beyond-ness. It is a pattern of fantasy that the love story provides. Like the perfect image of the Lacanian mirror stage, the reality (fantasy) of the love story conceals the contradictions and flaws of the real life (world) and its anxiety temporarily. This fantasy doesn't challenge audiences to question their own life. It does not allow any new desire to go beyond the fantasy. A similar pattern of fantasy operates in religious sermons. Popular preaching promises Christian audiences a happy life by believing in (loving) God. Preachers strongly claim that nothing in the world can satisfy people but God. God as a god of absolute power and knowledge will give people the meaning of life and fulfillment, whole-ness. In this kind of sermon, God (Jesus) takes the place of an object of love which will complete the subject. The fantasy of happiness and wholeness is maintained while anxiety and uncertainty are repressed. Likewise, the fantasy of completion doesn't allow beyond-ness.

However, within the biblical narrative, there is a woman possessing a hole (a lack) which is the deadly sickness of her beloved brother. She waits for Jesus's coming to heal him. In vain, he dies. However, as soon as Jesus arrives, he miraculously brings her brother back to life. Up to here, we can expect a typical happy end. Her problem is solved, she expresses her gratitude to him, and people around her applaud her. She experiences a union with Jesus as the Messiah and the Savior of life. Readers will gain a moral teaching from her such as if one has faith in Jesus like her, he/she will experience union with Jesus and will have a happy, whole life. How-ever, this is not a picture that the passage of John 12:1–8 presents. After her brother Lazarus is raised from the dead, Mary of Bethany anoints Je-sus's feet with an expensive perfume and wipe his feet with her hair. One disciple accuses her of her being immoral. Her desire expressed in this scene is an enigma. Furthermore, the desire of the narrative is ambiguous which leaves readers in anxiety.

In this chapter, I read Mary of Bethany's desire in John 12:1–8 from the perspective of Lacanian sublimation. First, I describe her enigmatic and erotic act of anointing Jesus in the pericope, which has led to various interpretations among scholars. Second, I briefly introduce the *Ethics of Psychoanalysis*, Lacan's seventh seminar. Third, through a study of char-acters and characterization as literary criticism, I investigate how Mary goes beyond the limit of the fantasy of love (union), driven by death drive while Judas is in opposition to her. I explore how she refuses Jesus as an object of love but raises him to an object of the *Real* like Antigone's transgressive love.

ENCOUNTERING DESIRE AND MARY'S ENIGMATIC ACT OF ANOINTING

The chapter 11 provides the immediate context of the pericope of Mary's anointing, Jesus's beloved friend Lazarus, who lived in Bethany, has a deadly disease. Jesus intentionally stays two more days where he is after being informed that Lazarus is sick by Lazarus's sisters Martha and Mary. Then, Jesus returns to Bethany with his disciples after Lazarus has died and meets and converses with Martha and Mary. He then calls Lazarus from the tomb; Jesus raises him from death. Because of Jesus's miracle, many Jews come to believe in Jesus. However, the chief priests and Pharisees conspire to kill Jesus because of this miracle. Knowing the danger he faces, Jesus withdraws to a desert area called Ephraim (11:54). With the approach of Passover, the Jews coming to Jerusalem look for Jesus, wondering if he will appear in the midst of this threatening situation.

Context of the Pericope

In John 12:1–8, Martha, Mary and Lazarus gather together again in Bethany due to Jesus's miracle of raising Lazarus and a dinner is held to celebrate the new life that Lazarus has with Jesus. Their home in Bethany is less than two miles away from Jerusalem (11:18). The indoor meal setting suggests a private, intimate atmosphere of gathering with beloved family and friends, though it may have been "semi-public," with outside guests drawn to Lazarus after the miracle.[1]

In the context of this dinner setting, in the presence of gathered guests, Mary of Bethany anoints Jesus's feet (not his head) with expensive perfume and wipes his feet with her hair. Unlike the normal practice of anointing in her time, Mary uses both an excessive amount of extravagant-quality perfume. Moreover, her strange, scandalous, and abnormal body gestures create an image of deviation and ambiguity. Her desire is enigmatic. Her anointing meets severe criticism by Judas Iscariot, probably one among other guests around the table, for the stated reason that the money for the expensive perfume could be used for almsgiving. However, rebuking Judas, Jesus approves her by enigmatically saying that her act is in preparation for his funeral rite.

Compared to the story of Lazarus in chapter 11, "the last and the greatest miracle story in the Gospel of John,"[2] the story of Mary's anointing seems theologically insignificant and unextraordinary.[3] Her anointing is often reduced to her desire to offer "thanks for the resurrection of

1. Barrett, *Gospel According to St. John*, 409.

2. Haenchen, *John 2*, 56.

3. Carson, *Gospel According to John*, 425.

Lazarus."[4] Moreover, this pericope is often compared with the anointing story in the Synoptic gospels (Matt 26:6–13; Mark 14:3–9; Luke 7:36–38). Unlike Mark's and Matthew's accounts, which indicate theme of Messiahship and kingship of Jesus by anointing Jesus's head, or Luke's story, which emphasizes themes of sinfulness and forgiveness,[5] it seems embarrassing that there seems to be a lack of significant theological themes or moral lessons in John's story.

Various Interpretations

Well-known male biblical commentators frame Mary's enigmatic anointing as conventional images of a woman of faith, such as an expression of humility.[6] In other readings, Mary's act becomes the ideal model of discipleship articulated as the "expressing of loving faith."[7] Her nonconforming, unfamiliar act is thus sanitized into a stable image within fixed frameworks of Christian faith. Her excessiveness and ambiguity are excluded or "castrated" in these interpretations; her desire is alienated as something normalized. The implied desire (lack) expressed by the narrative is repressed by the symbolic order of the interpreters. The conservative interpretation allows only images which can be legitimately circulated within the order and structure of the institutionalized church.

The dominant patriarchal readings of Mary's anointing underwent some changes (cracks) beginning in 1970 when feminist biblical criticism emerged alongside women's liberation movements.[8] In the hermeneutic trend started by Brown and based on his historical assumptions of the Johannine community, Mary (rather than her act), as well as other women in John's gospel, is read as a deviation from the fixed feminine images of virtue and faith imposed by the patriarchal church. Her desire is read as following Jesus as an "intimate disciple" which functions as a "primary

---

4. Haenchen, *John 2*, 84.

5. Brown, *Gospel According to John*, 450.

6. Bultmann, *Gospel of John*, 414; cf. Carson, *Gospel According to John*, 427–28: "As a sense of the woman's self-perceived unworthiness" and "the utmost in self-humbling devotion and love." It is interesting to see that male commentators use humility in this situation. Humility is often portrayed as a feminine virtue, thus framing Mary's actions within traditional patriarchal understandings of gender and attendant virtues.

7. Brown, *Gospel According to John*, 454. "The expression of an unwavering faith and love" (Beasley-Murray, *John*, 209). Or Moloney says, "Superabundant generosity, reflecting her love" (Moloney, *Gospel of John*, 349).

8. Conway, "Gender and the Fourth Gospel," 221.

category for John."[9] From the time of Brown's interpretation, Mary has been portrayed as a fixed disciple.[10]

Both Sandra Schneiders and Elisabeth Fiorenza assume an existing historical Johannine community, following the hypothesis of Brown,[11] and juxtapose the account of Mary in John with the account in Luke 10:38–42, where she listens at Jesus's feet. These authors understand Mary's act as a kind of eucharistic ministry and identify Mary as a "true disciple . . . as counterpart to the unfaithful disciple of Judas,"[12] or as one of the students of Rabbi Jesus, among the "active members of the school who devoted themselves to sacred study and discussion,"[13] which was not accessible for Jewish women. In these interpretations, in the community of equality between man and woman, Mary's ambiguity is colored by ideals or pre-existing roles and the position of men in the church. Due to their desire to find a historical precedence for women's ordination, feminists' reading of Mary's action did not go beyond the desire of "the Other," the desire of feminist theologians of the late twentieth century.

LACAN'S ETHICS OF PSYCHOANALYSIS AND MARY'S DESIRE BEYOND PROHIBITION

Then, what is her true desire if "man's desire is the desire of the Other" according to Lacan? In his seventh seminar, *The Ethics of Psychoanalysis*, Lacan says that people come to psychoanalysis to look for a cure; they want to feel happy. Analysts must confront such "demands of happiness."[14] The belief that analysis should lead to happiness has its roots in traditional ethics, such as Aristotle's *Nicomachean Ethics* or "the ethics of happiness." According to Aristotle's ethics, happiness (*eudaimonia*) is the ultimate goal for human beings.

---

9. Brown, *Community of the Beloved Disciple*, 190–91. In the appendix, "The Role of Women in the Fourth Gospel," Brown claims that women in the Johannine community had different roles from other first-century churches. He identifies the Samaritan woman and Mary Magdalene as a "quasi-apostle," while he depicts Mary and Martha as intimate disciples.

10. Fehribah, *Women in the Life of the Bridegroom*, 83.

11. Conway, *Men and Women*, 18–26.

12. Fiorenza, *In Memory of Her*, 330–31.

13. Schneiders, "Women in the Fourth Gospel," 42.

14. Lacan, *Ethics of Psychoanalysis*, 292.

Lacan's Ethics on Desire

For Lacan, a problem of *Nicomachean* ethics is that it suggests a complete, final picture in the life—that there will be somewhere completion, perfect happiness, fulfillment, wholeness, one final answer, one absolute truth, and one stable, finite universe etc. On this presupposition, ego psychology (which had been derived from Aristotle's happiness ethics) encourages clients to "aspire to happiness" or to have "a sense of oneness or completeness" as their goal of treatment. Lacan explains this desire as nothing but an illusory function of the imaginary order constructed in the mirror stage. Oneness of love or completeness of harmonious sexual relationships and roles between men and women, achieved through an active man and passive woman is impossibility.[15] It is in fact a product of unconscious fantasy that the operation of two mental apparatuses (pleasure principle and reality principle) brings about.

The subject of fantasy, as a slave to moral laws operating within human psychical structure (i.e., the superego), does not dare to desire beyond the limits of the moral law (symbolic order). It desires only an object socially acceptable, established, and familiar, and all ideals that the Other defines. This desire is "conventional."[16] It is an alienated, castrated desire since it is structured and programmed; by repeating what society values and recognizes as good through identification, it serves to maintain the status quo. This is what Aristotle thought of as happiness: desiring only within the limit of the pleasure-reality principle. What Lacan wants to say is that Aristotle's ethics is merely ethics within the pleasure-reality principle.

Lacan suggests that there is another, more important principle operating in the human psyche than the pleasure principle, which is the death drive. The subject under operation of the death drive desires an object forbidden by the law of prohibition of incest.[17] It is an object of *the Real* (*Das Ding*), an unknowable, alien, "strange, even hostile" object that the symbolic order attempts to repress.[18] The death drive is a psychical tendency to desire a crack, hole, emptiness (the *real*) which fantasy attempts to hide. The subject resists being conformed with the desire of the Other (social norms) even up to desiring death itself (or a symbolic death).

15. Lacan, *On Feminine Sexuality*, 82.

16. Ruti, *Singularity of Being*, 49.

17. Lacan, *Ethics of Psychoanalysis*, 67.

18. Lacan, *Ethics of Psychoanalysis*, 52.

Ethics of Transgression

In Lacanian approach, the ethics of psychoanalysis urges the subject to desire beyond prohibition; it is an ethics of transgression.[19] The subject is asked to confront their own desire.

In *Ethics of Psychoanalysis*, Lacan suggests that sublimation is one way of transgression. It is a process of elevating an object of desire, bound to the pleasure principle to the status of *das Ding*. Courtly Love is introduced as a "paradigm of sublimation."[20] In Courtly love, in spite of the knight's love, admiration, and fidelity toward the lady, his union with the lady is never achieved. It is pivotal that the woman as object of desire is never accessible. The knight's desire is to spend one night with the Lady. However, even though he deserves it after the difficult "love trial," its fulfillment is continuously delayed; more precisely, it is forever impossible. The lady is, in a sense, already a lost object.[21]

Her inaccessibility and absence make her like *das Ding*. For Lacan, love is narcissistic because it is a desire to complete—to become One by filling a fundamental lack in the divided subject.[22] However, Lacan sees the impossibility of fulfillment of this relationship, which he often expresses by saying, "there is no such sexual relationship" since the Other is also a lack in being. In fantasy, the imaginary female object functions to lure a subject and veil the lack in the Other. In this sense, courtly sublimation exposes the impossibility of love; it teaches that the female object of desire (object a) in a love relationship is the subject's narcissistic projection which covers the emptiness of *das Ding*. Thus, sublimation elevates the female object which veils the emptiness of *das Ding* "to the emptiness that represents it."[23] The lady, as an inaccessible, distant object, does not repress desire in the knight, but she is the cause of maintaining his desire because the prohibition of the law paradoxically causes the subject to desire beyond.

---

19. Freeland, *Antigone*, 33.
20. Lacan, *Ethics of Psychoanalysis*, 128.
21. Kesel, *Eros and Ethics*, 177.
22. Lacan, *On Feminine Sexuality*, 6.
23. Saint-Cyr, "Creating a Void," 17.

LACANIAN ANALYSIS OF ANTIGONE IN RELATION TO *DAS DING* AS AN ANALOGY FOR MARY

In the last section of *Ethics of Psychoanalysis*, Lacan introduces Antigone as a hero of transgression to its zenith and as a figure who "does not give up on her desire."[24] She is an image, an incarnate model of the death drive—absolute destruction.[25] Briefly speaking in the tragedy as the daughter of Oedipus, Antigone claims a proper funeral for her brother Polynices who betrayed the nation and died in battle, in opposition to the prohibition of her uncle Creon against burying Polynices. Creon orders Antigone to be buried in an empty tomb as a punishment for conducting this funeral rite.

Antigone is "autonomous" (possessing her own law) in relation to Creon's law.[26] Her autonomous subject is expressed in her explanation to Creon for the reason why she buried Polynices. She simply says, "That's how it is because that's how it is."[27] Her explanation does not depend on the discourse of the Other to persuade or appeal to him. She does not feel a need to persuade him. Antigone knows exactly the illusion, the fantasy of the "good" and the goods of country that Creon's law fabricates, and she traverses the law by transgressing it. By doing so, she not only reveals the "arbitrary brutality" of Creon's law, but her act also results in changing the political order and the collapse of Creon's rule.[28]

Antigone's enigmatic bond with her brother in relation to Creon's law, does not lie in her opposition to the law itself. "Her choice comes from another place"—beyond the law.[29] Her attachment to her brother lies in Polynices's irreplaceability and uniqueness (or her bond to Polynices) as Antigone's object of love.[30] Lacan pays attention to what Antigone further says about Polynices to Creon:

> My brother may be whatever you say he is, a criminal . . . but he is nevertheless what he is, and he must be granted his funeral rites. . . . As far as I am concerned, the order that you dare refer me to doesn't mean anything, for from my point of view, my

24. Shepherdson, *Lacan and the Limits of Language*, 51.

25. Lacan, *Ethics of Psychoanalysis*, 282.

26. Lacan, *Ethics of Psychoanalysis*, 282.

27. Lacan, *Ethics of Pyschoanalysis*, 278.

28. Shepherdson, *Lacan and the Limits of Language*, 76.

29. Shepherdson, *Lacan and the Limits of Language*, 76.

30. Lacan, *Ethics of Psychoanalysis*, 279; Kesel, *Eros and Ethics*, 217.

brother is my brother. If it were anyone else with whom I might enter into a human relationship, my husband or my children for example, they are replaceable.[31]

From the perspective of Creon and his law, Polynices is evil, criminal, an enemy of state.

However, Antigone claims that he is an object beyond good and evil, not to be represented by any concrete values and virtues corresponding with any moral discourse of a socio-linguistic system, such as Creon's law.[32] "My brother is my brother": he is unable to be articulated within a chain of signifiers, a tautology that reveals a hole in the chain of signifiers and expresses his unique being, his Thingness. He, and Antigone's bond with him, is beyond the reach of the law (signifier). Antigone's desire aims at the irreplaceable Thing in the Real. Her desire goes beyond the pleasure principle which allows a subject only to detour around *das Ding*, creating a safe distance, pursuing an endlessly metonymic displacement of objects of desire. This is the pure desire of suffering and death: the death drive.[33]

In what follows, through literary criticism of the characters and characterization, I will investigate how the narrative presents Mary's desire for Jesus as death drive like Antigone's desire and how it presents Mary's anointing elevating Jesus as an object of *das Ding* in line with courtly sublimation.

LACAN'S SYMBOLIC ORDER (LAW) AND CHARACTER AND CHARACTERIZATION IN BIBLE

R. Alan Culpepper popularized literary criticism of the Gospel of John, though he was not the first one to use this method.[34] Instead of looking at the text for historical evidence for the world behind the text, seeking an idea of what the Johannine community would be like, literary criticism focuses on the textual world as "a mirror in which the reader can see the world in which they live," and considers the gospel a "narrative text."[35] Analyzing the text literally brings awareness that women's pres-

---

31. Lacan, *Ethics of Psychoanalysis*, 278–79.
32. Lacan, *Ethics of Psychoanalysis*, 279.
33. Lacan, *Ethics of Psychoanalysis*, 282.
34. Culpepper, *Anatomy of the Fourth Gospel*.
35. Culpepper, *Anatomy of the Fourth Gospel*, 5.

ence is not just marginal, but rather female characters play central roles in "theologically complicated passages" in John.[36] In other words, "their status as women" matters.[37] The prominence of women in the Gospel of John is intentional for its theology.

Concerning literary apparatus, John's gospel has a certain distinctiveness compared to the synoptics. The gospel frequently uses irony, metaphor, symbolism, misunderstanding, contrast, and a cast of various characters to shape the narrative and theology.[38] One of the most conspicuous features is the presentation of various kinds of characters in particular situations.[39] Each character has a "unique story" in the Gospel of John.[40] Contrast is a key literary device used in the gospel to describe characters. The contrast between characters is especially used in this pericope to make a theological point between Mary and Judas.[41] Mary (and Jesus) is depicted as a character of death drive like Antigone through sublimation process, while Judas is a character of the pleasure principle and oppressive symbolic order. The narrator uses methods of telling and showing differently to emphasize the contrast between two characters. Telling is when the narrator gives information about characters directly so that the reader can understand the story easily, while the technique of showing is when, through the characters' actions and words, the reader can gather information and deduce the conclusion.[42]

Though several characters appear in the pericope, I will only look at characters which play an important role in the narrative: Jesus, Mary, and Judas. Though Mary precedes Judas in the pericope, I will look at Judas before Mary as Judas being a representative of oppressive symbolic order (law).

---

36. Seim, "Role of Women in the Gospel of John," 57.

37. Conway, *Men and Women*, 30.

38. O'Day and Hylen, 7–12; Culpepper, *Anatomy*, 151–202. See also Koester, *Symbolism in the Fourth Gospel*; Lee, *Flesh and Glory*.

39. Since Culpepper's *Anatomy*, there have been several studies on character and characterization of John. Bennema's research especially shows the characters in john are not flat but complex and dynamic. See Bennema, *Encountering Jesus*.

40. Bauckham, *Gospel of Glory*, 15.

41. Collins, "Who Are You?," 140.

42. Thatcher, "Jesus, Judas, and Peter," 435.

Lacan's Symbolic Order and Characterization of Jesus

Jesus is the protagonist of the Gospel of John and lends a reliable and authoritative voice to the narrator's narration. Jesus knows all things, even the thoughts, feelings, and intentions of others.[43] His theological discourse and actions are in line with what the narrator introduces in the prologue. The narrator often explains Jesus's enigmatic teachings. The narrative depicts Jesus as revealing the *Real* (God). By often using "I Am" (ἐγώ εἰμι) to define himself, Jesus identifies himself with God who reveals her name to Moses as "I am who I am" (Exod 3:14), a tautology unable to be defined by a chain of signifiers; there is a hole (void, mystery) in God.[44]

Jesus reveals God who is ineffable, beyond human understanding and description. Moreover, the narrative shows that Jesus constantly creates cracks in the symbolic order (for example, his violation of sabbath observance in John 5 and 9 in healing the paralyzed and the blind on the Sabbath). His presence hints at beyondness—beyond the symbolic order of Jewish traditional belief and practices. Jesus's non-conforming, deviant, enigmatic acts and words cause anxiety and conflict among the Jews. He trespasses the law and decenters the authority of Moses. Moreover, he does not depend on people's recognition—"Jesus does not entrust himself to them" (2:24)—nor does he seek the glory of human beings (5:41).

Jesus is presented as "autonomous" in relation to the law and established traditions and norms, as "speaking" but not "being spoken." He is in a position beyond the law. His death is his choice. Like Antigone, Jesus is fully aware of his fate and goes straight toward it.[45] His transgression threatens the stability that the Jewish belief system provides. By doing so, he reveals the excessiveness of God (i.e., the paradox or mystery of God). In the same way, Mary who anoints Jesus is a twin image of death drive with Jesus in the narrative, which I explain later.

From the beginning of the pericope, Jesus's prominent presence is felt. In verse one, his proper name is mentioned repeatedly, emphasizing that the event is centered around Jesus. In the pericope, Jesus's body is the specific focus: his body posture is depicted as reclining, and the object of Mary's performance (anointing and wiping) is part of his body—his feet (πόδας) are mentioned twice in verse three. This focus invokes Jesus as an embodied, mortal human. Moreover, it alludes *the Song of Songs*.

---

43. Thatcher, "Jesus, Judas, and Peter," 34.

44. Lacan briefly mentions "I am who I am" in *Ethics of Psychoanalysis*, 81.

45. Lacan, *Ethics of Psychoanalysis*, 278.

Here in the pericope, Jesus is an object of Mary's performance. He is not only aware of his impending death but he also intends not to avoid it since he comes to Bethany (near Jerusalem). Without refusing to receive Mary's performance, he allows her to conduct such an extraordinary, enigmatic performance on him. By correcting the misunderstanding of Judas, a male disciple, Jesus defends Mary, a Jewish woman. Actively siding with the woman would have been unthinkable in first-century Jewish society. From this, Jesus is characterized as unconventional, deviating from Jewish culture. Moreover, Jesus knows Mary's intention, which the narrator does not explicate. Jesus alone functions as authorial interpreter of Mary's enigmatic performance. In this pericope, Jesus once again goes beyond the limit of the Jewish law system and Moses's authority. In alluding to Moses's command for the poor in Deuteronomy 15:11, Jesus distorts the original intention and meaning of the command (importance of almsgivings) to pinpoint and emphasize his own impending death.

Lacan's Symbolic Order and Characterization of Judas

Judas is introduced with the adversative particle δέ ("but," "on the other hand") in verse 4 after the narrator's depiction of Mary's performance and its effect, contrasting Judas with Mary. While the narrator respects Mary's own space in silence through the method of "showing," the narrator intervenes dramatically in the narrative to directly "tell" information which the readers may not alone be able to infer from the Judas's words to Mary (v. 6).[46] Indeed, the narrator functions oppressively here in that she forces her negative view of Judas on the readers; the narrator opens no space for divergent interpretations.[47]

Before the narrator directly presents Judas's criticism of Mary, the narrator introduces him as "one of disciples, Judas Iscariot, who was later to betray him" (v. 4).[48] The narrator thus identifies him as a disciple, an important status among Christians. Judas has a firm social position unlike Mary, who is introduced only in terms of her performance. However, the narrator also shows that status is simply an empty signifier. Not only

46. The narrator presents Judas through the technique of "telling," "showing" (Judas's speech act) and "telling" consecutively.

47. In fact, within the gospel, Judas is the only disciple of whom the narrator reveals his internal thought and motivation (Culpepper, *Anatomy*, 23).

48. "One of the disciples" also implies that other disciples share Judas's sentiment about Mary. See Carson, *Gospel According to John*, 428.

is Judas presented as antagonist who will betray Jesus, but he is also exposed as a contradictory character (one in the inner circle of Jesus who betrays Jesus).[49] This designation of Judas begins even before this pericope, as 6:71 tells us "Judas, the son of Simon Iscariot, who, though one of the Twelve, was later to betray him." The narrator sneakily exposes within Judas, who functions as representative of the symbolic order, a hole which the symbolic order always attempts to conceal.[50] In that same chapter (6), Judas is identified with the devil by Jesus (and confirmed by narrator). Jesus later identifies the Jews who stand in opposition to him as children of devil (8:44). Before the pericope at hand, the narrative builds up the character of Judas as sharing common features with the Jews who are faithful servants of the Jewish religious system, only desiring within the limit of the symbolic order according to the pleasure principle, by identifying both Judas and the Jews with the devil.

Like the Jews who don't understand Jesus throughout the whole Gospel of John, Judas does not comprehend Mary's performance and is disturbed by her. He expresses hostility, saying, "Why wasn't this perfume sold and the money given to the poor? It was worth a year's wages" (v. 5). However, Judas's actions appear to fit within the established norms of Jewish society; if there were no comments on Judas's personality and intention, his objection to Mary may sound pious. His complaint about Mary wasting perfume may be legitimate since caring for the poor and leading a modest life (against luxury as love of wealth) are important virtues and devotional practices within the Christian tradition.[51]

Even more importantly, the historical and theological background of the word πτωχός and the view of poverty (and almsgiving) which πτωχός connotes, indicates that in the time of Jesus, almsgiving was one of the most emphasized acts of service to God within the Jewish law system (especially after the destruction of the temple).[52] When Judas mentions

49. Conway, *Men and Women*, 152.

50. Lacan pays attention to a defect that the reality (fantasy) has. Since the reality constructed of moral, logical discourse is a "linguistic reality," it is structurally lacking as language (signifiers) is structured by interval or gap; the signifier needs another signifier to produce a meaning not that the signifier refers to the signified (meaning). In other words, there is something that reality fails to repress or censor, which Lacan calls the *Real*. See Kesel, *Eros and Ethics*, 28, 79.

51. Rhee, *Loving the Poor, Saving the Rich*, xiii.

52. In the apocryphal Book of Tobit, Tobit equates acts of charity to the poor to service to God at the temple. Such identification of almsgiving as service to God can be found in the Book of Sirach which openly compares alter sacrifice and charity. Anderson, *Charity*, 19–21.

the poor and helping the poor with money from selling the perfume with which Mary anoints Jesus, he does not simply mean a service to the poor to alleviate their poverty; he means probably a service to God, devotion, a way of piety which has the effect of atoning for sin.[53] More precisely, he is suggesting almsgiving is *the* devotion that Mary "has to" do for God. It is *the* legitimate way, perhaps the *absolute* way, of service to God. The standard she must follow is violent and oppressive since it does not allow different ways. Without such commentary, any character or reader who shares the same symbolic order would agree with Judas in opposing the extravagant, wasteful Mary whose act threatens and confuses.

This, however, is the point that the narrator wants to make: Judas may sound right, but he is too conventional and too conservative in pursuing God (Jesus). Judas obsessively pursues the Jewish law system, believing that there is no hole (no excessiveness of God) in the system. Deviation, transgression, or otherwise desiring beyond the system is prevented. Relying on the oppressive, hegemonic system, Judas attempts to tame and limit Mary by defining what is proper piety for Mary (and probably for all women generally) and attempts to put her back into a legitimate place already assigned by the system. He demands conformity like Creon does to Antigone.

The truth about Judas is further exposed by the plain "telling" of the narrator: "He [Judas] did not say this because he cared about the poor but because he was a thief; as keeper of the money bag, he used to help himself to what was put into it" (v. 6, NIV). In order to expose Judas's greed, the narrator identifies Judas as a thief (κλέπτης). The narrator parallels Judas with the hired hand that Jesus criticizes in his teaching on the Good Shepherd (10).[54] The hired servant is a thief (10:1, 8) who does not care about (οὐ μέλει περὶ) the sheep (10:13) as Judas is a thief who does not care about the poor. The thief's hidden intention is "to steal, kill and destroy" (10:10). Likewise, Judas's hidden intention is stealing money from common purse.

By revealing Judas's greed, the narrator renders Judas's objection to Mary as unjust. Simultaneously, the narration shows how hypocritical and fictitious in nature are the Jewish religious system and its authority which Judas clings to. In claiming the central devotion of almsgiving (caring

---

53. The idea of meritorious, "atoning almsgiving" in Second Temple Judaism shaped the deed of charity as a privileged devotion of post-temple Judaism (CE 70) and early Christianity (Downs, *Alms*, 5; Anderson, *Charity*, 18).

54. Michaels, *Gospel of John*, 669.

about the poor), Judas means nothing; he simply repeats a meaningless, empty signifier to cover his greed with piety! The narrator thus implies that many legitimate pious activities and services to God can be meaningless signifiers, giving people a certain, stable, legitimate status in the system. In contrast with Mary and her death drive, Judas is characterized not only as one who has conservative desire in pursuit of God, operating under the pleasure principle, but also as representative of the system who unintentionally exposes the fictitious, empty nature of the system.

Lacan's Symbolic Order and Characterization of Mary

In the pericope in chapter 12, Mary appears in verse three, after the setting of dinner for Jesus is established. The narrator shows her action with three different verbs; λαβοῦσα (having taken a pint of pure nard); ἤλειψεν (anointed); ἐξέμαξεν (wiped).[55] Mary's performance can be divided into two actions: (1) anointing the feet of Jesus with nard, and (2) wiping his feet with her hair. These two distinctive actions define who Mary is in 11:2 in the context of Lazarus's death and resurrection. Interestingly, the actions are characterized by smell and body gesture. Concerning the conspicuously olfactory motif in her performance within the verse three,[56] there appear several words related to a sense of smell such as μύρου (ointment, perfume), νάρδου(nard), ὀσμὴ (smell, fragrance). Smell is not commonly evoked in the Bible, but one of three main areas where the language of olfaction is used in the Old Testament is the portrayal of sensual love relations.[57] The example of this kind olfaction is used in the Song of Songs in which sensual, erotic relations between lover and beloved and their desire for each other are metaphorized in terms of perfume and spices.[58]

55. More precisely, since λαβοῦσα is a participle, ἤλειψεν (anointed) and ἐξέμαξεν (wiped) are the two main verbs to describe her action.

56. Aside from Paul's writings, this is the only verse in the New Testament to contain the word ὀσμὴ (Kurek-Chomycz, "Fragrance of Her Perfume," 334–35). The word μύρου (ointment) occurs twice more in the pericope: in Judas's criticism (v. 5) and Jesus's defense of Mary (v. 7). In conjunction with John 11:2, where Mary's anointing first mentioned in the story of Lazarus, μύρου appears five times within chapters 11–12. The pericope also describes the quantity and quality (value) of the perfume; λίτραν μύρου (a pound of perfume); νάρδου πιστικῆς (pure, genuine nard); πολυτιμου (expensive, costly) all in verse 3. Verse 5 specifies τριακοσίων δηναρίων, "worth three hundred denarii; a year's wage" (NIV), indicating both the excessive amount and extravagant quality of perfume used by Mary.

57. Green, "Soothing Odors," 1.

58. Green, Aroma of Righteousness, 65–66.

Mary's actions of anointing the feet of Jesus and wiping his feet with her hair have two distinctive connotations: (1) a romantic sensual connotation in ancient literature,[59] and (2) expressing grief for the death of beloved and funeral rite.[60] With the sensual, feminine usage of smell and body gesture, it is not hard to find parallel between Mary's anointing and Song of Songs 1:12, "So long as the king was at table, my spikenard gave forth its smell" (in LXX, "ἕως οὗ ὁ βασιλεὺς ἐν ἀνακλίσει αὐτοῦ νάρδος μου ἔδωκεν ὀσμὴν αὐτοῦ").[61] The references to the table (reclined on the table), nard and smell create a strong connection between these two passages. Mary's act seems to allude to the Song of Songs and be an expression of her desire (love) for Jesus in excess and extravagance.

However, her actions are done in silence, and she is indifferent to the presence of the other. Her sensual performance breaks conformity with the Jewish law system. She offers no explanation of her performance, nor does she react to Judas's harsh criticism of her wasting expensive oil. She appears as a person who does not care about the Other or social recognition. In a moment of unusual silence, the narrator offers no explanation for her character (personality), motivation or meaning to help the reader to understand the pericope. The narrator only reports the effect of the anointing: "the house is full of fragrance."[62]

Mary's performance is simply reported as if its effect seems to transfer her to an alien, unknown world operating outside the fixed symbolic order as smell/fragrance is silent, but mobile, uncontainable, and transgressive.[63] The readers (and those present in the scene) are left in confusion and uncertainty to interpret her action without clear guidance of the narrator.

59. Brant, "Husband Hunting," 218. In Athanasius's writings, there can be found a close parallel of anointing of feet with erotic connotation in that men's feet were rubbed (anointed) by mistresses (Coakley, "Anointing of Bethany," 247; Tilborg, *Imaginative Love in John*, 198).

60. Lee, *Flesh and Glory*, 205; Brant "Husband Hunting," 217; Tilborg, *Imaginative Love in John*, 198.

61. Along with other scholars, Winsor insists that some specific words are used as "markers" in the pericope, especially in verse 3 (i.e., "hair, reclining, extremely precious nard ointment, feet, scent"), function to remind the implied readers of the whole text of the Song of Songs and its theme of intimacy between the lover and beloved, through "metonymic allusion." See Winsor, *King Is Bound*, 19–26.

62. It is worth noting that the narrator's report that "the house is full of fragrance" is unusual because it occurs only in this pericope and is absent in the similar anointing stories in the synoptics.

63. Harvey, *Scenting Salvation*, 7.

The narrator thus attempts to show that Mary's desire for Jesus (her *jouissance*) is beyond comprehension (feminine *jouissance*). The narrator wants the reader to experience her enigmatic performance instead of understanding and theologizing it. By not admitting any legitimate interpretation through the symbolic order of the Jewish religious system nor providing any other authorial interpretation, the narrator places Mary in a vacuum of social norms and tradition. She is not an ideal image of faith; she is an object beyond what readers want to be identified with as a model for faith, that is, nothing but a narcissistic object in Lacanian terms. Her desire remains unknowable, alien, anxiety-provoking to the readers; she represents emptiness.[64]

Mary's performance immediately merits sharp criticism and hostility from Judas. In front of Mary's ambiguous performance of desiring, unable to understand her, Judas, as representative of the Jewish symbolic order (elaborated later), cannot bear such deviation and violation. Judas attempts to control her and return her to a proper religious role, i.e. piety of almsgiving (12:5). However, her performance in turn exposes Judas's hidden intention which is greed, though the exposure is done through the mouth of the narrator (12:6). As with Antigone's autonomy—her transgression leading to the crumbling of Creon's dominion—Mary's enigmatic performance results in revealing the hypocritical, fictitious nature of the oppressive symbolic order (represented by Judas) and deconstructing its hegemony. After the narrator's exposure, Mary appears again in the form of proper noun now when Jesus intervenes the situation and rebukes Judas by saying, "leave her alone" (v. 7). It is Jesus who respects and defends her deviation from the desire of the Other. Jesus allows Mary to remain in a place beyond the symbolic order, that is, the realm of the *Real*. Then, Jesus offers explanation of her performance: she did it for his funeral.[65] In other words, as an object of desire he is not accessible, like the lady in Courtly love. Then, I will describe Mary's desire as accessible sublimation.

64. Lacan says, "The Thing will always be represented by emptiness, precisely because it cannot be represented by anything else" (*Ethic of Psychoanalysis*, 129).

65. "ἵνα εἰς τὴν ἡμέραν τοῦ ἐνταφιασμοῦ μου τηρήσῃ αὐτό." This Greek sentence is not easy to translate. Several different interpretations exist: (1) "in order that she may keep it for the day of my burial"; (2) "[she has done this] in order to keep it for the day of my burial"; (3) "Let her keep it for the day of my burial" (Carson, *According to the John*, 429). Lee is wise to say that in the pericope, Jesus "is linking Mary's action to Jesus's death and burial," instead of fixing an exact meaning of the wording (Lee, *Flesh and Glory*, 202).

Lacanian Sublimation concerning Mary's Desire and the Dominant
Narratives

Mary's deeply sensual performance of anointing and wiping demonstrates her adoration of Jesus as messiah-lover, adopting the tradition of
the Song of Songs, while avoiding the safe categories of Christian dogmatic faith[66] or the Mosaic Law System.[67] She seems to desire Jesus as
messianic lover. If Mary desires Jesus as an object of love, then Jesus is
merely an object of fantasy in which she is made complete with him. Jesus
is still an ideal object which can be enjoyed socially, with a proper place
in the symbolic order, so she who is identified with him also will have a
proper place in the symbolic order. Whether he is desired as ideal husband, lover or messiah, Jesus is nothing but a narcissistic object operating
in fantasy. Her desire is bound to the object.

However, the narrative implies that her desire deviates from social expectation through the sublimation process as explained by Jesus.
Through Jesus, who reveals her intention, her gesture of erotic love turns
into a funeral rite. It is revealed that the Messiah or lover she pursues and
desires is in fact a dying or dead messiah; love will never be complete. Re-
call Mary's anointing and wiping each have two connotations: an erotic
connotation and a funerary one. In Mary's performance, two different
meanings are intermingled. Of course, though she is silent about her motivation (as she is not obliged to explain anything like Antigone), Jesus's
omniscience in the Gospel leads the reader to believe Jesus has faithfully
explained her motivation.

In contrast to scholars following Brown, who claims that Mary
is unconscious of Jesus's death and unaware of the significance of her
performance as burial, I follow the reading of others who see that Mary
is clearly aware of his impending death based on their reciprocity and
close relation.[68] She knows of his death, yet still she pursues him as he

66. Mary never expresses her desire in the "conventional language" of the early
Christian church as Martha does in chapter 11: "You are the Christ, the son of God,
who was to come into the world" (v. 27). See O'Day and Hylen, *John*, 298; Brown, *Gospel According to John*, 433. This messianic profession of faith is uttered by other people
in the gospel, such as Nathanael or the crowds (1:41, 49; 6:14). Even Peter offers the
same confession of faith in the Synoptics.

67. Within this system, people look forward to "second Moses, or a new Moses."
Moses becomes a fixed standard (norm) against which to judge true messiah by the
Jews; the anticipated deliverance by the messiah should be a "repetition" of Moses's
deliverance (Glasson, *Moses in the Fourth Gospel*, 20).

68. Brown, *Gospel According to John*, 449. However, some scholars also argue that

is, similar to Antigone's desire to bury her brother Polynices. Jesus, as the ephemeral, dying messiah whom Mary adores, is an object with no value or position in society. His paradoxical actions and words, as well as his impending death, defy the social expectations of the messiah. He is an object she should not be identified with: he is a crack, a rupture, a hole. He is an unrealistic object to desire: an empty vapor. By adoring a dead or dying messiah, Mary elevates Jesus to the object of the *Real* (the status of *Das Ding*).

The narrative implies Mary's sublimation process; it shows how the meaningful/ideal object of desire (Jesus as messiah or lover) turns out to be emptiness, nothing (dead messiah /lover). Many characters in the Bible have a pattern of fantasy wherein their lack is exposed and then it is satisfied, such as the anointing story in Luke, where a woman's immoral state is revealed and then Jesus forgives her, just like a happy-ending love story. Mary, however, is different in that her lack is exposed and instead of attempting to fill the lack with an ideal object, she desires the lack and remains in the lack as it is. By desiring a dead messiah (emptiness) she is identified with emptiness, as a person becomes what she desires. As she desires the object of the *Real* (*das Ding*) she is transferred to realm of the Real (death drive).

CONCLUSION

Mary does not desire happiness or feeling of completion and union with Jesus in anointing him. In spite of the demand of Judas to be conformed to the desire of the Other through almsgiving, Mary faces her own desire: desiring a vaporous, empty Jesus who does not have any meaning in the hegemonic religious, social order of her time since he is going to die. By pursuing her own desire, like Antigone who is situated in the empty tomb, Mary is not hesitant to go straight into the zone between two deaths, biological death and the death of the subject of being by a signifier (alienation). The second death means the "point where the false metaphors of being (*l'étant*) can be distinguished from the position of Being (*l'être*) itself."[69]

Mary is the first character who comes to know Jesus's impending death. See Moloney, "Faith of Martha and Mary," 493; Hoskyns, *Fourth Gospel*, 416.

69. Lacan, *Ethics of Psychoanalysis*, 248.

This is a destruction of the symbolic universe with which the subject is born and identified. This is the place of *ex nihilo*: all meanings and values (signification) are emptied, and a new signifier (new desire) can emerge. This love story of Mary's anointing disappoints readers who expect happy feelings but are left with discomfort and anxiety. The story, lacking a proper happy closure, invites readers to recognize their own fantasy and to traverse it. The text demands readers to become a desiring subject who desires to desire.

9

"There Is No Other of the Other"

A Lacanian Approach to *Dominus Iesus*

Heejung Cho

Jacques Lacan was a French psychoanalyst who made significant contributions to the theory and practice in the field of psychoanalysis. Lacan's work focused on the relationship between the self and the other, the nature of desire, and the construction of identity within linguistic and cultural contexts. His work continues to be influential not only in the theory but also in the practice of psychoanalysis, philosophy, literary criticism, cultural studies and so on.

Lacan's contribution in understanding others can be a useful tool in analyzing some of the complexity present in understanding non-Christian traditions within the Catholic Church, particularly expressed in the Vatican Declaration *Dominus Iesus*. *Dominus Iesus* addresses the relationship between Christianity and other religions, asserting the unique role of revelation in the life of Jesus Christ in God's plan of salvation. It emphasizes the uniqueness of Christ's salvific work and the necessity of the Church for salvation, thereby implying that the non-Christian traditions lack the access to the full truth. The position observed in *Dominus Iesus* appears to presume the ultimate otherness of the non-Christian traditions because it excludes the possibility of various traditions' access to the truth by genuine exchange and communication among traditions.

Whether the non-Christian traditions have access to full truth is not the focus of this essay and deserves a treatment in more in-depth research of its own. The focus of this paper is on *Dominus Iesus*'s position on understanding non-Christians as others. *Dominus Iesus* associates pluralism with relativism, and this is problematic because relativism is understood as one of the threats for Christianity. Pope Benedict XVI, previously Cardinal Ratzinger who was also the head of Congregation for the Doctrine of the Faith (CDF) when *Dominus Iesus* was issued, officially recognized relativism as one of the greatest threats that Catholic Christians were facing at the time. Most of understandings of Catholic teachings are shaped by the cultural and linguistic context, and there are elements of relativistic approach in some practical understandings that are contextually established. Cultural understandings are relative in its own nature. For instance, Catholicism in Latin America would have its own practices and rituals with a focus on the theme of liberation that are relative to their cultural contexts. Thus, relativism in and of itself does not pose a threat to Catholic theology.

According to *Dominus Iesus*, only Catholic Church is in possession of full truth revealed in the life of Jesus while other religions are in grievously deficient status. The stance observed in *Dominus Iesus* suggests that non-Christian traditions are ultimately in the position of "others" which cannot be part of the subject that is Catholic Church. Therefore, perceiving and understanding non-Christians as the ultimate other is what is problematic, making constructive pluralism with everyone helping to constitute the fuller truth by contributing an impossible concept.

This essay will focus on *Dominus Iesus*'s understanding of non-Christian traditions as others and demonstrate that *Dominus Iesus*'s description of non-Christians as others appears to be in the imaginary order from a Lacanian point of view. In doing so, this essay will proceed in three parts. First, I will provide a brief overview of the context observed in *Dominus Iesus* and its understanding of non-Christian traditions as others. Second, I will focus on the concept of otherness in the imaginary order from the perspective of Lacan and examine how otherness in the imaginary order stays as an image in a mirror reflection that only reflects the subject's desires. Third, I will analyze the issue of relativism in *Dominus Iesus* in light of the fear of fragmentation. Fourth, I will discuss the otherness in the Symbolic order and elaborate on Lacan's statement that there is no Other of the Other. This essay will conclude that *Dominus Iesus*'s understanding of non-Christian traditions is in the imaginary order and that its claim and aspiration of Christian unity is understood as phallus or an *object petit a* that indicates the absence of it.

AN OVERVIEW: *DOMINUS IESUS* AND ITS BACKGROUND

Dominus Iesus[1] is a declaration issued by the Congregation of the Doctrine of the Faith (CDF) of the Roman Catholic Church, under the leadership of Cardinal Joseph Ratzinger, who later became Pope Benedict XVI. This declaration was released in the year 2000, and addresses the unicity and salvific universality of Jesus Christ and the Roman Catholic Church. This document caused significant discussions and debates, especially in the area of interreligious dialogue, as it reaffirmed the stance of the Catholic Church on the necessity of the Church for salvation and the uniqueness of Jesus Christ as the mediator between God and humanity.

    Dominus Iesus addresses several theological issues, and one of them is relativism. It states that relativistic theories are used to justify religious pluralism (DI 4); however, it does not provide an explanation for this claim. *Dominus Iesus* appears to assume that, in understanding religious pluralism, there is a presupposition of "relativistic attitudes toward truth itself, according to which what is true for some would not be true for others" (4). Thus, the declaration asserts that the "truth of faith does not lessen the sincere respect which the Church has for the religions of the world, but at the same time, it rules out, in a radical way, that mentality of indifferentism characterized by a religious relativism which leads to the belief that one religion is as good as another" (22).

    Pluralism and relativism are neither the one and nor same; however, *Dominus Iesus* appears to make assumption that one leads to the other. Despite the fact that they are closely related, pluralism and relativism need to be distinguished as their implications are different. Pluralism acknowledges the existence of diverse religious beliefs and practices, suggesting that different beliefs and traditions can coexist harmoniously, contributing to the richness of human understanding of God. Thus, pluralism can be understood as recognizing the presence of religious expressions in various cultures while affirming the uniqueness of Jesus Christ and the

---

1. CDF, *Dominus Iesus*.

Catholic faith. On the other hand, relativism posits that truth is relative to individual perspectives or culture contexts. This can be interpreted as a challenge because it may suggest that all religious traditions in various cultures are equally true or valid, undermining the idea of uniqueness of revelation in the coming of Jesus Christ.

The tendency to associate religious pluralism with relativism in *Dominus Iesus* shows that there are different ways of understanding others. Pluralism suggests that others are contributing to constitution of richer meanings as we understand different cultures and religious, and therefore, different views and perspectives can come together on a higher level. This means that others' understanding can help enrich the meaning to be fuller, and in this sense, others' understanding and it can be brought together on a certain level. However, relativism implies that truth is relative and conditional to cultures and perspectives, and this becomes problematic for the Roman Catholic Church, because the relativist's claim becomes a stumbling block for the claim of full truth within the Catholic Church.

Relativism poses a particular threat for Roman Catholic Christians especially when it is married to an exclusive perspective of Catholic Church which suggests if one is right the other one must be wrong. In this way, others' understanding cannot become part of the subject's understanding. This means that the others stay as others and there is no possibility of understanding others' perspective in a fundamental sense. Thus, the claim that relativism presents a threat for Christianity reveals the presupposition that non-Christian traditions are ultimately in the position of other, implying that the constructive collaboration between different traditions is not a possibility.

THE OTHERNESS AND LACAN'S MIRROR STAGE

At this point, I would like to turn to the concept of other in the perspective of Lacanian psychoanalysis. The concept of the other holds significant importance and complexity in Lacan's theory because the other represents a fundamental aspect of human subjectivity and have influences and implications on the subject's identity and sense of self. In a general sense, the other means the external world, which includes people, society, cultures, languages and institutions outside of the self. However, Lacan's understanding of the other is more than just the external world, as it moves beyond an objective reality, but includes symbolic construct that plays a significant role in the development of the self.

One of the central ideas of the other in Lacan's theory includes the mirror stage. In the year 1936, Lacan presented a paper entitled "Le stade du miroir," which is later translated into English as "The Mirror Stage." It remains one of the most referenced works of Lacan's texts. It was translated in 1968 in the Marxist journal *New Left Review*, and played a significant role in the development of Lacan's Imaginary order. Dany Nobus describes the solidness of Lacan's mirror stage:

> The mirror stage has always been viewed by Lacan as a solid piece of theorizing, a paradigm relating its value to explain human self-consciousness, aggressivity, rivalry, narcissism, jealousy, and fascination with images in general. In a sense, this does not come as a surprise when it is appreciated that the 1949 Mirror Stage article was not something Lacan had concocted at a moment's notice, but a pearl which he had carefully cultured for some thirteen odd years.[2]

Lacan bases his theory in experimental psychology, which suggests the development of the sense of self through observing the mirror image of self.

This is different from the traditional psychology of the time which argued that self-awareness arises from the infants gradual and increasing awareness of its own physical body. The infant had a level of individual awareness to become aware of its own body in the first place. It was later added to the traditional approach that the infant must not only gain awareness of his or her own body and bodily functions, but also to develop an awareness of the environment and the external world at the same time. It is only then the infant will be able to differentiate himself or herself from the external environment. This means that for a person to identify himself or herself as a coherent and autonomous self, he or she has to distinguish himself or herself from others and from the external world.

Lacan's mirror stage elaborates on one's sense of self in observing one's own image in the mirror which is part of the external world. According to Lacan, the mirror phase occurs roughly between 6 and 18 months. It corresponds to Freud's stage of primary narcissism when the subject is in love with the image of themselves and their own bodies, and

---

2. Nobus, *Key Concepts of Lacanian Psychoanalysis*, 104.

this precedes the stage of the love of others.[3] During this stage the infant is fascinated with his or her own image and tries to control and play with it. When looking at the mirror, the infant is initially confused with the image with reality, but he or she soon recognizes that the image as his or her own image.

During the mirror stage, the infant introjects the image as his or her body which has the total form through seeing the image in the mirror. This idea of totality or the image of the body however, is in contrast to the infant's experience of his or her own body, because he or she has not developed the sense of the full control over the body yet. The infant still feels his or her body fragments and not yet united; however, the image in the mirror provides him or her with a sense of unification and wholeness. The mirror image therefore anticipates the development and mastery of the infant's body which is in contrast to the infant's experiences. Although the infant identifies with the mirror image, the image is alienating that it is not the infant himself or herself. Therefore, the sense of self in its wholeness is acquired in identifying with the mirror image. Lacan describes the mirror stage:

> The mirror stage is a drama whose internal thrust is precipitated from insufficiency to anticipation—and which manufactures for all the subject, caught up in the lure of spatial identification, the succession of phantasies that extends from a fragmented body-image to a form of its totality that I shall call orthopaedic—and, lastly, to the assumption of the amour of an alienating identity, which will mark with its rigid structure the infant's entire mental development. Thus, to break out of the circle of the *Innenwelt* into *Umwelt* generates the inexhaustible quadrature of the ego's verification.[4]

In this moment of disagreement between the infant's fragmented sense of self and the imaginary autonomy, a conflict occurs between within the infant's sense of self.

According to Lacan, the subject is established as a rival to himself or herself when the image of wholeness and unity is posited in opposition to the experience of fragmentation. The same rivalry established extends to the subject's future relations with others. Benvenuto and Kennedy put it, "the primary conflict between identification with, and primordial rivalry with, the other's image, begins a dialectical process that links the ego to

---

3. Thurschwell, *Sigmund Freud*, 79–94.

4. Lacan, *Écrits: A Selection*, 5.

more complex social situations."[5] According to Lacan, one has to be recognized by another, because one's image is mediated by the gaze of the other. This means that the other becomes the guarantor of oneself, and therefore one is dependent on the other as the guarantor and witness of one's own existence. At the same time, one and the other are in rivals to each other.

The mirror stage is helpful in unpacking the way non-Christian traditions are viewed as others in *Dominus Iesus*. Despite the hope for Christian unity, we now live in the world of religious pluralism. The pluralistic world is recognized in *Dominus Iesus*, and this becomes a problem for Christians because the world does not have the Christian unity as they learn from the doctrine within the Church. The revelation expressed in the coming of Jesus is unique to Christian faith. Jesus came into this world to bring people together, not to create division within the world. However, what Christians experience is not consistent with what they learn from the teachings of the Church. Christians experience division and fragmentation of the world with various religious traditions; on the other hand, the teachings of the Church expressed in doctrines do not reflect their experience. However, they understand the hope for Christian unity is what the world should pursue, and the current fragmentation only creates a sense of alienation in their Christian identity.

In this way, the experience of division and fragmentation can be compared to the sense of underdeveloped self and the concept of Christian unity to the mirror image as a whole and united body in the mirror stage. Moreover, Christians can experience a sense of competition or rivalry with others. In the mirror stage, the rivalry arises from the perceived idealized image presented by the reflection, and the infant strives to attain or surpass this image. This competition with the mirror image, representing the gaze of the other, develops as the desire to achieve a sense of wholeness and mastery.

For Christians development of Christian identity, despite the sense of rivalry, the gaze of other is crucial in constructing the sense of self and others. The rivalry in the mirror stage emphasizes the complex interaction between the internal self-image and external perception, which contributes to shaping one's ongoing psychological development and relationship with other.

---

5. Benvenuto and Kennedy, *Works of Jacques Lacan,* 58.

THREAT OF RELATIVISM IN *DOMINUS IESUS* AND FEAR OF FRAGMENTATION

As explored above, the mirror stage demonstrates the disagreement between the infant's fragmented sense of self and the imaginary sense of self with wholeness and mastery. Based on the image of wholeness and unity which is in opposition to the experience of fragmentation, the subject then also develops a sense of rivalry to himself or herself. This rivalry relationship with self continues to develop as a sense of rivalry with others in the subject's future relationship.

The mirror stage and the disagreement between introjected self (ideal ego) and the Ego Idea[6] can be helpful in explaining the Christian identity and the threat of relativism. The stance of *Dominus Iesus* shows the dynamic of rivalry in the disagreement between the experience of fragmentation and the ideal image of Christian unity. The sense of rivalry extends to the others, thereby stating that "it is also certain that objectively speaking they [various religious traditions] are in a gravely deficient situation in comparison with those who, in the Church, have the fullness of the means of salvation" (DI 22). From the perspective of Lacan, the sense of rivalry is based on the idealized image that reflects the Christians' desire of wholeness and unity, and therefore does not reflect the reality in its context. In what follows, I would like to analyze the threat of relativism and the fear of fragmentation observed in *Dominus Iesus*.

There is a background to the association of pluralism and relativism. Cardinal Joseph Ratzinger, the Pope Emeritus Benedict XVI, who was the Prefect of the Congregation of Doctrine of Faith at the time of *Dominus Iesus,* expresses his concerns about a "dictatorship of relativism."[7] Ratzinger's concerns are indicated in his homily, *Pro Eligendo Romano Pontifice,* which he delivered to the cardinals before entering the conclave that elected him Pope.

Today, having a clear faith based on the Creed of the Church is often labeled as fundamentalism. Whereas relativism—that is, letting oneself be "tossed here and there carried about by every wind of doctrine"— seems the only attitude that can cope with modern times. We are building a dictatorship of relativism that does not recognize anything as definitive and whose ultimate goal consists solely of one's own ego and desires.[8]

---

6. Lacan, *Desire and Its Interpretation,* 28–29.

7. Ratzinger, "Mass *Pro Eligendo Romano Pontifice.*"

8. Ratzinger, "Mass *Pro Eligendo Romano Pontifice.*"

At this point, questions arise with regard to pluralism and relativism. Does *Dominus Iesus* equate relativism with pluralism? Where does this fear of relativism come from? Does this fear reflect the Church's anxiety based on fragmentation or is it based on the nature of relativism? If it is based on relativism, if there is a notion of religious pluralism that does not presuppose religious relativism, does that change the Christian understanding of religious pluralism?

Dominus Iesus asserts that relativism is the greatest doctrinal threat to Christian society. According to the declaration, relativism denies the uniqueness and universality of Jesus Christ and the claim that Catholicism is the one true religion. Ambrose Ih-Ren Mong asserts that *Dominus Iesus* was influenced by Ratzinger's understanding of other forms of relativism, such as National Socialism, and Marxism, which made him aware of the inherent dangers of relativism.[9] The tendency observed in *Dominus Iesus* to associate relativism with pluralism appears to have been influenced by Ratzinger's understanding of religious pluralism. Mong argues that "while Ratzinger has argued convincingly about the danger of the tyranny of relativism, there is a tendency in his writings to equate religious pluralism with relativism, which results in his dismissal of theology not grounded in the Platonic and Augustinian tradition."[10] Hence *Dominus Iesus* assumes that religious pluralism in an Asian context entails a relativistic understanding of religions.

This tendency may also stem from Ratzinger's reading of John Hick, who he considers "a prominent representative of religious relativism."[11] In "Relativism: the Central Problem for Faith Today," Ratzinger is tackling the relativist contention that correct judgments of fact and value cannot be made. This is a philosophical departure point that denies the possibility of divine revelation being fully disclosed in the coming of Jesus Christ.[12] In the same way, Ratzinger is critical of those theologians influenced by European post-Enlightenment philosophy who privilege reason as the primary source of authority and legitimacy, thereby granting equality to all religions and at the same time denying the possibility of absolute divine truth in any religious tradition. That said, *Dominus Iesus* does seem to assume and present a structural connection of relativism and pluralism.

9. Mong, *Dialogue Derailed*, 146.

10. Mong, *Dialogue Derailed*, 146.

11. Ratzinger, *Truth and Tolerance*, 121.

12. Ratzinger, "Relativism."

In searching for an understanding of religious pluralism that does not assume relativism, a fuller definition of relativism is essential. However, relativism is an ambiguous term and it is challenging to come up with a single definition. Barbara Herrnstein Smith writes, "If relativism means anything at all, it means a great many things. It is certainly not, though often treated as such, a one-line 'claim' or 'thesis,' for example, 'man [sic] is the measure of all things,' 'nothing is absolutely right or wrong,' 'all opinions are equally valid,' and so forth."[13]

In her book *Relativism*, Maria Baghramian defines relativism as "the view that cognitive, moral or aesthetic norms and values are dependent on the social or conceptual systems that underpin them and consequently a neutral standpoint for evaluating them is not available to us."[14] Other definitions of relativism, constructed according to different perspectives, include that of Maurice Mandelbaum, who understands historical relativism as "the view that no historical work grasps the nature of the past (or present) immediately, that whatever 'truth' a historical work contains is relative to the conditioning processes under which it arose and can only be understood with reference to those processes."[15] For his part, sociologist Karl Mannheim defines relativism as "the approach that recognizes that all knowledge is socially dependent, bound to the location of the thinker."[16] This definition is based on his understanding of "the inevitable relativity of all human truth."[17] These are a few examples of the attempts to define relativism, where oftentimes, the definition depends on the field of study in which it is used.[18]

Joseph Ratzinger also enters the discussion with a definition of relativism, which he sees as an attitude of modern times that does not recognize anything as definitive, and that accepts changeable moral and religious standards.[19] He presses the term further to precisely identify the dangers of a relativist view and to highlight the importance of protecting the core values of Christian faith. Gediminas T. Jankunas asserts that

13. Smith, "Relativism, Today and Yesterday," 228. Please note that the gendered language is a reflection of the time in which the text is written.

14. Baghramian, *Relativism*, 1.

15. Mandelbaum, *Problem of Historical Knowledge*, 19.

16. Baum, *Truth Beyond Relativism*, 36.

17. Baum, *Truth Beyond Relativism*, 36.

18. There are multiple meanings for the term relativism in contemporary academic philosophy. On the variety of definitions, see Herre and Krausz, *Varieties of Relativism*.

19. Ratzinger, "Mass *Pro Eligendo Romano Pontifice*."

"Ratzinger spent his life analyzing and speaking out against relativism,"[20] and that Ratzinger's address on relativism in 1996 was the first time the term "relativism" appeared in a document conveying the Magisterial teachings of the Roman Catholic Church.[21]

There is a cautious tone in Ratzinger's homily where he expresses his concerns about the modern situation of pluralism. He describes the contemporary situation as buffeted by a multiplicity of winds of doctrine. How many winds of doctrine have we known in recent decades, how many ideological currents, how many ways of thinking? The small boat of the thought of many Christians has often been tossed about by these waves—flung from one extreme to another: from Marxism to liberalism, even to libertinism; from collectivism to radical individualism; from atheism to a vague religious mysticism; from agnosticism to syncretism and so forth.[22]

Within this description of "multiple winds of doctrine," relativism is seen as an attitude of being tossed and carried about with every changing ideology, and the phenomenon of relativism as a whole is seen as a form of dictatorship. The definitions of relativism are varied and inconsistent. Moreover, relativism appears to present inherent fallacies, especially in its epistemology. Some proponents of relativism suggest that knowledge is socially dependent in a context of changeable standards of truth and this means that one can never access what is true. Moreover, associating pluralism with relativism is within the context of Europe and does not represent religious pluralism in the entire world. In a way, considering relativism as a threat reflect the reality in a European post-enlightenment philosophy, thereby indicating that it is based on the idealized image of its own context.

THE SYMBOLIC ORDER: "THERE IS NO OTHER OF THE OTHER"[23]

Lacan introduced the concept of the imaginary, symbolic and real orders in understanding the human experience and the structure of subjectivity. These three orders are interconnected and constitute the framework

20. Jankunas, *Dictatorship of Relativism,* xi.

21. Ratzinger, "Relativism."

22. Ratzinger, "Mass *Pro Eligendo Romano Pontifice.*"

23. Lacan, *Écrits,* 292–325.

through which individuals perceive reality and construct their identities. The imaginary order is associated with the mirror stage that was explored previously. It is early stages of human development when the infant experiences a moment of self-recognition when they see their reflection in a mirror. The recognition of the self-image in the mirror creates an image of wholeness and unity, which becomes the bases of the sense of self.

However, the image in the mirror is an idealized image of self which is characterized by identification, resemblance, and the formation of representations. This image also bears a fundamental misrecognition, because the image is based on idealization and illusion that conceals the inherent fragmentation and lack within the self. The disconnect between the idealized image and the existential experience of fragmentation brings about a sense of rivalry of oneself with its own image, which later develops into the rivalry with others in the world. In this essay, in their process of constructing Christian identity, I demonstrate that the understanding other religions from a Christian perspective parallel with the subject in the mirror stage.

The symbolic order for Lacan is the realm of language, culture and social structures. This order is the domain of shared meanings, norms, and systems that govern social interactions and organize experience. It is based on the presupposition that there is an unconscious structure that determines the individual's social position and regulates their relationships without their being aware of it. Lacan holds that language is the primary symbolic system which plays a central role in shaping the identity of subject and mediating the subject's experience with the external world.

This symbolic order is also characterized by the gaze and desire of the Other with the capital O, and the Other represents the collective social and cultural frameworks that influence and shape the identity of the subject.[24] It is through the symbolic order that the subject gains perspective by accessing social reality and constructs their sense of self within the context of the society. Lacan makes an important distinction between the little other and the big Other, and calls this distinction a "twofold alienation."[25]

> There is the other as imaginary. It's here in the imaginary relation with the other that traditional *Selbst-Bewusstsein* or self-consciousness is instituted. ... There is also the Other who

24. Lacan, *Four Fundamental Concepts*, 67–74.
25. Lacan, *Psychoses*, 241.

speaks from my place, apparently, this Other who is within me. This is an Other of a totally different from the other, my counterpart.[26]

The lower case other refers to imaginary other explored in the mirror stage. This is the other as an image in the mirror who the infant presumes will completely satisfy his or her desires of mastery. The subject considers this other as a whole, united or coherent self, because as reflections of the subject this image gives the sense of being complete and whole being despite the inner feelings of fragmentation. On the other hand, the big Other represents the absolute otherness that one cannot assimilate to his or her subjectivity. The big Other is the symbolic order as language in which one is born into and must learn to articulate one's own desire. It is also the discourse and the desires of those around the subject, through which one internalizes and reflects one's own desire.

Lacan holds that our desires are always inextricably influenced by the desires of others. According to Lacan, desire remains beyond the necessity of need or the appetite for satisfaction. After all, "desire is something that gives back the margin of deviation marked by the incidence of the signifier on needs"[27] The unconscious desires and wishes of others flow into the subject through language and discourse. Therefore, desire is inescapably shaped and molded by language. According to Lacan, there is no such thing as the unconscious without language. Thus, the subject can only come into being through others in relation to the Other.

In the Symbolic order, Lacan asserts that the Other with a capital O is not an individual person but a symbolic framework that is language, and goes on to say that there is no other of the Other. For Lacan, language precedes individual's consciousness because the speaking subjects are born into the system of language. In other words, language does not necessarily reflect reality but rather one produces one's experience within the constraints of the system of language. Lacan states that "the unconsciousness is structured like a language."[28] In other words, language conditions the nature of one's experiences.

Moreover, language is not an absolute and fixed system but evolves with one's attempts of mediation via signifier and signified. In this way, the language speaks through us rather than we speak through language.

---

26. Lacan, *Psychoses*, 241.
27. Lacan, *Ego in Freud's Theory*, 223.
28. Lacan, *Écrits*, 414.

Lacan defines the unconscious as the discourse of the Other. The big Other with the capital O is language. As the symbolic order, the Other can never be fully assimilated to the subject. The big Other represents a radical and ultimate otherness which contributes to the forming of one's self. We are born into language through which the desires of others are articulated and through which we articulate our own desires. Lacan calls this bound with language a circuit of discourse.

> It is the discourse of the circuit in which I am integrated. I am one of its links. It is the discourse of my father, for instance, in so far as my father made mistakes which I am condemned to reproduce. ... I am condemned to reproduce them because I am obliged to pick up again the discourse he bequeathed to me, not simply because I am his son, but because one can't stop the chain of discourse, and it is precisely my duty to transmit it in its aberrant form to someone else.[29]

According to Lacan, we cannot escape from the order of language and discourse. As subjects, one can never fully grasp the symbolic totality that constitutes the entire world, but the totality has a structuring force upon everyone within the world. Lacan states that there is no Other of the Other, and emphasizes the idea that there is no ultimate authority or transcendent entity that can fully guarantee the meaning or provide absolute knowledge in the symbolic order. In Lacan's own words,

> Let us set out from the conception of the Other as the locus of the signifier. Any statement of authority has no other guarantee than its very enunciation, and it is pointless for it to seek it in another signifier, which could not appear outside this locus in any way. Which is what I mean when I say no metalanguage can be spoken, or more aphoristically, that there is no Other of the Other.[30]

This means that there is no ultimate symbol outside the symbolic order that functions as a final reference point. For Lacan, the symbolic order is inherently incomplete and the subject continues to generate meaning that can be captured by the signifier and the signified although with its limits.

The distinction between the small other and the big Other in Lacan can help indicate the otherness observed in *Dominus Iesus's* understanding of non-Christian religions. *Dominus Iesus* appears to claim that the otherness is radical by saying that non-Christian religions are in gravely

---

29. Lacan, *Ego in Freud's Theory,* 89.
30. Lacan, *Écrits,* 310–11.

deficient situation that can never have access to the full truth that the Church holds. However, the religious otherness is still within the realm of language which can be articulated, and it falls under the small other in the mirror stage. As explored earlier, the religious otherness expressed in *Dominus Iesus* reflects the disagreement between the ideal image of Christian unity and the lived experience of fragmentation in the context of religious pluralism.

Lastly, the Real order is the domain of the un-symbolizable and the unrepresentable meanings. It is that which resists symbolization through linguistic expression. According to Lacan, the Real is that which is there at first before the symbolic functioning began, from the standpoint of the symbolic itself.[31] The real is in the realm of ineffable that cannot be expressed any language or cultural mediation. It is characterized by the encounter with the limits of language and the inherent impossibility of fully capturing or comprehending reality.

Within the real order are experiences of trauma, anxiety, and the irreducible gap between language and lived experience. Despite the challenges caused by ineffable nature, the real has a profound influence on the subject. There are inexplainable symptoms come up in the process of psychoanalysis, and they fall into the realm of the real order. The real represents surplus that cannot be integrated into symbolic framework.[32] It constitutes a disruptive force that destabilizes the subject's identity by undermining the illusion of coherence and mastery.

According to Lacan, the real does not exist because it is that which resists symbolization absolutely. Lacan states that the real precedes language. We can have a glimpse of the real in the concept of *Das Ding*, which is "the thing [which] is characterized by the fact that it is impossible for us to imagine."[33] In other words the real is beyond the signified and thus unknowable in itself. This echoes with the concept of the *object petit a* which is used as a placeholder for the object-cause of desire, representing the Other's lack as the lack itself.[34] It is from this perspective that Lacan says that there is no Other of the Other. Lacan's understanding of the Other can be interpreted as to suggest that understanding non-Christians as others may be an empty signifier which does not have content.

31. Lacan, *Four Fundamental Concepts*, 66.

32. Lacan discusses the excess and the unattainable nature of the Real in *Ethics of Psychoanalysis*, 177–83. See also Lacan, *On Feminine Sexuality*, 2–9, 63–77.

33. Lacan, *Ethics of Psychoanalysis*, 54.

34. Lacan, *Four Fundamental Concepts*, 103.

The otherness exists in the imaginary order as the reflected desires in the mirror stage, and in the symbolic order as the signifier; however, it does not exist in the real order because the difference as the *objet petit a* is an empty concept that precedes the language and never can be grasped. Thus, the real is that which enlightens the infant about the lack of wholeness and unity of the body in the mirror stage. The infant recognizes the disconnect which he or she cannot clearly pinpoint or conceptualize through the symbolic order. The experience of lack is genuine and yet it is ineffable, thereby creating a sense of anxiety and irreducible gap between language and the experience.

The three orders, imaginary, symbolic and real, interact dynamically and shape the subject's experiences of reality and sense of self. These orders also help understand the stance on non-Christians observed in *Dominus Iesus*. The disconnect between the idealized image and the lived experience of fragmentation in the imaginary order parallels with the disagreement between the idealistic hope of Christian unity in the world and the lived experience of religious pluralism. The disagreement also creates a sense of rivalry between the self and the image, and others. The symbolic order helps to understand how there is no Other of the Other but only more chain understanding of signifier/signified in further illumination of meaning. The real order indicates that there is ultimate absence that cannot be mediated or articulated by language, and Lacan uses the terms to use as a place holder that only indicates the absence such as *object petit a*. That which is lacking and is creating the gap between the idealized image and the lived experience.

CONCLUSION

This essay was an attempt to analyze the understanding of non-Christians observed in *Dominus Iesus* from the perspective of Lacan. Lacan presents the imaginary, the symbolic and the real orders as a way to understand how the subject constructs one's identity in the world. Lacan states that there is no Other of the Other, and explains that there is no such thing that is beyond the signification of the language. The otherness expressed in *Dominus Iesus*'s view on non-Christian religions exists in the imaginary order as the reflected desires in the mirror stage.

Dominus Iesus appears to understand religious pluralism in association with relativism It does not differentiate between pluralism and relativism; however, when religious pluralism is understood without assuming relativism, various aspects of different traditions can contribute to a more holistic understanding of truth. In this way, religious pluralism in an Asian context can serve as a resource for Christian theology. *Dominus Iesus* suggests a classicist view of culture, which views a culture can be introduced to people from a top-down approach. *Dominus Iesus* views religious differences as mostly contradictory, while in a different context, they can be understood as complementary through the discernment of the Spirit.

Although it can be difficult at times, recognizing others and the influence of the others is crucial in one's own identity, and this applies to Christian identity within the history of the Church. The Roman Catholic Church's teaching has always developed with the gaze of the other in the picture. The axiom "outside the Church, no salvation" had been widely believed up until the time of the Second Vatican Council. However, the climate of a post Vatican II Church subsequently became the starting point for many contemporary theologians to contribute to the shift from a position of exclusivity to a position of inclusivity within the Roman Catholic Church. Fast forward a few decades, we realize that no one can be saved alone and we need to help one another. As shown in the history of the Church, the relationship with the other is inevitable element in this world, and there is hope in understanding others as partners with whom meaningful collaboration can be achievable.

10

Subversion of Desire and Transgression

A Lacanian Analysis of Margery Kempe's Holiness

Jiyoung Ko

THINKING ABOUT THE MEDIEVAL holy women who devoted their life to the divine, what comes to mind is a fixed image of a woman wearing a habit, characterized by elegance, moderation, and quietness, staying in an enclosed convent, praying incessantly. However, there is an exceptional figure who is bizarre and enigmatic both from the perspectives of her time, and from our modern eyes. Her name is Margery Kempe, an English lay woman, her religious actions in public seem somewhat funny, ugly, hectic and loud, leading audiences to think of her as spiritually immature or mentally insane. Her performances of piety were dramatic, exaggerative, excessive.

In this chapter, I explore Margery's spirituality of pursuing her own desire without succumbing to the desire of the Other, a concept of desire which Jacques Lacan suggests in his *Ethics of Psychoanalysis*. First, I briefly explore Margery Kempe's life and her bizarre performances in the context of the oppressive medieval religious system (i.e., the symbolic order of her time) in which norms (ideals) of female holiness were reproduced in relation to female sexuality and the body. Then, I will give an explanation of Lacan's idea of ethics of Psychoanalysis and death drive. Second, I explore her particular way of imitation of Christ's suffering "shame" in the context of medieval affective piety in terms of theology and Lacanian sublimation, especially Sadean sublimation. Finally, I examine the thematic parallels and deviations between Margery's conflict with a secular authority in chapter 46 of her book and the legend of Saint Katherine of Alexandria. With this literary approach, I will demonstrate how Margery identified herself with Saint Katherine of Alexandria and how she transgressed and went beyond the norm and pursued her own desire in line with Lacanian ethics.

MARGERY KEMPE AS A LACANIAN SUBVERSIVE SUBJECT PURSUING HER DESIRE

Margery Kempe was considered for a long time to be a holy sister or holy anchoress based on a small portion of her prayer left in the church from the sixteenth century. However, when her autobiography was rediscovered in 1934, everybody was shocked and embarrassed. Since then, she has been considered "the most controversial of the late medieval mystics."[1] Against the image of a submissive anchoress, she was an autonomous and independent enough woman to write (or to fabricate?) her own spiritual experiences known as the first English autobiography.[2]

On the surface, Margery Kempe seems to desire the conservative ideals of female holiness typical of her time. However, the images that she takes from her imitation of the virgin saints are not at all acceptable, not admirable to the society, either. Moreover, she constantly deviates from and exceeds the norms of female saints: she performs in public as a show-off what she should have done secretly in her convent room. In order to understand her anamorphic performances, it is necessary to examine them from a different perspective.

---

1. Lochrie, *Margery Kempe and Translations of the Flesh*, 1.

2. There is a large amount of scholarship on the authorship of the *Book of Margery Kempe*, which Margery dictated to two different scribes. This issue is not central to my project; however, my position in this research paper will be in line with that of Sarah Salih who says, "If there is a distinction between 'Kempe' and 'Margery' it is not that between author and character, but between the writing and the written selves of autobiography. Margery, like Augustine, constructs herself in time and in narrative, reassembling it through the process of memory, as the old woman in Lynn tells the story of her younger self" (Salih, *Versions of Virginity*, 170–71).

Margery Kempe's Life

Margery was born in Bishop's Lynn around 1373 to a rich merchant family. Her father served as mayor several times and held membership in the Guild of the Holy Trinity. Margery married John Kempe, who was from a less prominent merchant family. For a certain period of her life, Margery was not just the wife of a merchant but also independently ran a brewery and mill. After she gave birth to the first child, she suffered a mental illness for six months, assumed to have been postpartum psychosis, during which she had an extreme fear of death and hell. With her first vision of Christ, however, she recovered and continued her previous luxurious lifestyle, showing off her wealth. Soon after, her business failed, and she adopted an ascetic life, wearing a hairshirt. Over time, she took several dangerous pilgrimages to holy places in England, Continental Europe, and the Holy Land. She eventually negotiated with her husband from sexual intercourse by paying off his debt, and eventually she could keep her chastity. In Rome, she experienced a mystical wedding with God held in heaven witnessed by other saints.[3]

Dramatic Performances in Public

Her passionate religious performances for her love of Christ consisted of the extensive intense visions of and locutions with Christ, endless intercessory prayers for the souls of fellow Christians, and several pilgrimages. However, these are just one part of the whole picture. In public, she wept unceasingly and cried boisterously during sermons and while on pilgrimage, disturbing other pilgrims and humiliating her company such as her husband and servants. She often wore a white dress in the street, which was a symbol of virginity in her time and unfitting for a married mother of fourteen children. As a lay woman, she also taught and lectured to both ecclesiastical and secular male authorities which often placed her in conflict with them. She was arrested several times and became an object of inquisition as heretic—accused of being a Lollard, one of the followers of Wycliffe—though she always successfully defended her orthodoxy.

Her public confrontation with authority, craving for attention and consequent excessive pursuit of humiliation and shame are often considered signs of Margery's spiritual immaturity, evidenced by her lack of the humility or obedience which holy women were expected to display

---

3. See chapter 35 in Kempe, *Book of Margery Kempe*.

in her time. Moreover, aside from the fact that Margery was an enigma to her contemporaries, modern scholars who value monastic apophatic spirituality seem uncomfortable with or annoyed by her extraordinary religious practices and unusual claims of sanctity.[4] For example, David Knowles devalues her spirituality saying that she "is clearly not the equal of the earlier English mystics in depth of perception or wisdom of spiritual doctrine, nor as personality can she challenge comparison with Julian of Norwich."[5]

It is not surprising that she has been often used as an object of modern psychological research. Anthony Ryle diagnoses her symptoms as "hysterical personality organization with occasional psychotic episodes."[6] Trudy Drucker claims Margery experienced epilepsy or migraines and argues that Margery's desire for self-induced pain "resulted from pathologic distortion of the sexual impulse."[7] Dale Peterson simply identifies Margery as Schreber in the twentieth century, whose memoirs Freud used for his work.[8]

It is probably possible to explain her extraordinary behaviors through modern psychology without end. However, such studies do not adequately consider the difference between Margery's time and our era of modern psychology. With no consideration of Margery's desire, behavior, and life as "a child of her times, religious, social and personal,"[9] such claims are purely anachronistic. As Catherine Mooney points out attempts to "pathologize premodern individuals according to modern constructs" misses the point of the author's own writing.[10] Since Margery mentions in her autobiography that the purpose of writing is to present herself as a model of sanctity for readers ("a mirror amongst them"), her eccentric behavior (suffering shame) should be understood as a form of expressing her faith.[11]

4. McGinn, *Varieties of Vernacular Mysticism*, 472.

5. Knowles, *English Mystical Tradition*, 139.

6. Anthony Ryle quoted in Medcalf, *Later Middle Ages*, 114–15.

7. Drucker quoted in Porter, "Margery Kempe and the Meaning of Madness," 43.

8. Peterson, *Mad People's History of Madness*, 8.

9. Porter, "Margery Kempe and the Meaning of Madness," 44.

10. Mooney, "Interdisciplinarity in Teaching Medieval Mysticism," 65. Mooney's ideas in this essay, such as the need to read authors on their own terms, the importance of not pathologizing affective piety, and the importance of theological and historical groundings above psychological diagnostics can be seen clearly in my approach to Margery.

11. Since 1990 with Caroline Walker Bynum's works such as *Holy Feast and Holy Fast* (1987) and *Fragmentation and Redemption* (1991), the book has gained renewed

However, in spite of her claiming of her sanctity she has been read all the time as spiritually immature, or mentally ill. She is considered abnormal. More exactly, she was not conformed to the norms of holiness in her time.

Norms of Holiness during the Late Medieval Period

The discourse of holiness in the time of Margery functioned as a closed system refusing and repressing any excess or beyond-ness. Within such an oppressive system, only a conventional subject's desire to the divine is permissible; any deviant, disordered, or chaotic spiritual practices not conformed to the norms are excluded and oppressed. Such a system of discourse is so conservative that only what is expressly approved is repeated and reproduced within the system. Furthermore, the criteria for what is normative and the ideal for female holiness are determined by an androcentric, patriarchal cultural system. Female sexuality and the body in particular have been great barriers to access to holiness throughout church history.

The *Book* suggests that, as a lay woman maintaining an active sexual life with her husband and bearing fourteen children, Margery was prohibited from accessing the higher paths of sanctity reserved for virgins. Being married was regarded as a lower form of holiness than celibacy; sexual experience and procreation in matrimony were seen as obstacles to being elevated toward the spiritually higher mystical life for women. Medieval women who wanted to gain the highest place in heaven (nearer God) could only do so by maintaining their virginity. The *Book* explicitly depicts female sanctity in connection to virginity as one of the most oppressive norms of the day. Margery often cries and weeps in prayer because of her lack of virginity. She prays to Jesus in chapter 22:

---

attention and support from feminist scholars who claim that Margery's spiritual experience in particular and those of medieval women in general need to be understood with new models of feminine spirituality replacing the dominant patriarchal model which denigrates women's experience as inferior and marginal. Among others, Karma Lochrie contends that Margery's spiritual experience, and her own writing of it, is subversive in that Margery uses the social cultural position of women as flesh (vs. the "masculine" spirit) with all of its negative connotations ("pervious, excessive and susceptible") as a privileged place of "bodily access to the sacred" (Lochrie, *Margery Kempe*, 4). Using Judith Butler's gender theory, Sarah Salih sees that Margery subverts the hegemonic use of the spiritual paradigm of female virginity by "remaking" herself a virgin through her public performance. Salih, *Versions of Virginity*, 180.

Oh Lord, virgins are now dancing merrily in Heaven. Shall I not do so? Because I am not a virgin, lack of virginity is really a great sorrow to me; I think I wish I had been slaughtered when I was taken from the baptismal font so that I could never have displeased you and then you, blessed Lord, could have had my virginity without end. Oh dear God, I have not loved you all the days of my life and I regret that so bitterly![12]

Jesus consoles her sense of unworthiness as a woman who had children and still had sexual relations with her husband due to her communication with Him. However, he does not contradict her feeling, saying, in her autobiography chapter 21, "Though the state of maidenhood is more perfect and more holy than the state of widowhood, and the state of widowhood more perfect that the state of wedlock; yet daughter I love you as well as any maiden in the world." Margery's own lament of her loss of virginity further agitated people around her. Wearing a white robe (a symbol of virginity) made her an object of mockery by people she met in pilgrimage and an inquisition target for religious authorities. For example, in the *Book* chapter 52 upon seeing Margery, the Archbishop of York asked, "Why are you going about in white? Are you a virgin?" Within such an oppressive symbolic order, where virginity was the ideal for female sanctity, Margery's desire was a desire for impossibility—not in the sense that she desired to reclaim her virginity, but in the sense that she sought sanctity that was impossible for a married woman to achieve.

The medieval theological idea of virginity as the ideal for female sanctity evolved from patristic Christianity.[13] It was intensified in the medieval period. In the time of Margery three religious hierarchical representations of women's status were established according to the thirteenth-century treatise *Hali Meiðhad* (Holy Maidenhood). Since this book was addressed to anchoresses, it was biased toward virginity. The author says, "For marriage has its reward thirtyfold in heaven; widowhood, sixtyfold; virginity, with a hundredfold, surpasses both."[14] A high valuation of virginity or chastity above marriage was all-pervasive in the medieval mind (not only in the religious context); the existence of

12. Kempe, *Book of Margery Kempe*, 49.

13. The early church Fathers developed the idea of the superiority of virginity over marriage, considering any sexual activity as "evil." Their thought was influenced by misogynistic medical views and contemporary Greek philosophy, such as Neo-Platonism and stoicism, and they brought such influences into their own interpretation of the Bible. Bullough, "Medieval Medical and Scientific Views of Women," 499.

14. Evans, "Virginities," 25.

instructions for counterfeiting virginity through remaking hymen in medieval medical texts demonstrates how virginity was a source of anxiety and preoccupation for medieval women.[15]

However, the ideal of medieval virginity also had another connotation: women should be enclosed within a cell; the female body should be separated from the world.[16] Religious women and their activities were restricted to living in a nunnery or anchorage. Their enclosure in a cell or anchorage as a "spiritual space" protected female bodies from potential dangers and evil from the outside world[17] and prevented women from becoming a source of evil, that is, seducing males.[18]

Margery acknowledges within the *Book* that, as a married woman, her path to sanctity without being a virgin (chastity and enclosure) was impossible within this conservative, hierarchical, oppressive religious system in which the female body, inside and outside, was controlled and regulated. Some scholars read an attempt to recover her virginity as the major project of her spirituality.[19] This would mean that Margery Kempe was under the operation of the pleasure principle and reality principle, possessing a conservative desire of maintaining the status quo, at the mercy of the symbolic order in Lacanian terms.[20] These scholars understand Margery as a person who strived to identify herself with the ideal model established within the hegemonic symbolic order and repeating the desire of the Other. If this is the case, Margery's desire is not truly subversive, but a mere variation on convention. I disagree with this idea.

LACAN'S *ETHICS OF PSYCHOANALYSIS* AND MARGERY'S TRANSGRESSION OF DESIRE

In *The Ethics of Psychoanalysis*, Lacan claims that human desire is deeply transgressive, which is a significant point to make in relation to ethics.[21] That is, the desire which attempts to keep the law (symbolic order) eventually turns into a desire to transgress the law. Such transgressive desire, which Lacan calls the death drive, makes humans maintain their desire.

15. O'Faolain and Martines, *Not in God's Image*, 143.
16. Bernau, "Virginal Effects," 24.
17. Nichols and Shank, *Distant Echoes*, 52.
18. Padden, "Locating Margery Kempe," 5.
19. Salih, *Versions of Virginity*, 181.
20. Ruti, *Singularity of Being*, 49.
21. Lacan, *Ethics of Psychoanalysis*, 207.

Lacan develops the notion of the death drive into something related to the symbolic order: "symbolic death" (not biological death). Needs are always contaminated by the Other, the speaking mother's culture. The body is thus already structured; it conveys messages, and drive's satisfaction is polymorphous-perverse in nature.[22]

Margery's Jouissance to Transgress the Law

This is to say, drive, with its non-conforming, deviating nature, is the only way that a subject can transgress a limit and prohibition of the pleasure principle.[23] Lacan sees the drive's polymorphous-perverse nature as the true nature of human desire of transgression in relation to the self and the world.[24] Since drive goes beyond the pleasure principle into the realm of *jouissance*, every drive can be called a death drive.[25] The death drive is a tendency of the unconscious for the subject to go straight to *das Ding* without making a detour around it. It is a subject's desire to transgress the limit and prohibition of the symbolic order of which the subject's existence is at the mercy.[26] With the concept of the death drive, tendency to transgress the law, Lacan contends that moral law (symbolic law) does not serve "the good" as traditional ethics supposes; on the contrary, it is "an instrument of evil, transgressive *jouissance*."[27]

Lacan seeks the possibility of a new level of the ethics of psychoanalysis in this transgressive nature of desire. The weight of the ethics lies in *das Ding* (*jouissance*). Ethics does not remain within the boundary of the pleasure principle, but rather should go beyond the pleasure principle toward the Real object, *das Ding*, the prohibited object, a *jouissance* which "serves no purpose."[28] By transgressing prohibition and traversing the construction of fantasy, the subject is asked to confront their own desire. Margery went beyond the oppressive symbolic order directly facing the impossibility (i.e., the *Real*). Her desire for Christ attempted to excel the sanctity of virgins rather than attempting to regain the state of virginity.

22. Lacan, *Ethics of Psychoanalysis*, 4, 92.
23. Lacan, *Four Fundamental Concepts*, 183.
24. Lacan, *Ethics of Psychoanalysis*, 4.
25. Lacan, *Écrits*, 719.
26. Lacan, *Ethics of Psychoanalysis*, 212.
27. Kesel, *Eros and Ethics*, 125.
28. Lacan, *On Feminine Sexuality*, 3.

As a married woman, Margery's impossible sanctity gave her a strong motivation to pursue a more excessive, idiosyncratic way to heaven (death drive), through which she could create a way to surpass the virgins' holiness by accumulating more spiritual assets through affective piety. However, she accrued these spiritual assets through pursuing shame in public, especially engaging in conflicts with male authorities.

The Thing (*das Ding*) as Affective Piety of Margery's Sublimation

Affective piety allowed especially medieval women including Margery Kempe to go beyond the oppressive, hierarchical symbolic order. Affective piety was one of popular forms of devotion throughout the late Middle Ages,[29] characterized by a way of meditation using the human capacity for imagination and emotions, such as tender affection and compassion, focusing on the human Jesus, especially the passion of Christ, and bodily imitation of Christ's suffering.[30] This piety developed alongside the medieval theological trend of emphasizing the human Jesus.

Devotion to the passion of Christ and bodily mortification, within the broader context of affective spirituality, was especially popular among late medieval women.[31] Among medieval biological medical views of women and their bodies, Galen's view in the second century—in line with that of Aristotle—was the most popular among medieval physicians and texts. According to Galen, the male was dry and hot while woman was cool and moist, and from this view he drew the misogynistic understanding of woman as passive, imperfect and deformed.[32] In the context of medieval misogyny, male and female types were often constructed in terms of soul (intellect) vs. body, active vs. passive, rational vs. irrational, reason vs. emotion, and self-control vs. lust.[33]

Male writers in the medieval period appropriated this gender dichotomy as a symbol for their spiritual lives. They often used the feminine image of being "powerless, poor, irrational, without influence and authority," for their religious conversion, which meant denying all power, prestige and wealth they once had.[34] However, women appropriated the

---

29. Kieckhefer, "Major Currents in Late Medieval Devotion," 75.

30. Atkinson, *Mystic and Pilgrim*, 129–30; Lochrie, *Margery Kempe*, 13–14.

31. Bynum, *Holy Feast and Holy Fast*, 26.

32. O'Faolain and Martines, *Not in God's Image*, 120–21.

33. Bynum, *Fragmentation and Redemption*, 151.

34. Bynum, *Fragmentation and Redemption*, 178.

asymmetry between genders in a positive way, associating themselves with the physical and bodily. They saw their physicality as a point where they could identify with the humanity of Christ.[35] For female theologians such as Hildegard of Bingen and Julian of Norwich, women were the symbol of humanity, expressed in Hildegard's claim, "Christ's humanity was to Christ's divinity as woman is to man, and *mulier* represented humankind, fallen in Eve, restored in *ecclesia* and *Maria*."[36] Therefore, they saw themselves as a more proper model of imitating Christ in his humanity and especially in his suffering. In line with this view, they pursued sanctity (being closer to God) by engaging in extreme bodily manipulations and desiring bodily illness, along with expressing overcharged emotions.

Such identification with the suffering Christ through their own bodily suffering led late medieval women to oppose the oppressive religious system in which encountering and experiencing God was considered as something predictable and repeatable only in the virginal, enclosed female body.

According to Lacan, suffering is excessive in a sense that "it involves forcing an access to the Thing (*das Ding*)."[37] Suffering (pain) is what the human psyche attempts to avoid through the operation of the pleasure-reality principle as a defense of the ego; it is related to the realm of the *real (jouissance)* that the symbolic order represses and is unable to be articulated within a chain of signifiers like "trauma."[38] It defies representation and cannot be tamed or domesticated. The idea of a bodily God who suffers is paradoxical, excessive. Experiencing the suffering Christ through actual suffering cannot be predicted or repeated with a formula; the encounter is contingent. In other words, desiring the suffering Christ for medieval women was, in Lacanian term, a sublimation process, elevating the object of desire (fixed concept of God) to the dignity of *das Ding* (object in the *Real*).[39]

35. Bynum, *Fragmentation and Redemption*, 175.

36. Bynum, *Fragmentation and Redemption*, 171.

37. Lacan, *Ethics of Psychoanalysis*, 80.

38. Lacan, *Four Fundamental Concepts*, 167, 55.

39. Lacan, *Ethics of Psychoanalysis*, 112.

Sublimation for Freud and Lacan

For Freud, sublimation means satisfaction of a drive without repression.[40] In *Civilization and Its Discontents*, Freud describes sublimation as a process by which the sexual drive, which would cause suffering in a subject by aiming at a socially forbidden object, can find satisfaction through the artist's creative works or the scientist's intellectual research.[41] This amounts to the displacement of the forbidden object of drive with socially accepted and valued ones. Here, social recognition is an essential element for the process of sublimation. While Lacan accepts Freud's notion of sublimation as substitution of objects, he points out the contradiction in Freud's notion of sublimation, in which satisfaction through socially established objects is nothing but a form of repression of a drive (an individual's pleasure) that Freud sees as a defense system of civilization.[42] Instead, Lacan sees sublimation in terms of an object in the Real beyond the imaginary-symbolic order, "beyond the signified." Sublimation is a kind of process helping a subject to go beyond the symbolic system. In other words, for Lacan sublimation is a process that relocates an object to the status of *das Ding*.[43]

Thus, desiring the suffering God through the process of undergoing suffering transgresses expectations and pre-established norms. In *On Feminine Sexuality*, Lacan expresses such medieval female mystics' experiences as "experiencing it but knowing nothing about it at all."[44] Experiencing and encountering God by desiring the suffering Christ transfers a subject to the realm of the *Real*, revealing God beyond the hierarchical, institutional medieval religious system which only produced a "tidy, moderate, decent, second-rate place for women and for the laity."[45] In the midst of this hegemonic oppressive system of spirituality, medieval women used affective piety as a means of negotiating their own revolt against the established order. However, affective piety was still largely relegated to the private sphere, preserving the public order of things.

---

40. Lacan, *Ethics of Psychoanalysis*, 110; *Four Fundamental Concepts*, 165.

41. Freud, *Civilization and Its Discontents*, 26.

42. Lacan, *Ethics of Psychoanalysis*, 94.

43. Evans, *Introductory Dictionary of Lacanian Psychoanalysis*, 201.

44. Lacan, *On Feminine Sexuality*, 76.

45. Bynum, *Holy Feast and Holy Fast*, 243.

Margery's Body and Shame, and Its Sublimation

Margery's unique desire for God grows out of and deviates from the tradition of affective piety. Margery chose to pursue extreme shame[46] as a socially-experienced affect in the form of imitation of Christ, rather than more typical severe forms of private physical bodily suffering.[47] Shame, as a social affect, however, is not totally removed from bodily suffering. In medieval terminology, shame was associated with the naked or blushing, especially female, body.[48] Shame was experienced through the blushing face and was thought to spring from the body when it was exposed to an audience, when it became a spectacle or the object of the gaze of another. Thus, shame was a kind of bodily suffering. Therefore, some scholars' claim that Margery's spirituality transformed bodily asceticism to social and emotional suffering, as if these were phenomenologically distinct, would not be completely accurate.[49] While other medieval women manipulated or tortured their bodies for the imitation of Christ, Margery manipulated the situations where her body was exposed to the public as a spectacle to maximize public shame.

More importantly, if desire for the suffering Christ can be understood in terms of a sublimation process for medieval women, Margery's pursuit of shame and humiliation can be explained as an extreme case of sublimation.

46. Shame is one of the dominant emotions in the *Book*. Although there are several passages in the *Book* where the reader may note Margery's experiences of shame without the appearance of the word "shame," throughout the *Book* the Middle English noun *shamis* or *schame*, referring mainly to the emotion caused by an awareness of disgrace or dishonor, and the adjective or adverbial forms of "ashamed" (*a-schamyd*) occur explicitly and extensively. In the modern English translation, these words appear nearly fifty times in the *Book*. The word in the adjective form describes the shameful emotion experienced primarily by Margery but also by other people around her due to her extraordinary, heroic, eccentric behaviors (e.g., her husband and her maidservant) and people whom Margery lectures and rebukes for their faults. Occasionally, the experience of shame is so strong that those who experience it immediately flee from the situation. Furthermore, the noun form of the word "shame" consistently occurs with the words "despite," "scorn" and "reproof" throughout the *Book*. With the combination of these words, the text clearly shows the intensity of shame that Margery feels. Lewis, "Schame."

47. Saint Francis pursued humiliation. Angela of Foligno had a similar desire for extreme shame, so that she imagined walking naked around the street and putting pieces of raw meat and fish around her neck. Dickman, "Margery Kempe," 164. Many scholars agree that Margery pursued the piety of shame. See VanGinhoven, "Margery Kempe."

48. Allen, "Waxing Red," 191.

49. Salih, *Versions of Virginity*, 170.

Lacan points out the limitation of the courtly sublimation, that is, the issue of identification and idealization.[50] If bodily suffering is idealized, the subject falls into the trap of the Other's recognition, just as some medieval women (like Julian of Norwich or Katherine of Alexandria) became idealized and their practices of bodily suffering were praised. Therefore, they were subsumed into the symbolic order.

Lacan therefore suggests another way of sublimation which avoids idealization and recognition by the Other: Sadean sublimation.[51] Lacan praises the Marquis de Sade because of his own transgressive, perverse writings, which demonstrate nonconformity to and utter resistance against established social norms.[52] Sade's philosophy is revealed in Sadean characters' reversing the moral law by "extolling incest, adultery, theft, and everything else you can think of." Sadean perversion helps us to better understand the death drive—that there is a certain will to transgress, that is, a drive, operating beyond the level of the pleasure principle in humans who live under the limits of the symbolic order.[53]

Moreover, Lacan pays attention to the fact that Sade became an object of social criticism and reproach through his experimental writings,[54]

50. Courtly love, in its idealizing of the Lady, is narcissistic. In courtly love, the subject's ideal (his fantasy) is projected into emptiness. Idealization does not allow a subject to go beyond and reach the destructive *das Ding* itself, but, as a mirror has a limit "that cannot be crossed," courtly love leads a subject to be confined to his own imaginary, fictional ego projected into a mirror (emptiness). Lacan, *Ethics of Psychoanalysis*, 151.

51. Baek, *Lacan, Lacaneul Inganhak*, 274–76; Lacan, *Ethics of Psychoanalysis*, 200.

52. For Lacan, there is a sublimation of experiencing the emptiness of the Real, without identification with the Other, which confines a subject to an imaginary image and symbolic position. Lacan locates extreme transgression in the "perverse" nature of the Marquis de Sade's literature. Baek, *Lacan, Lacaneul Inganhak*, 262–66. However, this does not mean Lacan literally praises and enjoys Sade's fantasy—his descriptions of crimes, including cutting a woman's body. Rather Lacan considers them boring. Here the word "perverse" does not refer to the psychical structures Lacan later coined surrounding with neurosis and psychosis, though Sade's work probably helped Lacan to develop the theory of perversion. Kesel, *Eros and Ethics*, 191.

53. Lacan, *Ethics of Psychoanalysis*, 78–79.

54. Lacan sees that true value of Sade's work lies in its experimental nature. Lacan clarifies his point by saying: "Sade's work belongs to the order of what I shall call experimental literature. The work of art in this case is an experiment that through its action cuts the subject loose from his psychosocial moorings—or to be more precise, from all psychosocial appreciation of the sublimation" (Lacan, *Ethics of Psychoanalysis*, 201). Experimental literature which aims at challenging and resisting the existing, repetitive art forms and attempting to introduce new forms, results in the destruction of artists' and audiences' understanding of the self and the world. Baek, *Lacan, Lacaneul Inganhak*, 276. Practicing such experimental art, the artist cannot help but be in a contradictory position with respect to dominant social norms and power. The artist should bear social stigma or notoriety.

instead of receiving any social approval or compliment. Through his works, he experienced social expulsion. Sade followed the sublimation process up to a point where his ego was totally destroyed in relation to the symbolic order; he achieved social notoriety.[55] By rejecting "the ego's pursuit of socially desirable goals,"[56] Sade experiences a decentering of the ego. Through Sade, what Lacan wants to claim is that by a process of sublimation, by elevating an ordinary object to the status of *das Ding* through creative work, a subject can encounter her own emptiness in such a way that the subject can start again with new a signifier: creation *ex nihilo*.

Like Sade, Margery's creative piety of desiring the suffering Christ did not lead her to become an object of identification nor idealization neither in her society nor even in the present. Through her excessive, nonconforming public performance, Margery became socially undesirable. Her actions placed her in direct opposition to the hegemonic, dominant socio-religious system. Through severe conflict with male authorities and public shame, she experienced social expulsion, not praise nor honor as other female saints. And this is in fact the goal of her performance: to gain and to accumulate as much shame as possible is to be closer to God in line with affective piety. The fact that her piety, her performance, was an object of mockery both in her time and also in our time—she is still considered an alien, bizarre, second-class mystic by dominant mystical scholars—suggests that Margery's desire was near death drive; she achieved (Sadean) sublimation.

MARGERY'S PERFORMANCE AS ANAMORPHIC IMAGES OF VIRGIN SAINTS

Anamorphic perspective in art is one technique for mastering emptiness by structuring space. Perspective gives an illusion of a stable, orderly space which veils the emptiness of the Real, which causes anxiety while fixing a subject's (spectator's) position.[57] However, the emptiness which is veiled by the illusion of perspective can reappear through the technique of anamorphosis, in a way to "reverse the use of that illusion of space."[58]

---

55. Baek, *Lacan, Lacaneul Inganhak*, 275.

56. Kirshner, "Toward an Ethics of Psychoanalysis," 1228.

57. Lacan, *Ethics of Psychoanalysis*, 140.

58. Lacan, *Ethics of Psychoanalysis*, 141.

Anamorphosis is a form of painting composed of simply distorted or undecipherable images which emerge as readable, as representing something, only when viewed from a certain "perspective" or angle or when they are projected on a cylindrical mirror. For example, in Holbein's painting of *The Ambassadors* there is a small, puzzling form resembling "fried eggs," which is recognized as a skull only when a spectator stands far to the right of the image instead of directly in front. Another example that Lacan gives is a cylindrical anamorphosis of the crucifixion copied from Rubens's work. Meaningless and senseless distorted images of irregular dots emerge as crucifixion after placing a cylindrical mirror on the surface on the image and standing at a certain angle to view it.[59]

Like anamorphic images, Margery's performances are only readable if the audience changes their position to see them from the perspective of affective piety as I said above.[60] Anamorphic images with the sudden encounter of the *Real* challenges the audience's trust in an absolute truth. What we believe as truth is in fact one perspective supporting our fantasy of Oneness and completeness. Margery's case shows that there is no absolute, complete way of pursuing God. Margery's "anamorphic" performances which do not give clear picture or absolute meaning, by borrowing and combining signifiers artificially and in a cunning way[61] from virgin martyrs' legends create distortion and deviation from the norm of holiness. They can be recognized only from the perspective of her desire to imitate Christ in shame.

MARGERY'S PUBLIC PERFORMANCES AS ANAMORPHIC IMAGES

From chapter 46 of the *Book* on, the narrative presents a series of consecutive trials of Margery with secular and church authorities. These confrontations with male authorities are presented in a similar way to those of the virgin martyrs, especially Saint Katherine of Alexandria. The narrative in fact intentionally and explicitly makes connections between Margery's trials and those of the virgin martyrs; the fact that among the

---

59. Lacan, *Ethics of Psychoanalysis*, 135.

60. Lacan, *Ethics of Psychoanalysis*, 135. Perspective is invented to domesticate (tame) the Real (emptiness, disorder), however, its reversed use, called "depraved perspective," allows a sudden encounter with mystery as soon as the subject departs from a given position. Saint-Cyr, "Creating a Void or Sublimation in Lacan," 17–18.

61. Lacan, *Ethics of Psychoanalysis*, 152.

virgin martyrs, the names of Saint Katherine appear throughout the *Book*: Saint Katherine's role is especially predominant in the text; her name appears six times. Most importantly, Margery's heroic public performance of teaching and preaching to male secular and church authorities with her biblical knowledge and wisdom is perhaps the most apparent similarity to Saint Katherine.

A short episode in chapter 46 where she confronts the mayor of Leicester, followed by a long portion of public interrogations by both secular and church male leaders up to chapter 52, functions to parallel Saint Katherine's initial confrontation of the pagan tyrant Maxentius and her consequent debate with fifty philosophers according to popular legends, especially found in Osbern Bokenham's fifteenth-century *Legend of Holy Women*.[62]

The passage where Margery was interrogated by the mayor of Leicester parallels Katherine's first encounter with the brutal emperor Maxentius in its presentation of both protagonist and antagonist. The pagan Maxentius in the *Book* is replaced with the mayor of Leicester, although the mayor is Christian. He is presented as the antagonist who expresses curiosity about Margery by asking where she comes from and what family background she has, in the exact manner that Maxentius asks Katherine. In replying to this question, Margery says "I am of Lynn in Norfolk, a good man's daughter of the same Lynn, who has been mayor five times of that worshipful town and alderman also many years."[63]

Margery presents herself in a pompous attitude emphasizing her father's social status as mayor of Lynn. Margery's presentation of her father's superior, respectful position in society is not intended merely to provide a helpless woman with safety and security in a patriarchal society. Margery intentionally follows Saint Katherine's answer to Maxentius, who said, "I was a king's daughter. He died long ago and left no children but me, so that I am his heir, and I am named Katherine. But although I was born in royal purple and instructed in the seven liberal arts, I set no store by my knowledge or my honorable birth."[64] Katherine presents her noble origin strategically to emphasize the superiority of God to worldly power and knowledge. Upon hearing this, the emperor tries to refute Katherine's faith in God by discrediting her through misogynistic claims that she cannot be trusted because she is a woman, "by nature a frail

62. Bokenham, *Legend of Holy Women*, 129.

63. Kempe, *Book of Margery Kempe*, 82.

64. Bokenham, *Legend of Holy Women*, 129.

creature, variable and unstable, fickle, false, and deceitful."[65] After hearing one further speech by Katherine, the emperor has her imprisoned.

When the mayor of Leicester's responds to Margery's pompous introduction of herself, however, the parallelism is broken. Against the implied reader's expectation, the mayor notices Margery's imitation of Saint Katherine and rebukes her, saying, "Saint Katherine told what kindred she came of and yet you are not like her."[66]

Margery's intention in imitating Saint Katherine is presented as intelligible to her contemporaries like the mayor. The mayor's contemptuous rejection of Margery's enactment of the saint denies not only that Margery's sanctity is equal to that of Katherine, but also (perhaps more importantly to him) denies his similarity to the brutal pagan Maxentius persecuting the Christian protagonist. Ironically, however, by noticing Margery's reenactment of Saint Katherine and by rejecting her claims of sanctity and threatening to imprison her, the mayor demonstrates and strengthens the connections between the two women.

Shame as a Anamorphic Way to Her Holiness

In the Book, the mayor pejoratively accuses her of being "a false strumpet, a false Lollard,[67] and a false deceiver of the people."[68] As Maxentius's resistance to the Christian faith is rooted in his misogyny ("a woman cannot speak truth"), the mayor expresses his rejection of the female public speaker and her public performance by falsely accusing her of being a prostitute and Lollard, connecting sexual promiscuity with heresy, a popular accusatory mode at that time.[69]

Margery further provokes the mayor by showing willingness to accept his false accusation instead of defending herself or asking for mercy,

---

65. Bokenham, *Legend of Holy Women*, 130.

66. Kempe, *Book of Margery Kempe*, 82.

67. In England in her time, John Wycliff's followers were called pejoratively called as Lollards. Lollard women were allowed to preach as well as proselytize. Margery was likely influenced by the preaching of the heretical Lollards without consciously realizing it. McAvoy, *Authority and the Female Body*, 179. Persons accused of being Lollards experienced great shame and stigma. According to Cole, "Lollardy" became a locus for "a new discourse of shame" (Cole, *Literature and Heresy*, 156). In this period of sensitivity about Lollardy, Margery was often accused of being a Lollard and examined for her heresy.

68. Kempe, *Book of Margery Kempe*, 82.

69. Arnold, "Margery's Trials," 83.

which increases her shame and slander at the hands of the mayor. By shaming Margery and sending her to prison, the mayor implicitly confirms the parallelism between her and Saint Katherine and between himself and Maxentius. Through the mayor, Margery's real intention of imitating Saint Katherine is accomplished in becoming the innocent victim of slander and shame. By appropriating Saint Katherine's first encounter with Maxentius in the legend, this passage presents how Margery follows the model of Saint Katherine's trial. Margery, like Saint Katherine, is depicted as autonomous in front of male authorities instead of following the stereotypical model of the passive, quiet, and obedient woman expected by society. Margery is presented with the mayor as equal in power by initiating the mayor's provocation and anger.

Margery reenacted the moments of confrontation of Saint Katherine by imitating her "in extremely literal and concrete" ways.[70] However, there is a clear discrepancy: Margery was not a virgin martyr in any way. She was just an ordinary married lay woman, perceived as simply another "woman on top" like Mrs. Noah[71] or a Lollard woman. While Katherine's confrontation eventually led her to victorious death in martyrdom and the assurance of her sanctity in heaven, Margery's heroic imitation of Saint Katherine in the public sphere was seen as nothing but a gesture of disruption of social and religious conventions. What she gained from this performance was not public recognition of her sanctity as a virgin, nor real martyrdom, but rather ridicule and shame and false recognition as a Lollard. From this, Gibson rightly says that Margery was assured of

70. Gibson, *Theater of Devotion*, 7.

71. In the late Middle Ages (in contrast to the early Middle Ages or the Reformation Era), women in the merchant-middle class had equality with men in various ways. Atkinson, *Mystic and Pilgrim*, 97.

Patriarchal ideology manifest in contemporary literature emphasized the domestic role of the merchant wife and her subjection to male authorities and brought special attention to the disruption of social norms that such women would bring. Aers, *Community, Gender, and Individual Identity*, 87; Wilson, "Margery and Alison," 225. Men's anxiety regarding female autonomy was also reflected in the popular theme of husband abuse in contemporary literature (mostly written by clergymen) and plays. In these stories, women with autonomy were often characterized as "foolish, vicious, or ridiculous" like Mrs. Noah, the husband beater. Mockery, humiliation and shame were employed as defense mechanisms against the fear of women's autonomy and their potential subversion to the social order. Atkinson, *Mystic and Pilgrim*, 98–101. Husband beating was a popular theme in many literary genres at this time, though in reality, wife beating was much more common in the Middle Ages. Masculine discourses ridiculing and shaming women holding power may have been an effective social convention/apparatus to restrict women's role to the domestic realm.

her sanctity through "martyrdom by slander" since real death by pagan emperor due to her Christian faith was unavailable to her.[72]

In Margery's time, imitating the virgin martyrs was a norm to structure women's sanctity and to limit women's diverse experiences of God. Margery imitated the virgin martyrs in pubic theatrically, ridiculously and excessively as a lay woman. She pursued an anamorphic appropriation of this spirituality and did not try to recover her virginity in conformity to the norm of her time as some scholars claim. Through the strategy to experience and endure extreme public shame, she desired to imitation of Christ as her unique way to achieve holiness.[73] Margery's desire of pursuing God was transgressive like Sadean sublimation. Her desire was "perverse" and subversive because her performances disrupted the hierarchical social order. More significantly, by doing so, she didn't gain praise but shame, that is social notoriety. She deprived herself of any possibility for social identification through her public performances of affective piety. She encountered her own emptiness so that she could start a new symbolic order.

CONCLUSION

Margery Kempe has been considered spiritually immature from the perspective of spirituality scholars and mentally ill from the criterion of modern psychology. She has been judged to be an aberration. However, from the perspective Lacanian desire, the abnormality of her performances was due to her transgressive desire, a desire to go beyond the conformist norms demanded by the oppressive, hierarchical, misogynic religious system of her time. Though she imitated the virgin martyrs, her true desire was not to become virgin like them, a socially desirable goal, which was impossible for her as a lay woman. Rather, by imitating them in a theatrical, pompous way, placing her in opposition to male authorities, she created a new signifier of piety—a new, particular way of imitation of Christ through suffering shame. She did not give up her own desire of pursing God.

72. Gibson, *Theater of Devotion*, 47.

73. For example, Salih sees the main motive of Margery's performative spirituality as recovery of virginity. Salih, *Versions of Virginity*, 181.

Part IV

Clinical Lacan

11

A Lacanian Clinical Case of Perversion
The Wheelchair Man

ALI CHAVOSHIAN

ONE OF THE UNIQUE approaches of the Lacanian clinic is about perversion. In this chapter, I will explain the structure of perversion as a clinical category for diagnostic purposes and its use in assessing a particular kind of perversion, referred to as foot fetishism. Clarifying Lacan's approach to perversion, I will compare it to different methods. Then, I will present a clinical case entitled the "wheelchair man" with some excerpts from the verbatim of the analytical sessions to explain further the mechanism and the dynamic structure of perversion.

LACAN AND DSM-5-TR

In the *DSM-5-Text Revision*, there is no mention of perversion, its symptoms, or the structural analysis of it. Instead, in the chapter on Paraphilic Disorders, there is a description of Fetishistic Disorder. The Diagnostic Criteria for the Fetishistic Disorder are:

> A. Over at least six months, recurrent and intense sexual arousal from either the use of nonliving objects or a highly specific focus

on nongenital body part(s), as manifested by fantasies, urges, or behaviors.

B. The fantasies, sexual urges, or behaviors cause clinically significant distress or impairment in social, occupational, or other important areas of functioning.

C. The fetish objects are not limited to articles of clothing used in cross-dressing (as in transvestic disorder) or devices specifically designed for the purpose of tactile genital stimulation (e.g., vibrator)

Specify:

Body part(s)
Nonliving object(s)
Other.[1]

Although the criteria mentioned above can help recognize Fetishistic Disorder, there are some shortcomings in the DSM-5-TR approach to Fetishism. First of all, as a diagnostic sourcebook for psychiatry, DSM-5TR does not offer any discussions regarding the etiology of fetishism, assuming some vague neuro-physiological and environmental factors in the formation of this category of mental disorder. It is evident, in general, that the DSM-5-TR has a symptom-oriented approach regarding classifications of mental disorders. Consequently, it offers medical intervention and treatment congruent to cognitive-behavior, family therapy, and even dynamic approaches for the removal and reduction of the symptoms, without providing an understanding of fetishism.

Contrary to the DSM-5-TR, Lacanian psychoanalysis is not a symptom-oriented approach but a structural approach concerning fetishism, which stands under the category of the structure of perversion. Lacan clarifies that the symptoms of fetishism can only be understood by examining the structure of perversion, and this approach requires comprehending the human developmental process, which starts from the birth of a human infant and its development. Moreover, in Lacanian psychoanalysis, the presence or absence of the symptoms are not required criteria for the diagnosis of perversion. Often, perversion can manifest

---

1. APA, *Diagnostic and Statistical Manual*, 797.

without symptoms and operates only within speech and intersubjectivity. Furthermore, we can consider perversion to be a way of being and living.[2]

Lacan and Developmental Psychology

Like many developmental theories, the Lacanian approach to human development relates to studying the human life span from infancy. Classical theories, such as Jean Piaget's cognitive development, Brazelton's infant observation model, Mahler's separation and individuation theory, Erikson's psycho-social development stage, Kohlberg's moral development, and Levinson's human development through the whole life, are referred to as staged theories, which explain human development within the cycle of life, from its beginning to its end.[3] The methods they apply include positivism, empirical data, and evidence-based *science* (emphasis mine). However, this approach needs to be revised to explain perversion. The structural point of view can be more useful to understand perversion.

Contrary to developmental models, Lacanian psychoanalysis approaches infancy and childhood retroactively, using clinical practice as a praxis for inferences for the diagnosis of perversion. It is a contingency-based method, called conjectural sciences (human sciences), posited against exact sciences, including positivism and natural sciences. According to Lacanian psychoanalysis, developmental theory cannot adequately explain what happens in the mind of a child in terms of fantasy, unconscious, infantile sexuality, including gender and sexual differentiation. Lacanian psychoanalysts define human development as subject and subjectivity, deeply related to the object. A subject's birth ontologically begins from a pre-subjective or pre-ontological state.

Lacan and the Object Relations Theory

Lacan spent his whole seminar on object relations theory from 1956 to 1957.[4] He acknowledges and critiques the object relations theory and explains its historical development in the seminar. He includes the

---

2. Khan, *Alienation in Perversions*, 121–24.

3. See Piaget, "Piaget's Theory," 703; Brazelton and Nugent, *Neonatal Behavioral Assessment Scale*; Mahler et al., *Psychological Birth*; Erikson, *Childhood and Society*; Kohlberg, "Claim to Moral Adequacy"; Levinson, *Seasons of a Man's Life*.

4. See Lacan, *Object Relation*.

theory of Otto Fenichel's preoedipal stage and that of Melanie Klein's paranoid-schizoid position, and examines the American object relations theory, including Heinz Kohut's controversies about the two analyses of Mr. Z.[5] Also, Lacan critiques the British School theories, such as Winnicott's transitional objects theory, Bion's theory on the Importance of Not-Knowing, and Fairburn's Endo psychic situation theory.[6]

Object relations theories generally emphasize the individual's subjective experiences about early objects, specifically primary caregivers, as the most significant aspects of their lives. The theory assumes that the subject's experience of objects in early childhood can be reconstructed through analysis. Reconstruction can occur in the analytical session when the analyst interprets the experience of transference in the analysand. Psychoanalysts within object relations theories believe this method leads analysis to catharsis, insight, and intellectual enlightenment.

Lacan sees the relationship between subject and object in a more complex way. He questions diachrony (historicity and linearity) in object relations theory, especially when it comes to the structure of perversion. The interruption in diachrony occurs through the unique mechanism of language called synchrony. The synchrony happens when the perverse subjects persist in promoting the sexual object of their illusion as they speak. In *Seminar IX, Identification,* and *Seminar XIV, The Logic of Fantasy,* Lacan introduces topography and mathematical set theory to demonstrate the spatiality and temporality of the perverse in terms of a way of experiencing the object, which tends to be indefinitely fantastic. Also, Lacan implies that the temporality and spatiality of the object's experiences are constantly shifting, and that experiences can be understood only retroactively.[7] Never can it be on time that the subject meets the object: it is either too soon or too late because of the illusory tendency or anxiety, respectively.

Next, I will explain the perverse subject's structure from Lacan's point of view and its relation to the illusory object of desire. To do so, we begin with the Lacanian clinical structure.

---

5. See Fenichel, *Collected Papers*; Klein, "Notes on Some Schizoid Mechanisms"; Kohut, "Two Analyses of Mr. Z."

6. See Winnicott, "Transitional Objects"; Bion, *Second Thoughts*; Fairbairn, *Psychological Studies of the Personality.*

7. Lacan, "Logical Time."

LACANIAN CLINICAL STRUCTURE

Lacan nosography consists of three discrete clinical structures: neurosis, psychosis, and perversion.[8] The structure does not simply consist of a collection of symptoms; instead, it describes the subject's position concerning self (intra-subjective or internal representation) and the Other (intersubjective interpersonal relations). According to Lacan, each structure is characterized by a different defensive mode of operation: neurosis by the defensive mode of operation of repression, psychotic by foreclosure, and perversion by disavowal.[9]

The structural analysis can also be used as a diagnostic criterion to place the subject in the categories of psychotic, neurotic, and perversion. These structures are mutually exclusive. For example, a perverse subject cannot be in the neurotic or psychotic structure at the same time. Within the structure of neurosis, we find anxiety, obsessional neurosis, phobia, and hysteria. Perversion includes sadism, masochism, voyeurism, exhibitionism, and fetishism. In psychosis, there are paranoia, schizophrenia, and manic-depressive psychosis. In terms of etiology, Lacanian psychoanalysis proposes that the critical period of hypothesis, the first few years of life, determines the subject's clinical structure. Lacan, in the seminar on anxiety, describes this period in terms of privation, frustration, and castration.[10]

Finally, Lacanian psychoanalysts, using the free association technique, find the neurotic a good candidate for analysis. The perverse poses difficulty in treatment and the psychotic is described as unsuitable for analysis. Certain modifications are needed to treat the psychosis to obtain a good result.

Clinical Perversion

Lacan starts to talk about perversion by critiquing Freud's early text, *Three Essays on the Theory of Sexuality*. In this text, Freud describes perversion as a deviation from natural and normative heterosexual genital intercourse. After his three essays, Freud continues to consider perversion as a deviation, which is universally rooted in the pre-Oedipal state

---

8. Lacan, *Four Fundamental Concepts*.

9. Lacan, *Identification*.

10. See Lacan, *Anxiety*.

and regarded as polymorphous perversity and manifested in forms of acts such as sadism, masochism, and fetishism.[11]

However, Freud in his essays on the Ego and the Id, while introducing his structural model of the unconscious, explains pervasion not only in terms of an "act" but also in terms of structure.[12] Following Freud, Lacan differentiates between the perverse "act" and the perverse structure. A perverse subject can still function within perversion with or without displaying the perverse act. Furthermore, Lacan removes the discussion of perversion from biology, moral law, and nature: "What is perversion? It is not simply an aberration in relation to social criteria, an anomaly contrary to good morals."[13]

The law is not moral law or socially approved heterosexual normative behaviors. The law is the Law of the Father or the Name-of-the-Father, represented by the phallus (prohibition) during castration. When the preverbal subject, who has enormous need and demand for love and pleasure, walks through language (linguistified), he must experience the limits of his wants and needs. The-Name-of-the-Father operates through language by saying, "No," meaning the prohibition or the dictum not to enjoy.

The speaking subject is a castrated subject who can never go back to the preverbal level. In other words, a castrated subject indicates a subject as the subject speaks. The pervert is aware of the law of the father and finds a conflict that his desire stands outside the already existing law. The perverse subject resolves this conflict by taking the law into its own hands through the Imaginary. This operation of the perverse is referred to as disavowal, a defense mechanism that the subject uses to avoid the anxiety of castration.

Lacan's analysis of clinical cases of perversion are discussed in *The Seminar of Object Relations* which includes Freud's cases in the dream of the young homosexual woman, Freud's transference analysis of the case of Dora, and Little Hans's phobia.[14] Also, in the seminar on transference, Lacan discusses Alcibiades's transference to Socrates in the scene of Symposium as perversion.[15] Alcibiades goes through all the impossible and possible ways to seek pleasure while expressing his affinity for Socrates.

11. Freud, "Instincts and Their Vicissitudes."

12. Freud, "Ego and the Id."

13. Lacan, *Freud's Papers on Technique*, 221.

14. Lacan, *Relation d'Objet*, 208–12.

15. Lacan, *Transference*.

Next, we will describe three constitutive moments: privation, frustration, and castration in the formation of perversion in general and fetishism (one type of perversion) specifically.

Fetishism in Perversion (Perversion of Perversions)

Lacan interprets Freud's view on fetishism that the fetishist subject persists in believing in the mother's phallus (symbolic penis).[16] For this reason, sexual excitement, pleasure, and jouissance depend on the fantasy of the presence of bodily objects such as a foot or non-bodily objects such as a shoe or a piece of underwear as a symbolic substitute for the mother's missing phallus. Contrary to Freud, who assumes perverse fetishism is part of the neurotic structure, Lacan sees perverse fetishism, like other perversions, as a separate structure in which the subject positions the self as an instrument of the object of drive for the enjoyment of the big Other.

"The subject here makes himself the instrument of the Other's jouissance."[17] This definition of perversion is described in Lacan's formula for perversion as $a <> \$$,[18] where *the objet petit a* (the illusory object) of desire takes over the subjectivity to fill the lack within the subject. While in the formula of fantasy for neurosis ($\$ <> a$), we see the opposite, an inversion of the subject to object, where the divided subject desires an impossible *objet petit a*. In the first formula, the perverse subject's lure guarantees the jouissance for the Other through control, invasion, shame, and causing guilt in the Other. The divided subject also uses the object to cover the lack of self and the Other. The perverse fetish operates within the linguistic field as well as within the visual field. The operation originates from the preverbal (pre-Oedipal) experiences of the triangle of the mother-child-phallus. The perverse subject recognizes the linguistic signifier prohibition of "No" within the symbolic but attempts to circle around it.

Next, I will describe the structural formation of perversion and fetishism, in particular, within the three moments of the castration complex: privation, frustration, and castration. This occurs within the triangle of the mother-child-phallus experience. Privation represents the Real of the Father, where the agency of the father is not born yet

16. Freud, "Fetishism," 149.

17. Lacan, *Écrits*, 320.

18. Lacan, *Écrits*, 774.

but kept within the mother-child-phallus matrix. Frustration represents the Father in the domain of the Imaginary in the absence of the mother feeding (absence the breast). Castration represents the father in the symbolic domain where the symbolic father takes the responsibility for the Name-of-the Father. The Name-of-the Father should not necessarily be the actual father. Anybody can fulfill this function.

The Formation of Perverse Structure (Fetishism) within the Castration Complex

Lacan spends a significant portion of his seminar on objection relations to explain the three moments of the castration complex, named privation, frustration, and castration.[19] The first moment, privation, takes place as the phallus (the signifier of lack) represents the Name-of-the Father (the law) in the domain of the Real. At this moment, meaning has not formed yet. Within the symbiosis of the mother (primary caretaker) and the child, the mother is the holding place for the Name-of-the-Father and has to announce its coming when it is needed. From the child's point of view, the mother is complete and provides him with all sorts of needs and demands for love. For example, when the child is fed, the child is satisfied. There is no differentiation between me and not me, and the child has no concept of inside and outside. With the triad of mother-child-phallus, the child assumes the child is the breast or the mother. Privation represents the Real of the phallus.

In the second moment, frustration occurs when the child is not fed due to the absence of the breast-phallus. The child finds out the mother is incomplete. The absence of the breast-phallus is traumatic, terrifying, and causes full anxiety. To compensate, the child hallucinates the breast-phallus or denies the lack of phallus when not fed. Fetishism is the denial of the phallus in the mother and an attempt to be the phallus for the mother by creating a fetishistic item (foot, shoe, underwear) within the symbolic domain. Here, perversion is the response to the Other (mOther) jouissance, while separation is a response to the desire of the Other.

The phallus operates within the Imaginary realm in frustration. According to Lacan, frustration also occurs at the moment of alienation when the divided subject is alienated from the self.[20] Before alienation,

19. Lacan, *Object Relations*, 84–85.
20. Lacan, *Four Fundamental Concepts.*

the child is a complete being within the matrix of mother-child-phallus with full jouissance. Frustration is a state of estrangement; it is an alienation from the previous fullness of being.

In the third moment, castration, the child is separated from the mother and accepts the prohibition of the Law of the Father. Consequently, the child postpones its jouissance by focusing on the relationship with others in the future. Castration is also the moment of separation from the mOther, where the paternal function plays a significant role in the transition.[21] Contrary to Winnicott and the American object relations theorist Mahlar,[22] it is not the child who experiences separation from the mother; instead, it is the mother who is separated from the child.

The mother introduces the Name-of-the-Father to the child. Through limit setting, the mother makes the transition available to the child. Moreover, for Winnicott, the transitional object represents the mother, while for Lacan, the transitional object represents something lacking in the mother.[23] In fetishism, the subject has not overcome the separation and remains in alienation and believes that the mother has no lack. This belief is the "fundamental fantasy"[24] where the subject assumes the mOther is not barred and has no lack. Encountering the lack of the mother is terrifying for the subject. In fetishism, the subject is aware of the law of the Father, but through disavowal, takes the law into its own hands and imagines that she or he can bypass the Law.

Finally, separation also takes place at the end of the analysis, where the subject traverses the "fundamental fantasy" by encountering the drive and the lack of its desire for union with the other. What follows is the presentation of a clinical case material concerning foot fetishism as a type of perversion.

CLINICAL CASE

In this section, we introduce Mr. K's foot fetishism, the case of a wheelchair man. This section includes a referral, excerpts verbatim, and an analysis.

21. Verhaeghe, *On Being Normal*.
22. Mahler, *Psychological Birth*.
23. See Winnicott, "Transitional Objects," 5; cf. Lacan, *Object Relations*, 145.
24. See "Direction of the Treatment and the Principles of Its Power," in Lacan, *Écrits*, 489–542.

Referral

Mr. K. is a thirty-two-year-old white male who is in a wheelchair due to an early childhood accident that happened while he was in the car with his family. He has no use of his legs and has a tube in his chest to facilitate breathing. He was referred for analysis by his mother, who is an academic and intellectual. His mother believes that his previous treatment was not "effective."

Mr. K. admitted that he is a foot fetishist. He is an artist of abstract painting and drawing. He said when he drew, he felt "better." He presented many of his works in the sessions, but due to confidentiality, they are not presented in this chapter. Mr. K's obsession with foot fetishism manifested in his artwork. Mr. K. claimed he did not have a problem and came to analysis only because of his mother's request. His mother stated that her son's situation became more exasperated after his involvement in a legal matter.

Four years ago, Mr. K. had threatened his caretaker, a young woman, with a gun and forced her to perform a sexual act (fellatio) while he was "kissing" her on her toes. It was unclear where and how Mr. K. acquired the gun. According to the court papers, he claimed the incident was "all a game," which was orchestrated by the young caretaker, and he was frustrated because he could not achieve orgasm. After the court trial, Mr. K. was found guilty and sentenced to house arrest, and the court required him to three-years of court mandated therapy treatment for sexual assault and criminal acts. Mrs. K. is concerned her son may "lose control" and commit the "sexual assault" again.

Excerpts from Mr. K's Early Sessions

> I don't know if Dr. C., my previous doctor, told you about me. But this is what I can say about myself: I am a mean son of bitch. I did all kinds of bad things in my life. I was on the street mostly, dealing drugs and sometimes using it. I know a lot of women on the street. People know they should not mess with me. Like Kimberly, the girl (referring to the young caretaker), the bitch borrowed some money from me and didn't want to pay back. So, she ended in getting not only hurt but giving head (oral sex).

The theme of "street" was repeated many times in subsequent sessions. Ironically, after any "street" talk, Mr. K. shifted to more proper language with sophisticated vocabulary. His phantasy was to be a street person of a "macho type" with a tough guy persona. It was evident he was from an affluent family and had gone to college and earned higher education.

According to Lacan, a subject with the structure of disavowal in perversion has a particular relation to language.[25] The use of language in perversion suffers from duality and contradiction. Mr. K. uses two styles of language and shifts at any moment he wishes. This indicates his narcissistic omnipotence and omniscience within the Imaginary domain where he can bypass the law. He knows the law: "My father is always in the house, but he is quiet and hardly saying anything." He attempts to reject it. The law can be accepted in the public domain but rejected in private without any continuity.[26] Similarly, when it comes to describing his parents, Mr. K. has two different styles of language presentation. Concerning his mother: "I adore my mom. She is the greatest woman. She sacrificed everything for me." In another session, he said, "the bitch is crazy. She is very controlling, and I hate her for it."

Overall, Mr. K. grew up with a controlling mother, and all decisions about her son and household activities needed to meet with her approval, contrary to his father, who was passive, quiet, and distant. Two specific and vivid memories repeatedly appeared in the analytical session when Mr. K. spoke in free association. One event occurred when Mr. K. was six years old (before the car accident). He would go to his parents' bedroom at night while his father and mother were "dead sleeping." He (Mr. K.) would then look at his mother's feet with "astonishment and adoration" and then "smell, touch, and kiss his mother's 'right'" foot.

According to Mr. K., he was fantasizing that his dead sleeping father could do nothing or he would stay outside and watch while he slept with his mother all night. In one of these nightly performances, Mr. K. was caught when his mother and father woke up. He said, first, he was shocked and fearful, then went to an extreme state of anxiety. He managed to run away and locked himself in a small storage in the backyard. The mother went out the yard and asked him to come out. She reassured him he would not be punished. Mr. K. refused to come out and spent the whole night in the storage room. Ironically, during his sexual assault

25. Lacan, *Noms-Du-Père*, 18.

26. Verhaeghe, *On Being Normal*, 77–95.

against the young caretaker, Mr. K. repeated the same behavioral pattern of going to the storage room while sitting in a wheelchair, locking himself in, and refusing to come out before the police arrived. Apparently, during the assault, the young caretaker managed to run away and call the police.

The second incident with his mother occurred while he was a teenager. Mr. K. described the incident in which his mother caught him looking at Playboy magazines and masturbating. He said, "The psycho is so mean-spirited," referring to his mother. "She slapped me on the face as though I shouldn't have any desire for sex."

In both incidents, Mr. K. felt panicky, facing tremendous anxiety and stress. These memories continuously manifested in the analysis, especially when Mr. K. could not sexualize the sessions. In the long term, repetition helped Mr. K. to notice the limits of disavowal and his transgression against the Law of the Father.

In most sessions, Mr. K. was very resistant to any comments, questions, or interpretations. He was happy when I was quiet, like his "dead father." He tried to lure me in, soliciting a response. He would describe in detail all fetishistic tendencies, fantasies, and his porn watching and wanted to be sure that I had heard every single word. There was no consistency and long-lasting transference experience toward me as the "subject supposed to know" since he felt that he was the operative of the Law and could control the Father-analyst. Therefore, he knew how to have pleasure beyond prohibition.

At the beginning of the analysis, Mr. K. was allowed to express himself with whatever came to mind, and the analysis operated as a containment apparatus with active listening. Mr. K. was content and said, "I feel I have a voice and space here." For Mr. K., I was the analyst with "no desire," like the castrated dead father who would allow him to be with his mother alone so that he can deny the lack in himself and his mother, with the condition that his mother does not have the phallus, and he can be the phallus.[27]

Right in the middle of the analysis, "Che vuoi (say more)" and punctuation were introduced in the sessions. Also, I asked Mr. K's mother not to call and not to inquire about her son's analysis. Mr. K. was pleased with "Che vuoi," but he disliked the punctuation and was furious that his mother could not have information about his sessions. To "Che vuoi," "What do you want?" "Say more," Mr. K. responded with

---

27. Lacan, *Relation d'Objet*, 212.

excitement. He continued to sexualize the sessions and always came up with new narratives to describe the incident with the young caretaker or his childhood memory of the foot fetishism that happened in his parents' bedroom. But the punctuation, cut through variable sessions, made him anxious and angry. In one session, he said punctuation reminded him of the interrupted sex with the young caretaker, Kimberly. He emphasized that "Kimberly seduced me to have sex with her. . . . She was giving me a 'blow job,' and I began to 'kiss her on the toes,' and at that moment she started to move around her body and wanted to leave. I could never have a 'decent orgasm.'"

Mr. K. constantly resisted the limit setting, including punctuation and variable sessions, and remarked: "You remind me of the judge in the court. There is no difference between you and my probational officer." He threatened several times that he would leave the analysis by saying, "I am here at my mom's request. I never wanted to be here." As the analysis continued, he attempted to defend himself against my intervention by somaticizing the sessions. Below is an excerpt of the verbatim transcript from the middle part of the analysis: "I don't feel good. I don't know what is wrong with me. I was ill last week. Perhaps I am allergic to something. I don't know what I am allergic to. I think I had hay fever. I don't use any prescribed meds. But I buy meds. From the drug store nearby. I don't think I am physically ill now."

As Mr. K. continued our sessions, he began to talk about the feeling of sensation in his body. Prior to this, he had always identified his body with his wheelchair, where he could feel "nothing." He appeared to be less omnipotent and omniscient. As the analysis continued to the fourth year, Mr. K.'s speech became more within the symbolic realm than the Imaginary. He talked about his problems with daily function and his disability.

He had remorse concerning the incident related to his caretaker, saying, "It was all wrong what I have done to Kimberly." Mr. K. entertained the idea of moving out of the house where he lived with his mother: "I rely on my mother too much. I think I can make it my own." During the analysis, he resolved his legal problems and did not engage in any more sexual assaults or criminal acts. He was much at ease with his physical disability.

But at the end of the analysis, Mr. K. continued to remain within the perverse structure. During the analysis, he managed to distance himself from the world of the Imaginary and stay within the symbolic. His structure of perversion was well established during his early oedipal stages, and similar to the neurotic and psychotic, a shift to another structure is difficult to make. The treatment of Mr. K. was challenging due to his disavowal mechanism and the difficulties that he presented during the transference. As Lacan believes, the perverse subject is reluctant to go deeper and works beyond the symptoms.[28]

Lacanian treatment ultimately focuses on facilitating transformations of the analysand to the level of drive. The drive is closely related to the repetition compulsion in demanding jouissance (enjoyment beyond pleasure principle) and wanting to go beyond the limits of jouissance. Mr. K.'s repeated obsessional fantasy of foot fetishism and desire to act upon his impulses represent an extreme example of returning to the infantile mode of drive, "the circuit of the drive."[29] According to Lacan, jouissance is "the satisfaction of a drive."[30] Within the circuit of the drive, the drive is partial, as well as the object. The object of the drive, one's body or others, is a moving object. The drive never fully meets the object but circles around it. However, Mr. K. often resisted having insight into his repetition compulsion. In the last part of the treatment, Mr. K. seemed to show more flexibility and willingness to go deeper in his analysis, even though it was anxiety-provoking and "painful."

SUMMARY

Mr. K. is a thirty-two-year-old white male in a wheelchair who engages in foot fetishism. His fetishism caused him to commit an act of "crime" and "sexual assault" against his female caretaker with a subsequent court trial and house arrest. He was brought to treatment for compulsion and the fear of committing the "sexual assault" again. He grew up in an affluent household environment with a "domineering" mother and a "passive" and "distant" father.

Mr. K. was diagnosed with foot fetishism, which must have been formed in early childhood. In the analysis demonstrated here, I used the Lacanian clinical structure of perversion as the main criterion for his treatment. Like in any object of obsession, Mr. K's foot fetishism was the main characteristic of his personality traits. His obsession with returning to the primary object of his desire (the mother) constitutes his

28. Lacan, *Psychoses*, 156.
29. Lacan, *Four Fundamental Concepts*.
30. Lacan, *Ethics of Psychoanalysis*, 209.

fundamental fantasy. Within the analytical treatment, Mr. K. resisted the treatment intervention by perceiving the analyst as the castrating father who intended to separate him from his mother.

Due to the defense mechanism of disavowal and difficulty in transference, completing the analysis of Mr. K. was impossible. However, after premature termination, he was able to manage his life more within the symbolic realm than the Imaginary. Also, he could reevaluate his fundamental fantasy of reunion with his mother. He was in control of his impulses not to commit "sexual assault." He had remorse for what he had done to his caretaker and felt responsible for it. Further, he left his parents' house for the first time and managed to live independently.

12

A Lacanian Clinical Case of Neurosis
The Melancholic Woman

Ali Chavoshian

In general, listening can be a crucial tool for treatment, but in the case of neurotic patients, it is essential for analysts to cultivate the art of listening, to understand the nature of listening. The art of listening to the patient of neurosis requires a thorough knowledge of understanding the structural position of the subject in relation to language, law, demand, desire, and jouissance. I, in this chapter, introduce the art of listening with neurotic patients as the most essential part of treatment, and explore principles and necessary concepts, which help to understand attentive listening. Also, I present a clinical case of a fifty-eight-year-old woman, suffering from the symptoms of depression and melancholia. With some part of verbatim, I will describe Lacanian analysis, which utilizes the transference in the clinical structure of neurosis, presenting some sessions through excerpts of a verbatim.

UNDERSTANDING NEUROSIS

As mentioned in the previous chapters, the diagnostic criteria for neurotic include the structural analysis of the psyche regardless of the manifestation of its symptoms such as depression or anxiety. The structural analysis focuses on the ontological subjective experience as one encounters the Other. Here, the Other represents law and language. The ontological experience is the structure of experience of being, expressed in language.[1] For example, the experience of being for the hysteric neurosis, a type of neurosis, is formulated as: "Am I a man or am I a woman?" or in the obsessional neurosis, another type of neurosis, it is formulated as: "Am I dead or am I alive."

In general, according to Lacan, there are three types of neuroses: phobia, hysteric, and obsessional.[2] The hallmark of all neuroses appears as a type of negation, referred to as "repression." Repression is the primary experience of a subject who has entered the signification of language. The signification of language is represented by the repressed signifier as "the representation of the representative"[3] where the affect is separated from the original trauma and displaced on a new experience.

Another hallmark of neurosis is castration. The neurotic subject has accepted the castration, meaning the affirmation of the "Name-of-the-Father," but holds a grudge against it by expressing doubt and uncertainty toward the Law (the Father). The neurotic subject holds concerns about the limit of *jouissance* and the inhibition of the drive. The subject seeks excess in *jouissance* through demand, desire, and objet petit a. In the context of the nature of neurotic, the art of listening should be unique; it is a special kind of listening to the subject, focusing on demand and desire with their complexities.

THE ART OF LISTENING

Listening, in general is the fundamental principle of analysis. All approaches to listening should concern the questions of "how" and "what." The question of "how" helps us to create a process-oriented treatment rather than a content-oriented treatment. The process-oriented analysis allows the analysand to present fluently the content. The question of "what" is related to listening beyond spoken words, as it is referred to listening beyond the symptoms. I will describe further the question of "how" and "what" as the fundamental principles of listening.

1. Lacan, *The Psychosis*, 288.
2. Lacan, *Écrits*, 168.
3. Lacan, *The Four Fundamental Concepts of Psychoanalysis*, 218.

Listening of How and What

How I listen to the analysand is one of the most crucial tasks of an analyst and then it is also important to know what hinders analysts from listening; yet these two are interlaced. The reason why listening is hard goes as follows:

1. Listening causes anxiety: While listening, most analysts experience anxiety. Then, it is within the ability of the analyst to learn how to hold, contain, maintain, and manage her and his anxiety.

2. Listening, for most, is related to the desire of the analyst rather than the desire of the patient-analysand: The desire of the analyst is the desire of the Other. The analyst, as the desire of the Other, is preoccupied with past training and certain knowledge of treatment modalities. Can the analyst empty oneself from this desire, and listen with an empty mind, staying within here and now at the experiences of listening? Removing desire requires that analyst should damage one's narcissism of knowing and disclaiming any knowledge. This removal creates analytical neutrality where there is no judgement or pre-formulation while listening to the suffering of the patient.

3. Listening is a state of encountering the fear of unknown: Nicholas of Cusa, the fifteenth-century theologian, introduced the term "learned ignorance," meaning "knowing that you don't know" and avoiding "passion for ignorance," meaning "not knowing that you don't know."[4] To know the truth of not knowing is perhaps the only way to hold anxiety and keep listening to the analysands.

Thus, listening is not an easy practice, yet it is as an art which requires a deep understanding of the analyst's desire, which comes as an obstacle in treating the patient.

Then, what I listen, as an analyst, is a necessary question to ask. The characteristics of listening or the question of "what" go as follows:

•   Listening is "Listening Not"[5] rather than Listening:
    Active or attentive listening goes beyond the sound of speech, including all kinds of sensory reactions, facial expressions, and body movement. The ears should function as the trained instrument that reflects the exact words of the speaker. Only skillful and "humanized

4. Nicolas of Cusa, *On Learned Ignorance*, 46.
5. Chavoshian and Park, "Listening Not in Spiritual Direction," 5–12.

ears"[6] can reflect the suffering of the speaker. Thus, the term, "listening with the third ear" signifies an alternative way of listening which goes beyond ordinary communication based on knowledge a priori. This listening is not a conversation with a friend over a cup of coffee or a response to comments, like a game of Ping-Pong.

- Listening is not equivalent to silence:

  Often, we tend to think that listening is keeping silence. The listener could be silent out of anger, confusion, boredom, or not knowing what to say. However, attentive listening is not just being speechless. Rather, the listening includes active reflection and inquiry for exploration, by saying to the speaker, "Say more" or "Che vuoi" (what do you want?) and simply repeating what the patients said.

PRINCIPLES OF THE ART OF LISTENING

There are fundamental principles of the art of listening, which are more orientation and attitude, not a skill set. For cultivating the mode of attentive and active listening, I will introduce some concepts such as the metaphor and the metonymy, and transference and countertransference.

The Metaphor and the Metonymy

Originally, Lacan borrowed the system of signs from Saussure's structural theory of signifier and signified in language.[7] However, he changed Saussure's system of signs to the system of signifiers. To understand the relationship between the signifier to the signified, Lacan further borrowed the concepts of metaphor (condensation) and metonymy (displacement) from Jacobson to demonstrate how they influence the speech of the analysand within the analytical treatment.[8] Metaphor as the substitution represents the mechanism of repression and the return of repression. The return of repression is an isolated symptom in the neurotic to the point that "the symptom is a metaphor."[9] But in metonymy, because of its combinatory factor, it represents the desire of the analysand. According to

---

6. Marx, *Economic and Philosophical Manuscript of 1844*, 98–114.

7. Saussure, *Course in General Linguistics*, 65–67.

8. Jacobson, "Two Aspects of Language," 95–114.

9. Lacan, *Écrits*, 175.

Lacan "desire is a metonymy."[10] The focus of analytical treatment should be listening to the desire of the analysand, not to the symptom.

Transference and Countertransference

Lacan refers to transference as the development of the relationship between the patient and the analyst. Neurotic transference includes a displacement of affect and ideas on the analyst. The patient attributes knowledge to the analyst as the "Other." The analyst is the "subject supposed to know."[11] The "subject supposed to know" is an imaginary projection of the patient to the analyst. In response, the analyst plays the role of a "dummy" and remains silent. The affective displacement is the imaginary nature of transference which includes transference love as positive transference and transference hate as negative transference. These transferences are compulsively repetitive (repetition compulsion), linked to the experience, and manifest in the analytic treatment.

Transference is like a double-edge sword. From one point, it closes up the opening of the unconscious, and from the other point, it allows the analyst to know that there is something hidden in the transference. It is the symbolic nature of the transference which is mainly the focus of the art of listening.[12] The symbolic transference is the patient's understanding of the repetition compulsion in developing an imaginary relationship with the analyst.

If transference is the patient's response, developed as the result of the analytical treatment, countertransference is the response of analyst to the patient's transference. Freud thought countertransference was antithetical to the analytical treatment, and when the analyst has affective reaction, judgment, and overall response toward the patient, she/he needs to go back to the coach to be analyzed again.[13] After Freud, Paula Heimann, Margaret Little, and Heinrich Racker all sought countertransference as an inevitable response to the transference.[14] They believe countertransference provides useful insights, both to the patient and the analyst.

10. Lacan, *Écrits*,175.

11. Lacan, *Four Fundamental Concepts*, 232.

12. Lacan, *Ego In the Freud's Theory*, 210–11.

13. Freud and Jung, *Freud/Jung Letters*, 231.

14. See Heimann, "On Counter-Transference," 81–84; Little, "Counter-Transference," 32–40; Racker, "Meanings and Uses of Countertransference," 303–57.

Lacan seldom talks about the concept of countertransference in his works. In one of his early works, as he attempts to revisit Freud's treatment of the young homosexual woman, he analyzes Freud's "countertransference" toward the patient.[15] In his later works, Lacan seldom uses the term countertransference. Instead, his focus is on the "desire of the analyst." When the subject is addressing the analyst as the "subject supposed to know," the analyst's desire must not be to play the role of knowing, but rather to remain ambiguous.[16] The ambiguity of the analyst's desire raises the question of "Che vuoi" ("what do you want from me?") for the subject. The question of "Che vuoi" will be addressed to the analyst. It brings up the fundamental fantasy of the subject within symbolic speech. The fundamental fantasy, as the reunion with the mother-analyst, emerges in the transference love and in the identification with the analyst.[17] It is an imaginary reunion. Ultimately, the patient traverses the fundamental fantasy and positions self within the symbolic speech as she/he sees the impasse to the desire and to the jouissance for the reunion.

A CLINICAL CASE: THE MELANCHOLIC WOMAN

The patient is a 58-year-old devout Muslim woman, referred to me by her faith leader, "Imam," (spiritual director). The reason for the referral was that the patient was displaying a wide range of clinical symptoms which was interfering with her spiritual work. Prior to coming to see me, the patient had had a stroke due to high blood pressure, just a month before. I also realized she was placed on psychotropic medications for delusional disorder prior to being discharged from the hospital. After her evaluation, I came to the conclusion that she was suffering from the symptoms of atypical depression with melancholic feature, common among the elderly population and delusional disorder is not warranted. The delusion is the result of the stroke, which normally would disappear in a short period of time. Therefore, I asked the treating psychiatrist to discontinue the patient's medications and then I began the treatment.

---

15. See Lacan, *Relation d'objet*; Freud, "Psychogenesis," 13–33.
16. Lacan, *Four Fundamental Concepts*, 274.
17. Lacan, *Écrits*, 854.

Presenting Problems

Patient has been preoccupied with the death of her mother for ten years. She also feels that God will punish her for raising a child "who has become a lesbian."

Excerpts from a Verbatim from the Middle Part of the Analysis

Patient: Hello, hello, how are you? I am so glad to see you and I am lucky that you are my doctor. I feel I can talk with you about all my problems because we are from the same faith and background. Before I start, I should ask you if you are OK. You seem to be pale and weak. Every week it is getting worse. Do you sleep and eat enough? Is your wife taking care of you?

(Short silence)

Well, last week was horrible as usual. First, I have been thinking about my mother and how much I miss her even though she died ten years ago. I can't accept her death. She lives with me every moment (crying and short silence). Then I couldn't sleep all night because I was thinking over and over what my mother told me. She told me once: "Your daughter is a lesbian and God will punish you for that" (continue crying, and a long silence).

Analyst: "Your daughter is a lesbian and God can punish you for that."

Patient: Yes, Mom thought I didn't spend enough time with my daughter and didn't raise her properly. But I didn't have a choice. I was a single mom and had to go to school and work. Our faith leader in the community is saying that it is not true. That is an old fashion way of thinking. Nothing in Koran is saying that. I read Koran several times. There are remarks about male homosexuality, but nothing about female. My daughter is [happy with] her sexuality. All the physicians are telling me that I have tremendous stress and my blood pressure is very high. They say if I have stroke and heart attack again, they may not be able to save me this time. (Suddenly she seems frighten and anxious and crying, in few minutes) I hope I won't go to hell when I die.

(Silence for a long time)

Analyst: Say more.

Patient: Considering what my mother said, it is a possibility. But my faith leader says, Allah (God) is forgiving. (Continues praying, saying, "Allahu Akbar"—God is great—with a gesture of asking for forgiveness.)

Then spoke in a lengthy way in detail about the concept of hell and heaven.

Clarification—the Patient's Atypical Depression, Melancholy and Application for the Listening

The above session indicates the patient's position is within the clinical structure of neurosis and her main defense mechanism is repression. According to the DSM-5-TR, the diagnostic criteria for major depression with subtypes and specifiers of atypical features and melancholic features are fully explained in behavioristic terms. A typical feature of depression and melancholy prevails in the elderly population. Patients suffer from a lack of sleep (morning blue), and repetitive thinking of the past experiences as visual images, extreme sense of loss, guilt, self-worth, and suicidal ideation.

Despite the literature that explains melancholic is to be placed within the category of psychosis due to its defense mechanism of foreclosure, there is evidence in the sessions that the patient is neurotic. The patient's gender, religion, and culture and her main use of repression is proper to put her in a suitable position for analysis where variable sessions, cut, and "Che vuoi" and listening can be utilized as analytical techniques.

Within the Lacanian categories of mental disorders, these features by themselves do not warrant the diagnosis of depression and melancholy. They are the symptomatic aspects of a larger category known as the neurotic clinical structure. The depressive features are located within the neurotic structure where the negation, repression, and castration have already taken place within the psychic structure of the patient. Regarding the melancholia, unlike the classic works such as Karl Abraham[18] and Freud,[19] who consider melancholy as the feature of psychotic depression, contemporary analysts such as Fink explain how melancholy should be considered within the discourse of subject in the clinical practice and its association to the primary defense mechanisms (repression in neurotic, disavowal in perversion, and foreclosure in psychosis).[20]

---

18. Abraham, *Notes on the Psycho-Analytical Investigation*, 37–156.
19. Freud, "Mourning and Melancholia," 243–58.
20. See Fink, *Clinical Introduction to Lacanian Psychoanalysis*.

Analysis of the Excerpts

The patient developed a positive transference to me by repeatedly mentioning that she was glad that we were from "the same faith and background." She also mentioned she would feel at home in the sessions, and
she would not want to do analysis with the American analysts because
they would not understand her. In fact, I am not from "the same faith
and background," and the patient knew it. But I would not confirm or
disconfirm her views about me. The patient related to me as the "subject
supposed to know" and I played the role of "dummy." As the transference
developed further, she would bring copies of citations, from the "Holy
Koran," concerning her daughter's homosexuality. She would hand me
the copies and asked me to read it aloud. Below is one example:

ٱلرِّجَالُ قَوَّٰمُونَ عَلَى ٱلنِّسَآءِ بِمَا فَضَّلَ ٱللَّهُ بَعْضَهُمْ عَلَىٰ بَعْضٍ وَبِمَآ أَنفَقُواْ مِنْ أَمْوَٰلِهِمْ
فَٱلصَّٰلِحَٰتُ قَٰنِتَٰتٌ حَٰفِظَٰتٌ لِّلْغَيْبِ بِمَا حَفِظَ ٱللَّهُ وَٱلَّٰتِى تَخَافُونَ نُشُوزَهُنَّ فَعِظُوهُنَّ
وَٱهْجُرُوهُنَّ فِى ٱلْمَضَاجِعِ وَٱضْرِبُوهُنَّ فَإِنْ أَطَعْنَكُمْ فَلَا تَبْغُواْ عَلَيْهِنَّ سَبِيلًا إِنَّ ٱللَّهَ
كَانَ عَلِيًّا كَبِيرًا

Men are the protectors and maintainers of women, because
Allah has given the one more (strength) than the other, and
because they support them from their means. Therefore the
righteous women are devoutly obedient, and guard in (the
husband's) absence what Allah would have them guard. As to
those women on whose part ye fear disloyalty and ill-conduct,
admonish them (first), (Next), refuse to share their beds, (And
last) beat them (lightly); but if they return to obedience, seek
not against them Means (of annoyance): For Allah is Most High,
great (above you all). (Surah An-Nisa 4:34)[21]

By asking me to read the above verse from the "Holy Koran," the
patient wanted me to intervene as "the Name-of-the-Father" to separate
her from her intrusive dead mother and prohibit her daughter from the
act of homosexuality. This would help her to reduce her "obsessive neurosis" symptoms of guilt, self-worth, and that would temporarily relieve
her from the pressure she was receiving from her persecutory mother.

The transference development further appeared in the excerpts
from the above as the patients raised her concerns about my health:
"You seem to be pale and weak. Every week it is getting worse. Do you
sleep and eat enough? Is your wife taking care of you?" The patient in her
"transference love" totally identified with me as her husband. The fact

21. The first English translation was published in 1934 in India.

is that she, herself, had been suffering from many illnesses, and she was pale and weak. Rather than talk about her medical condition, she must attribute her illness to me through the mechanism of projection, then identify with me as her husband whom she can take care of.

When the patient asked me questions concerning my health, I did not answer, rather I created a silence. The silence allowed the patient shift to her ruminating thoughts and the feelings she had for her mother. When the second silence occurred, I reflected exactly the patient's statement back to her: "your daughter is a lesbian and God can punish you for that." In response, the patient explained further the relationships with her daughter and her deceased mother. In the third moment of silence, I said to the patient: "say more," paralleling the "Che vuoi." In response, the patient's explanations were more detailed and expansive in a larger sense.

Case Formulation

The patient is caught up between two version of Islam, or two grand narratives. One narrative is represented by her mother stating that she will be punished by God for raising a "lesbian" daughter. Another narrative is represented by the spiritual leader that God is forgiving. None of the narratives are her own as they are presented to her. If we interpret the narratives in terms of the desire of the patient, we can say her desire is the desire of the Other. Meaning, her desire of wanting to know what is going to happen to her in terms her religious belief is based upon the narrative that is given by the Other.

During the sessions, she did not speak about her own desire, but rather she spoke of the desire of the Other. The goal is for her to be the author of her own desire and to speak of her own desire. Speaking one's own desire is recovering the drive. It means realizing that the enjoyment of the drive is partial and there is an impasse or lack in desire. This can be done when the analyst is listening, and the patient is speaking. We can never underestimate the power of listening in analysis and the power of speech. Speech moves in so many directions and creates so many possibilities, where in the beginning they seem fixed. This happens when a patient moves from the vertical, metaphorical, and the imaginary of empty speech to the horizontal, metonymical, and the symbolic of full speech. The art of listening was demonstrated through silences, reflections, and

"Che vuoi," and—in the later sessions—punctuation and variable sessions were introduced.

Analysis

This fifty-eight-year-old woman, a devotee Muslim, was referred to me for analysis. She was on psychotherapeutic medication for a primary diagnosis of delusional disorder. After a decrease, and finally discontinuation of her medication, the patient diagnostic was reformulated within the Lacanian neurotic clinical structure with the primary defense mechanism of repression. She continues to display the symptoms of atypical depression and melancholy.

The art of listening was introduced in the sessions. The patient managed to distance self from her symptoms by creating interspace and moving toward the "analytical third." As the analysis continues, the patient was also able to position herself within symbolic speech and understand the structurization of her desire, that her desire is the desire of her mother. She developed an insight of her own transference in the sessions.

Although the feature of the patient's melancholy was explained within the structure of Lacanian neurosis, it can also be explained according to Freud's classical paper on "Remembering, Repeating, and Working Through" (1914).[22] In this paper, Freud describes the infantile memory of early loss object relations in terms of "repetition compulsion" and "acting out."

Patients prefer to repeat an act rather than remember the original trauma. For example, it is common for patients to display no affect while talking about the most traumatic events of their lives, but when they are talking about, for example, the "weather," they will be crying. This split between the thought of the trauma and the related affect and attaching the affect to new events, is an example of the repetition and acting out. Further, the acting out can be described in terms of repression, repetition, resistance, and transference. The acting out is the reflection of the loss of the love object. But the infantile love object is ambivalent where it manifests itself through love and hate. The repetition of the memory of the love object is only one-sided.

It excludes the hate for the object. Only in "Remembering" can the patient speak about the hate of the object. As the analysis progressed,

22. Freud, "Remembering, Repeating," 145–56.

my patient was able not only to speak of the love of her object lost (her mother), but also her hate. She was able to remember the cruelty and hostility impinged upon her (the patient) by her mother and was able to express her hate and "disgust" that she had for the mother.

To describe repeating and remembering, Lacan uses "automaton" and "touché," terms introduced by Aristotle in the second book of *Physics*. Lacan's terms for the repetition compulsion is "automaton"[23] or the "instance of the letter,"[24] which explains the cause of repeating. For re-membering, Lacan uses the term "touché."[25] Touché is the moment of encountering with the Real, which is the gap, the absence, the unrealized, as for my patient it was the moment of encountering the "hate."

In the final analysis, the patient was able to separate herself from her mother. She was able to write her own desire rather than her mother's and accept her daughter's homosexuality. She was more tolerable and flexible in interpreting the "Holy Koran." As the results, she became closer to her daughter and her family.

23. Lacan, *Quatre Concepts*, 60.

24. Lacan, "Instance of the Letter," 412.

25. Lacan, *Quatre Concepts*, 59.

13

A Lacanian Clinical Case of Psychosis
Richard's Fear of Bugs

ALI CHAVOSHIAN

LACAN'S DISCOURSE IS FUNDAMENTALLY clinical. How we approach psychosis depends on the school of psychoanalysis. Lacan's understanding of psychosis is deeply rooted in the process of identification. This chapter begins with an introduction to Lacan's description of psychotic clinical structure as the diagnostic criteria for psychotic disorders. A clinical case of "Richard's Fear of Bugs" will be presented to demonstrate the Lacanian approach to the diagnosis and the treatment of psychosis. I will also show the analysis of the sessions with some excerpts from the verbatim transcripts. This chapter demonstrates certain modifications in the theory and technique required to treat psychotic disorders effectively.

LACAN'S APPROACH TO PSYCHOSIS

Lacan's interest in psychosis started early in his career when he was writing his doctoral dissertation.[1] The dissertation includes the case of Aimee, a psychotic woman whose concern was that people planned to harm her baby. Lacan believed that Aimee's paranoid psychosis was a

1. See Lacan, *Psychose Paranoïaque.*

problem of identification, a confusion of self and the other. After several years, Lacan, in his paper on the mirror stage[2] and its later reformulation implies that psychosis is a state sucked into the imaginary world, a world that remains not overwritten by the symbolic. Further, in the imaginary-governed version of the mirror stage, the psychotic fails to form ego-ideal and does not recognize desire in others. The psychotic imprisonment in the imaginary world creates an unstable and fragile sense of self and ego.

After his work on the mirror stage, Lacan dedicated his theme to Seminar III on *The Psychoses*.[3] In this seminar, Lacan explains that psychosis consists of having a psychotic structure, regardless of the symptoms of hallucination and delusion. In the structure, the Name-of-the-Father, the master signifier, is missing. The missing of the "Name-of-the-Father" from the symbolic universe means "foreclosure." In this work, Lacan also engaged in re-reading and re-evaluating Freud's case of Schreber to discuss the foreclosure of the "Name-of-the-Father."[4] Lacan's foreclosure is a distinct feature of psychosis, and it is different from neurotic repression. Here he refers to the foreclosure as "a function of the unconscious that is distinct from the repressed."[5]

Further, Lacan would associate "foreclosure" with a lack of symbolization, which occurs through the primary signifier of the "Name-of-the-Father" or the paternal metaphor.[6] It seems clear in the psychotic structure that the paternal metaphor is absent. The presence of the paternal metaphor, for example, for the neurotics, allows the subject to deal with some fundamental questions of life, such as the question of desire and being, law and boundary, and further accelerates the process of socialization and inculturation. In contrast, the absence of the paternal metaphor causes deep confusion for the psychotic subject in terms of the comprehension of law and boundary, and the desire of the other ("What do you want?") and the problem of existential identity ("Who am I?").

The lack of a paternal metaphor also makes psychotic speech antonymic and, at times, incomprehensible, full of autoreferential words and neologisms as though the psychotic subjects possess their own private languages. Regarding this characteristic of speech of the psychotic, Lacan

2. Lacan understood the mirror stage as formative of the I (ego) function revealed in psychoanalytic experience. See Lacan, *Écrits*, 445–48.

3. Lacan, *Psychoses*.

4. See Freud, *Schreber Case*.

5. Lacan, "On a Question," 445–88.

6. Lacan, "On a Question," 445.

explicates: "In many cases, certain words take on a special emphasis, a density that sometimes manifests itself in the very form of the signifier, giving it this frankly neologistic character that is so striking in the creations of paranoia."[7]

In 1975–1976, using the Borromean knot, which is composed of the three rings of the symbolic, real, and imaginary, Lacan explains the structure of psychosis, wherein the three rings disentangle. Symptoms for psychosis, as the fourth ring, function as the apparatus of holding all the rings together.[8] Recalling the discourse of the mirror stage that the psychotic is not fully overwritten by the Symbolic it is clear that this condition leads the psychotic to resort to the Imaginary domain, which is close to the Real. The irruption of the Real into the Imaginary without the symbolic safety net causes panic anxiety.

Some psychoanalysts emphasize the panic anxiety among psychotic patients. The leading British psychoanalyst Donald Winnicott described panic anxiety as a "fear of breakdown,"[9] and yet another British psychoanalyst Wilfred R. Bion described it as the "nameless dread" in his seminal article, "Attack on Linking."[10] Panic anxiety with an unthinkable fear of annihilation, along with unmediated jouissance of the drive (Other jouissance) means having an experience of encountering the Real of the death drive. The experience of the Real is similar to the experience of an unintegrated child who stays within the matrix of the mother's desire, and it manifests as a fear of being devoured at any time by a crocodile:

> The mother's role is the mother's desire. That's fundamental. The mother's desire is not bearable, just like that, that you are indifferent to. It will always wreak havoc. A massive crocodile in whose jaws you are—that's the mother. One never knows what might suddenly come over her and make her shut her trap. That's what the mother's desire is.[11]

Lacan explains the fear of a devouring mother here using a crocodile image.

7. Lacan, "Other Psychoses," 4.

8. Lacan, *Sinthome.*

9. Winnicott, "Fear of Breakdown."

10. Bion, "Attacks on Linking," 308–15.

11. Lacan, *Other Side of Psychoanalysis.*

A CLINICAL CASE

Richard is a twenty-eight-year-old white male who is short, stocky, overweight, and has poor personal hygiene. He was brought to my attention from another ward building for evaluation while I was working as a clinical psychologist-analyst at the Central Virginia Training Center (CVTC). CVTC was a state psychiatric hospital located in Lynchburg, Virginia. The hospital is closed now, but at that time, it housed two thousand female and male patients with more than three thousand employees. The hospital campus was the largest hospital in the US. CVTC was an inpatient hospital with several buildings. In this part, I will introduce his case and the treatment, which focuses on the interdisciplinary approach where the psychological and psychiatric teams and the medical, recreational, educational, and speech pathologists worked together.

Initial Contact

Richard was brought to my office building by two male attendees from a more restrictive ward, a locked-up building. Before entering the room, Richard was hesitant to come in. He took one step forward and two steps backward. Richard was taking steps in slow motion, very rhythmically and artistically, like the movement of an astronaut in space. He stayed in front of the door and would not come in, but continued his movement without looking at me or the attendees. I pointed to the attendees that they should not intervene. Instead, I got up from my chair, stayed on Richard's right side, and imitated his movements. Then, I intentionally made an error. Richard stopped me and, without saying anything, showed me that there is one step forward and two steps backward, not two steps forward and one step backward. After a few minutes of this game, I managed to lead Richard to his chair, and finally, he sat on the chair.

Richard stayed quiet during the evaluation while staring at the ground, but when asked any questions, he would get agitated and rock back and forth, repeating the words, "night, bugs, canteen, floor, window screen." As his anxiety increased, he would rock back and forth faster and repeat the exact words faster. I started rocking back and forth with Richard, saying: "night, canteen, bugs, floor." Richard looked at me for the first time and immediately corrected me, saying, "No, no, no. It is night, bugs, canteen, floor, window screen, not night, canteen, bugs, floor, window screen." I stopped the evaluation and told the attendees that Richard could return to my office in two days. I told them he should come from his residential building to my office.

It was clear that Richard had lost orientation toward time, place, and person. In his preverbal condition, he managed to create his private action of rocking back and forth and a private language, mentioning a few words in an orderly manner to secure himself from psychotic panic, anxiety, and nervous breakdown. He remained unregistered within the symbolic realm due to the foreclosure of the primary signifier, the "Name-of-the Father." He had to take refuge in the imaginary world and devise his deeds and words to ward off the horror and anxiety of the Real.

Except for his movements and verbal words, he mainly appeared catatonic. The catatonic muteness was a defense against the symbolic domination of the order in my office, the rules and disciplines of the hospital that I represented, which was similar to the Law or the Name of the Father. After I validated his behaviors and verbal words, he seemed to be more interactive with me through gestures and eye contact. His corrections to my errors indicated that the precision of his private words and behaviors was highly significant for his survival.

The Background Information of Richard

Richard grew up with a mother who was suffering from schizophrenia. They lived in a poverty-stricken environment. His biological father was unknown. Although he had the symptoms of delusion and hallucination with a psychotic structure, the records did not mention his symptoms. The reason for the omission of symptoms was that prior to seeing me, his treatment strictly included behavior modification technique for two years.

Through reading his file, I gathered the following information:

His original diagnosis included Intellectual Developmental Disorders (under Neurodevelopmental Disorders) with borderline severity and Autism Spectrum Disorder:

1. History of psychotropic medications: They used Loxitane, Thorazine, Melleril, Artane for aggressive and self-abusive behaviors.

2. Behavior problems were characterized by his speaking about bugs attacking him. Sometimes, he said he was a bug, or others were bugs. Often, he said the bugs were crawling all over his skin to the point that he had to pick at his skin. This caused severe wounds all over his body, and he hit himself and others.

3. Behavior treatment included DRO (Differential Treatment of Other). Patients would be rewarded for any behavior except the targeted behavior.

4. Reinforcement of Incompatible Behavior—The patient would be reinforced for incompatible behavior, such as playing basketball rather than picking his skin.

5. Four-point restraints (tying up a patient on a bed) and time out (isolation).

6. The goal and object of the treatment were to decrease and eliminate the verbalization of bugs, picking skin behavior, and hitting self and others.

Because the treatment focused on the behaviors and symptoms, Richard had never had an opportunity to talk about his fear of the bugs. His hallucinations and delusions seemed repressed, while his psychotic structure remained intact. I agreed to work with Richard on the condition that I performed psychoanalytical treatment and asked the training treatment team and staff to cooperate with my treatment.

Summary of Sessions

Richard came for the first session two days after the initiative session, but instead of coming into my office, he passed by my office. He continued to pass by my office daily as his schedule would allow him. I noticed two patterns: Richard was always on time and wanted to ensure I had seen him. I was out of the office on two occasions that week. Richard would wait very nervously until I returned so I could see him and make eye contact with him. In the meantime, when the director of the building asked if Richard had attended his treatment, I responded: "Yes, he just started."

After a week, I left some papers, crayons, and pencils outside my door and put the name "Richard" at the top of the pile of papers. Richard came and took the papers. The next day, he brought them back and left them behind my door. I noticed the drawing of the bugs. Richard continued coming near the office, bringing his drawings, and leaving them outside my office. After a week, Richard came into my office and handed me his drawings. I told Richard we would start tomorrow, so he should come to my office, and if he wanted, he could sit and do his drawings. Richard did not respond, but he was in my office the next day. He took the chair at the corner, and in so doing, he took distance from my desk and continued drawing. I told him he could write whatever came to his mind at the top of his drawing page. He wrote: "This is a bug, you are the bug, I am the bug, and everybody is a bug." His drawings looked bizarre and awkward with dismembered bodies, mostly arms and legs, and in the margin, he put many dots along with a screen window on the wall, a bed, papers, and books. Due to confidentiality, I do not present the drawings here. However, I found that Richard would use only red and black colors. Richard repeated the same pattern of behaviors and drawings for hours and days.

After another week, I asked Richard if he would talk with me about his drawings. He was anxious and suspicious and uttered the same order of the words as he did in the initial session: "Night, bugs, canteen, floor, window screen." As I became more acquainted with Richard's living environment and daily activities, I realized that those words represented Richard's subjective experiences during his stay in the hospital. The screen represented his delusion and hallucination of the bugs coming through the window at night. The experiences of the canteen (the hospital café) included R&R (required relation), a technique used to place Richard on the floor of the canteen when he would scream due to severe anxiety.

As time passed, Richard started talking in complete sentences and would make eye contact with me, but was still distrustful: "I shouldn't talk to you; you are one of them—bugs. It would help if you didn't tell any staff about our sessions. Last night, I dreamed that they (the bugs) were coming from my window through the screen. I screamed and ran out of my room." As I read the entry notes from Richard's file for that day, I noticed that Richard had run out of his room not last night, but in the morning while having breakfast. Similar incidents indicate that Richard confused reality and his waking hours with dreams. Obviously, Richard lived a dream-like life during his waking hours.

Change the Environment

Because one of my meetings took place in the building where Richard resided, I could see Richard's room for the first time. Of course, Richard was there. Richard's room was in the basement. The basement was a ward (living room) with twenty-five patients living together—a male-patient residential building where everybody had his own room, locked up with close supervision. Richard's room looked like a small prison cell, like a dungeon with a screen window and a single bed, on the bare cement floor. According to the staff, there was always fighting, yelling, and screaming among patients.

After observing Richard's living conditions, I immediately requested that Richard transfer to a less restrictive environment with improved living conditions. Richard moved to our building, the Social Skill Center, an open and unlocked building. In the meantime, I fully trained the clinical team, staff, and other patients on relating to Richard when speaking about his fear of the bugs. Rather than stopping, criticizing, and judging him, they should listen to him. Ironically, the patients in our building had no problem understanding what I meant compared to the staff. The patients were more sympathetic toward Richard.

Richard seemed to have a smooth transition to his new living condition. In his daily session, he was more creative, poetic, and articulate about his delusion and hallucination. As Richard was willing to talk and use the entire session, his skin problem (picking off his skin) disappeared. He was neither self-abusive nor aggressive toward others. Richard would take care of his hygiene and feed himself. He had great reading and writing skills, which manifested during the sessions. He walked into the campus library by himself and read there for hours.

I encouraged him to continue going to the library and incorporate his reading into his sessions. Richard would bring books into our sessions and read loudly. He had problems reading one particular novel, Franz Kafka's *Metamorphosis*. He seems terrified to mention the character Gregor Samsa, who woke up one morning and found that he had been transformed into a "monstrous vermin." When asked what about the character made him terrified, Richard said, "Sometimes I think I am him. Because I don't know who I am or where I am going, either, I can be attacked anytime by monstrous vermin." He identified with Gregor Samsa.

Further Analysis of the Sessions

At this point in Richard's treatment, I assumed that psychotic transference and the use of myth would be effective in the treatment of psychotic patients. As I mentioned earlier, Richard grew up with a mother who was suffering from schizophrenia, and his biological father was unknown. Richard's medical and psychological records describe that the mother's relationship toward Richard was "distant" and at times "devouring" and "suffocating."

Richard was separated from his mother twice. First, due to a neighbor's intervention, who had reported to Child Welfare Services that the mother was unstable and could no longer care for her child, Richard was placed in an orphanage for two years. When the mother became more stable and had a job, she brought Richard back home. The second time was when Richard was nine years old. The mother was unable to care for Richard again. At that time, Richard moved to his grandmother's and lived with her. He managed to finish high school. He was an excellent student and teachers often praised him for his reading and writing skills. Before finishing high school, Richard's mother committed suicide. The details of the suicide were unknown. Although Richard was not in the house at the moment of his suicide, he saw his mother's dead body in her bedroom. The reports indicated there was a pile of empty alcohol bottles on the bedroom floor, and the bedroom was infested with bed bugs.

Richard suffered clearly from severe trauma in childhood, but the details of his relations with his mother and possible abuse by his mother were imprecise, so it was unknown how this experience impinged upon him. He reflected an infantile mode of living with the experience of distancing and devouring from his primary caretaker, the mother. For Richard, the absence and presence of his mother is perceived as a double message, causing a primitive sense of ambivalent love, a love mixed with hate. In this mode of experience, there was no sense of inside and outside, "me" vs. "not me." In Richard's hallucination and delusion, the bug represented simultaneously the mother, Richard, and the analyst: "You are the bug, I am the bug, everybody is a bug." Richard could never overcome the ambivalent relationship he had developed with his mother during childhood. The separation did not occur due to the foreclosure of the "Name-of-the-Father," where the paternal metaphor did not intervene. The "Name-of-the-Father" is the primary signifier, the signifier per excellence, within the symbolic language, also referring to the "Other." It is the prohibition of "NO," a reaction to the incestual fusion of mother and child.

In the case of Richard, he didn't enter the symbolic language to talk about his childhood experiences; he resorted to the imaginary realm of delusion and hallucination of bugs. The myth around the bugs is an imaginary solution, the last resort for how Richard can distance himself from the Real, which would form a total psychological collapse. No matter how much pressure Richard received from the hospital in terms of behavioral modification treatments, psychotropic medication, four-point restraint, advice, and reasoning, he could not afford to lose his narrative concerning the bugs. His narrative of the bugs functioned as his survival mechanism to avoid encountering the horror of the Real, the "nameless dread," expressed as the mother's appearance and disappearance.

Richard articulated the myth of bugs in his transference experience by saying, "You are the bug." In this case, Richard's transference is a psychotic transference. He doesn't refer to me as though I am a bug or I look like a bug. He sees me literally as a bug, which causes severe anxiety. Therefore, he avoided his face-to-face sessions and spoke with me indirectly initially. A Kleinian school psychoanalyst, Hanna Segal, describes the experience within the psychotic transference as concrete, alive, and visual.[12] Using Klein's "paranoid-schizoid position"[13] and "depressive position,"[14] Segal differentiates between psychotic transference as a "symbolic equation"[15] vs. the neurotic transference as the symbolic proper. In psychotic transference, the symbol and the symbolized are the same, while in neurotic transference, there is the symbol, symbolized, and the subject who can interpret the experience. The Kleinian notion of the symbolic equation and the symbolic proper include reflecting the experience of the object that can be reconstructed within the transference experiences. However, for Lacan, the experience of the object is fantastic, and the symbolic equation is a linguistical experience. It is a raw experience with no meaning, yet it needs to be signified within the linguistic code.

Richard has no problem acquiring the English language, and I have seen that he has demonstrated his mastery of language by reading literary works. The appearance of the "Name-of-the-Father" is missing in the language as the mark of castration (separation from mother) within the symbolic language. In another sense, the symbolic language has a hole, and Richard has to create a private language to avoid encountering the hole. Initially, Richard only uttered a few orderly words, "night, bugs, canteen, floor, window screen," while rocking his body back and forth. These words functioned in Richard's private language, helping him to sustain himself from the anxiety of the Real. The behavioral approach to Richard's speech and bodily movements lead the clinicians in the hospital to conclude a diagnosis of higher functioning autism with

12. Segal, "Some Aspects of the Analysis of a Schizophrenic," 268–78.

13. Klein, "Notes on Some Schizoid Mechanisms," 99–110.

14. Klein, "Contribution to the Psychogenesis," 145–47.

15. Segal, "Notes on Symbol Formation," 391–97.

borderline intellectual developmental disorders (formerly known as mental retardation). This diagnosis was wrong. As analysis progressed, Richard demonstrated much artistic creativity and intellectual input into his hallucination and delusion. His rocking back and forth, self-abusive behavior (picking skin), and aggressiveness toward others stopped when there was a decrease in his psychotropic medications and a change in his living condition. Regardless of the appearance or disappearance of symptoms, Richard suffered from psychosis and paranoia, which resulted from a psychotic structure.

Treatment

Richard was caught up within the duality of psychotic transference, taking place between analyst-mother and Richard-subject in search of a non-separation objet petit a. He never developed the triangular structure of the mother-child-phallus. There is no mediation between him and the Other. He is afraid of the demand of the analyst (the Other), which would cause excessive and senseless jouissance. Unlimited excessive jouissance without a signifier and meaning places Richard in a prelinguistic experience with her mother, which terrifies him when he handles it. Therefore, Richard could perceive any statement of interpretation, exploration, recommendation, and guidance coming from the desire and the demand of the analyst for a cure as persecutory and harmful. If I say any word included in Richard's vocabulary, it implies a harmful action, which would occur during the session. For Richard, action and words were the same. As the session continued, Richard began to correct me many times on my choice of words.

Psychotic is a subjective daily life crisis with no signifiers support. There are some fundamental dilemmas for the patient concerning life and death, sexuality and identity, and the dilemmas of dealing with the paternal metaphor and authority. These crises come up more in transferential relations within the analytical session because analytical relations are an intense experience. A potential space should be provided when encountering psychotic transference so the subject can find its unique place about the Other.

Richard found a space where he continued to speak without my intervention, expressing himself with entire sentences and rich vocabulary. He began taking internal distancing from me and identifying with Franz

Kafka's character, Gregor Samsa. The process gave him a less fragile ego and a more solid and consistent imaginary structure. As a result, he was less vulnerable to the feeling of being overtaken by the invasion of drive and senseless jouissance by establishing a barrier against the Real.

The results indicated initiating a shift from psychotic transference toward neurotic transference where Richard attempted to position himself within the symbolic, detach himself from the transference relationship with the analyst-mother, and move toward the identification with Gregor Samsa. As a result, the Other was not so persecutory; instead, he gave him some support and security. Richard's psychotic crisis, in the first place, was the crisis of stability and function, as we could see through different phases of analytical work, shifting from breakdown to gradual stabilization.

As Richard was fully developed, he was able to accept the symbolic world, its terms, and its limitations. He could not only see that his delusion and hallucination were out of his reach, formed as a functional necessity from his past, but also that his symptoms were a product of his own creation, and he could be in charge of them. Richard's final discharge from hospitalization took place after four years of analysis with me. He found a job in a bakery and began independent living. He also attended community college, and his goal was to pursue further educational and professional development. I could not do more follow-up with Richard. The state hospital closed due to a budget crisis, and I also moved out of the state of Virginia.

SUMMARY

Richard, a twenty-eight-year-old male patient residing in a state hospital, had been in and out for eleven years. His original diagnosis included suffering from Intellectual Developmental Disorders (under Neurodevelopmental Disorders) with borderline severity and Autism Spectrum Disorder. Richard had been on significant tranquilizers for self-abusive behavior of picking skin, causing open wounds because of the fear of "bugs," and aggressive behavior toward others. Behavior modification (DRO & RIB) was the choice of treatment. In times of behavior crisis, time out, Required Relaxation (R&R), and four-point restraint were utilized.

Richard was added to my caseload for treatment because no treatment was effective, and his condition was getting worse. I accepted the case under the following conditions:

1. I start psychoanalytic treatment.

2. Staff and the interdisciplinary treatment team would be trained and supervised in executing my program treatment.

3. Significant decrease in psychotropic medication.

4. Rehabilitation in a less restrictive environment with more resources being available to him.

In his first evaluation session with me, Richard appeared to be catatonic with waxy mobility, only rocking back and forth and uttering sounds and words when asked questions. Richard seemed fragmented and full of anxiety when I asked about his background. Wilfred Bion defines this condition as "Attacks on Linking"[16] where diachrony and historicity in the psychotic would bring intolerable subjective images and memories and severe anxiety. One way to defend against the anxiety is a verbal attack on linking by stating a confused or unintelligible mixture of random words and phrases (word salad) and acting awkwardly. As treatment began, Richard avoided entering the office but made eye contact. He then started exchanging paper and crayons with me and left his drawings behind my doors.

Richard went through different phases of psychoanalysis for a period of four years. The beginning phase was a pre-analytical phase of treatment where I contained and validated Richard, never questioning his act. Richard eventually came to the office and stayed for full analytic sessions, starting with drawing, writing, uttering sounds and words, and ending in articulating complete speech with sentences and a rich vocabulary. His fear of bugs reflected his transference experience with me: "You are the bug," and later toward Kafka's main character in *Metamorphosis*. Richard demonstrated an artistic and creative myth describing his "fear of bugs" that could not warrant a diagnosis of Intellectual Developmental Disorders and Autism.

According to Lacan's structural analysis for the diagnosis of psychosis, Richard was functioning within the psychotic structure with the foreclosure of the "Name-of-the-Father" where he was not positioning himself within the Symbolic, but instead staying within Imaginary. The Imaginary is close to the Real. With proximity to the Real, Richard faced a subjective crisis of functionality and stability. As his speech developed, he managed to walk into the symbolic realm and protect himself against the Real.

16. Bion, "Attacks on Linking," 308–15.

Regarding the treatment, I did not use the punctuation cut and variable sessions generally used for analytical subjects within the neurotic structure. Instead, I mostly contained Richard in the sessions by listening, repeating his exact words, and asking him to repeat his previous words and statements. This treatment approach allowed Richard to be more present within the symbolic world regarding time, place, and person. As far as the treatment of psychosis is concerned, Lacan describes the role of the analyst as the "secretary of the insane."[17]

As the psychoanalyst listens to the psychotic subject, the analyst should remember that the psychotic speech is a "speech beyond the subject."[18] The "speech beyond the subject" is not containable for the subject due to the sheer anxiety of the Real. The analyst, who creates a holding environment, helps the subject to contain the anxiety and transition from a state of "breakdown" to the state of "breakthrough."[19] For Richard, this transition occurred within his transference experience in the final analysis phases. His transition from the psychotic transference to the neurotic transference, his distancing and separation from the mother-analyst, allowed Richard to accept the symbolic world and see his hallucinations and delusion not only beyond his reach but also as part of his creation. He was first discharged to live in halfway houses and community living, then to independent living as he pursued his academic and professional career.

17. Lacan, *Psychosis*, 206–13.
18. Lacan, *Écrits*, 479.
19. See Bollas, *Catch Them Before They Fall.*

Conclusion

We are living in an era of uncertainty filled with anxiety, in general, and after the pandemic in particular. Many people mention anxiety as their daily experience of dread, living in hypervirtual reality. Then, it is essential to engage critically with the following questions: What are anxiety and uncertainty, and how can we approach this interrelated topic? This volume includes issues of anxiety and uncertainty as the contemporary human condition moves and flows endlessly. The authors bring their lives situated in different environments, cultures, languages, and experiences yet explore the topic of anxiety in the era of uncertainty.

We live in the twenty-first-century global world, driven by the new high-technology culture, ecological crisis, and late capitalism. In this venue, human subjects do not feel confident about the future; then it is certain that people fall into anxiety. Jacques Lacan was very keen on the issues of human anxiety. In his seminar offered during 1962–1963 on anxiety, Lacan refers to anxiety not as *an emotion* but as an affect that is beyond all the doubt and is not deceptive. His profound understanding of anxiety indicates that anxiety is the fundamental question of being in the world and should not be narrowly defined within the concepts of human emotions. Also, contrary to the tradition of Freud, Heidegger, and Kierkegaard who believe anxiety may occur with the absence of an object, Lacan argues that anxiety cannot operate without an object. In other words, the anxiety we experience occurs only in relation to an object, a special kind of object, which is the object of lack, referred to as "object petit a." This object causes desire. Here, the object of lack could have a double meaning: on the one hand, it indicates a subject who has lack in oneself and looks outside to replace object petit a, and it also means the subject wants to be the object of desire of the Other to fill the lack, yet not certain it would happen. Anxiety happens when an object is replacing or filling this lack. In that sense, anxiety is "the lack of a lack," and the human subject ontologically deals with anxiety all the time.

Then, of importance is the fundamental function of lack while coping with anxiety. For Lacan, fundamental human lack can lead us to create an inner or potential space for creativity, aesthetics, and productivity. Inspired by the work of Lacan's theory of lack, many Lacanian theorists and social critics, such as Judith Butler, Slavoj Žižek, Gilles Deleuze and Félix Guattari, Chantal Mouffe, Jean Baudrillard, Alain Badiou, and Saul Newman, increasingly emphasize the concept of "constitutive lack" as an ontological claim in their multidisciplinary approach to their sociopolitical, clinical, cultural, and gender studies. The theorists view "constructive lack" as a motivational factor at the core of human subjectivity, opening up for an indefinite search for truth and knowledge.

Aligning with the ample literature from Lacan and his followers, we also delve into anxiety in the era of uncertainty, focusing on the constitutive lack. From our point of view, the time of uncertainty is the urgency to meditate on the human condition in the present time concerning the destruction of ecology, war, global poverty, and the potential for nuclear winter. Capitalism, called Neoliberalism in its final stage, forces the sacrifice of both human beings and nature for profit, creating crises in all aspects of our lives. These crises make us aware of a complete lack of a symbolic safety net, described as the crisis of *Umwelt*, unable to protect humans from everyday anxiety of living and uncertainty.

This book responds to this crisis by closely reading Jacques Lacan's seminars over nine years. Lacan's theory in each chapter functions as a lens to explain and appropriate their experience and various aspects of life situated in certain cultures and religions. By utilizing Lacan's discourses and his fundamental concept of anxiety, desire, "objet petit a," *jouissance*, and sublimation, each author from diverse socio-political and cultural environments articulates how deeply anxiety is embedded in the twenty-first-century world and how human subject experience it in culture and religion, and how somehow one experiences transformation or sublimation. Our learning community, the Lacan cartel, explicitly brought professional fields such as Lacanian psychoanalysis, spiritual direction, and expressive art therapy into the prison.

Lacan's psychoanalytic theory is fundamentally clinical. He utilizes many clinical cases of Freud as a way to claim his theory. Nevertheless, it is rare to find clinical cases of Lacanian approach. The three cases of psychosis, perversion, and neurosis demonstrate how Lacan's theories can be applied to clinical analysis.

Also, each author in this volume brought their academic interest, such as Medieval woman mystic Margery Kemp, a biblical character Mary who anointed Jesus in John's Gospel. Even in contemporary society, women struggle to gain their authentic voice and articulate their desires. Lacan's theory of jouissance and sublimation in relation to the death drive explains these women's struggle and the process of gaining their voice through negating conformity to society. Also, one chapter brings the paradox of Christian teaching as the fundamental cause of endless anxiety among Christians. The fundamental Christian teaching of salvation through faith and grace is permanently attached to or obeying the law. In this way, Christians suffer from anxiety: on the one hand, we are saved by grace, yet on the other hand, we should not sin. Almost the ontological paradox of Christian teaching perhaps explains deeply seated anxiety in Christian practice.

The other theme that this book includes is fantasy. Lacan explains the dynamic of fantasy as a tool to cover the real, which can be traumatic and terrifying. One chapter deals with one of the most popular romantic literatures, *The Phantom of the Opera*, which is situated in the anxiety-provoking setting of the Opera House in Paris. The fascination to the desirable object, leads three main characters to gain authentic desire, including *jouissance*. Also, the different area of phantasy this book include is fantasy of AI, particularly the sexbot. In this analysis, the author talks about the impossibility of having a perfect sex partner, using Lacan's sexuality and the position of male, emphasizing how the sexbot reflects a male's sexual fantasy. Regarding phantasy, readers would find certain aspects of fantasy are prevalent in the culture.

Further, one way to read Lacan in this book is to analyze the social symptoms that manifested as COVID-19. This analysis, performed in the beginning of Covid-19 pandemic, emphasizes more on the symbolic aspect of Lacan work, as he famously reports: "The unconscious is structured like a language." We cannot explain and analyze the anxiety and horror that human beings face during the pandemic with the symbolic order. The current symbolic system which supports capitalism and limitless confidence in success, development, and thriving, cannot comprehend or hide the horror of Real, palpable in the COVID body.

This edited volume involves a self-implicated nature. For example, a pastor's wife struggled to find her desire and identity, not living with a given or idealized identity provided by the Other. Also, in universal ecclesiology, the non-Western church or the discourse of the non-Western church is often considered not orthodox enough. However, in Lacan's view, "there is no Other of the Other." It means the big "O" of the Other is not a fully universal Symbolic and cannot contain globally all churches in a uniform manner. The view helps any church that has experienced colonial and Western dominance to claim an equal position.

Overall, this volume includes authors and Lacanian scholars who are mainly non-European. Our efforts were to damage the notion of Eurocentric Lacan by including non-European scholars from diverse cultural backgrounds to demonstrate Lacan's applicability in theory and technique to a wide range of topics at the global level. In disseminating Lacan in a multivalent and interdisciplinary approach, we try to tackle uncanny anxiety in the era of uncertainty.

Bibliography

INTRODUCTION

George, Sheldon, and Derek Hook. *Lacan and Race: Racism, Identity, and Psychoanalytic Theory*. New York: Routledge, 2021.

Lacan, Jacques. "The Cartel." *International Forums: School of Psychoanalysis of the Forums of Lacanian Field*, n.d. https://www.champlacanien.net/public/2/epCartels.php?language=2&menu=1.

———. "Excommunication." In *The Four Fundamental Concepts of Psychoanalysis*, edited by Jacques-Alain Miller, 1–16. Translated by Alan Sheridan. New York: Norton. 1998.

———. *The Object Relation*. Seminar of Jacques Lacan 4. Edited by Jacques-Alain Miller. Medford, MA: Polity, 2020.

Marriott, David S. *Lacan Noir: Lacan and Afro-Pessimism*. New York: Palgrave MacMillan, 2021.

Mills, Jon. "Lacan on Paranoiac Knowledge." *Psychoanalytic Psychology* 20.1 (2013) 30–51.

CHAPTER 1

Carrigan, Mark. "Choose Life: Some Notes on Lacan's Death Drive." *Mark Carrigan* (blog), December 28, 2022. https://markcarrigan.net/2022/12/28/lacans-concept-of-the-death-drive.

Fink, Bruce. *The Lacanian Subject: Between Language and Jouissance*. Princeton, NJ: Princeton University Press, 1995.

Hogle, Jerrold E. *The Undergrounds of the Phantom of Opera: Sublimation and the Gothic in Leroux's Novel and Its Progeny*. New York: Palgrave, 2002.

Lacan, Jacques. *Anxiety*. Seminar of Jacques Lacan 10. Edited by Jacques-Alain Miller. New York: Polity, 2016.

———. *Desire and Its Interpretation*. Translated by Bruce Fink. Seminar of Jacques Lacan 6. Edited by Jacques-Alain Miller. New York: Polity, 2019.

———. *The Ethics of Psychoanalysis 1959–1960*. Translated by Dennis Porter. Seminar of Jacques Lacan 7. Edited by Jacques-Alain Miller. New York: Norton, 1992.

———. *The Four Fundamental Concepts of Psychoanalysis*. Edited by Jacques-Alain Miller. New York: Norton, 1981.

———. *Identification 1961–1962*. Translated by Cormac Gallagher. Seminar of Jacques Lacan 9. Unpublished. http://www.lacaninireland.com/web/wp-content/uploads/2010/06/seminar-ix-amended-iby-mcl-7.nov_.20111.pdf.

———. *The Object Relation*. Translated by Adrian Price. Seminar of Jacques Lacan 4. New York: Polity, 2022.

———. "Seminar on *The Purloined Letter*." In *Écrits*, 6–50. Translated by Bruce Fink. New York: Norton, 2006.

Leroux, Gaston. *The Phantom of the Opera*. Kindle ed. Public Domain, 2012.

Moroncini, Bruno. "On Love: Jacques Lacan and Plato's Symposium." *European Journal of Psychoanalysis* 3.1 (2017). https://www.journal-psychoanalysis.eu/articles/on-love-jacques-lacan-and-platos-symposium-2.

Ormrod, J. S. *Fantasy in Lacanian Theory*. London: Pagrave Macmillan, 2014.

Said, Edward. *Orientalism*. New York: Vintage, 1979.

Shajirat, Anna. "The Gothic Fantasy of History: Fear and Loss in the British Long Eighteenth Century." PhD diss., University of Washington, 2017.

Sharoni, Josephine. *Lacan and Fantasy Literature: Portents of Modernity in Late-Victorian and Edwardian Fiction*. Boston: Brill Rodopi, 2017.

Webber, Andrew Lloyd, et al. "Angel of Music." Track 4 on *The Phantom of the Opera (Original London Cast Recording)*, March 19, 1987. https://genius.com/original-london-cast-of-the-phantom-of-the-opera-angel-of-music-lyrics.

Wilson, Japhy. "Anamorphosis of Captial: Black Holes, Gothic Monsters, and the Will of God." In *Psychoanalysis and the Global*, edited by Ilan Kappor, 164–69. Lincoln: University of Nebraska Press, 2018.

Wolf, Leonard, ed. *The Essential Phantom of Opera, Including the Complete Novel by Gaston Leroux*. New York: Penguin, 1996.

CHAPTER 2

Adams, Will W. "Making Daemons of Death and Love: Frankenstein, Existentialism, Psychoanalysis." *Journal of Humanistic Psychology* 41.4 (2001) 57–89.

Akagi, Akira. "Bishōjo shōkōgun: Rorikon to iu yokubō [The Bishōjo Syndrome: The Desire Called Lolicon]." *New Feminism Review* 3 (1993) 230–34.

Aoki, Beatriz Yumi, and Takeshi Kimura. "Sexuality and Affection in the Time of Technological Innovation: Artificial Partners in the Japanese Context." *Religions* 12.5 (2021) 296.

Baranoğlu, Selen. "An Analysis of Mary Shelley's *Frankenstein* and Robert Louis Stevenson's *Dr. Jeckyll and Mr. Hyde* in Relation to Lacanian Criticism." MA thesis, Middle East Technical University, 2008.

Berger, John, dir. "Women and Art." *Ways of Seeing* 1.2. London: BBC, 1972.

Bostrom, Nick. *Superintelligence: Paths, Dangers, Strategies*. Oxford: Oxford University Press, 2014.

Brandom, Russell. "AI Pioneer Accused of Having Sex with Trafficking Victim on Jeffrey Epstein's Island." *Verge*, August 9, 2019. https://www.theverge.com/2019/8/9/20798900/marvin-minsky-jeffrey-epstein-sex-trafficking-island-court-records-unsealed.

Broussard, Meredith. *Artificial Unintelligence: How Computers Misunderstand the World*. Cambridge, MA: MIT Press, 2019.

Cannon, Lincoln. "Mormon Transhumanism." In *Religious Transhumanism and Its Critics*, edited by Arvin M. Gouw et al., 53–74. Lanham: Lexington, 2022.

Cellan-Jones, Rory. "Stephen Hawking Warns Artificial Intelligence Could End Mankind." *BBC News*, December 2, 2014. https://www.bbc.com/news/technology-30290540.

Collings, David. "The Monster and the Imaginary Mother: A Lacanian Reading of Frankenstein." In *Frankenstein: Complete, Authoritative Text with Biographical, Historical, and Cultural Contexts; Critical History; and Essays from Contemporary Critical Perspectives*, edited by Johanna M. Smith, 323–39. 3rd ed. Boston: Bedford/St. Martin's, 2016.

Dobkin, Lawrence, dir. "Boy Meets Girl?" *My Living Doll* 1.1. New York: CBS, 1964.

Dworkin, Andrea. *Pornography: Men Possessing Women*. New York: Perigee, 1981.

Ellison, Harlan. "I Have No Mouth, and I Must Scream." *If*, March 1967. 24–28.

Fan, Ruiping, and Mark J. Cherry, eds. *Sex Robots: Social Impact and the Future of Human Relations*. Cham: Springer, 2021.

Freud, Sigmund. *Civilization and Its Discontents*. Edited and translated by James Strachey. New York: Norton, 2010.

———. *The Future of an Illusion*. Translated by James Strachey. New York: Norton, 1961.

———. *Totem and Taboo: Resemblances Between the Psychic Lives of Savages and Neurotics*. Translated by A. A. Brill. London: Routledge & Sons, 1919.

Gore, Edward. "The Technosexuality, Pygmalionist & Mind Control Fetish FAQ 3.0." *Pygmalion Syndrome*, 2003. www.p-synd.com/winterrose/wrindex.htm.

Hefner, Philip. *Technology and Human Becoming*. Minneapolis: Fortress, 2003.

Ko, Jiyoung. "Destruction and Creation Ex Nihilo: Mary of Bethany's and Margery Kempe's Spiritualities of Nonconformity from the Perspective of Lacanian Ethics of Desire." PhD diss., Graduate Theological Union, Berkeley, CA, 2022.

Kotze, Haidee. "Desire, Gender, Power, Language: A Psychoanalytic Reading of Mary Shelley's *Frankenstein*." *Literator* 21.1 (2000) 53–67.

Kurzweil, Ray. *The Singularity Is Near: When Humans Transcend Biology*. PDF ed. New York: Viking, 2005.

Lacan, Jacques. *Anxiety*. Translated by A. R. Price. Seminar of Jacques Lacan 10. Edited by Jacques-Alain Miller. Cambridge, UK: Polity, 2014.

———. *The Ego in Freud's Theory and in the Technique of Psychoanalysis*. Edited by Jacques-Alain Miller. Translated by Sylvana Tomaselli. Seminar of Jacques Lacan 2. New York: Norton, 1991.

———. *The Formations of the Unconscious*. Translated by Cormac Gallagher. Seminar of Jacques Lacan 5. Dublin: Lacan in Ireland, 2010.

———. *Identification*. Translated by Cormac Gallagher. Seminar of Jacques Lacan 9. Dublin: Lacan in Ireland, 2010.

———. "The Mirror Stage as Formative of the *I* Function." In *Écrits*, 75–81. Translated by Bruce Fink. New York: Norton, 2006.

———. *The Object Relation*. Translated by A. R. Price. Seminar of Jacques Lacan 4. Edited by Jacques-Alain Miller. Cambridge, UK: Polity, 2020.

———. *On Feminine Sexuality: The Limits of Love and Knowledge*. Translated by Bruce Fink. Seminar of Jacques Lacan 20. Edited by Jacques-Alain Miller. New York: Norton, 1998.

———. *RSI*. Translated by Cormac Gallagher. Seminar of Jacques Lacan 22. Dublin: Lacan in Ireland, 2010.

Leonard, Andrew. "The Tech Industry's God Complex Is Getting Out of Control." *Salon*, June 13, 2014. https://www.salon.com/2014/06/13/the_tech_industrys_god_complex_is_getting_out_of_control.

Levy, David. *Love and Sex with Robots: The Evolution of Human-Robot Relationships*. New York: Harper Perennial, 2007.

Liu, Jindong. "Social Robots as the Bride? Understanding the Construction of Gender in a Japanese Social Robot Product." *Human-Machine Communication* 2 (2021) 105–20.

Liu, Lydia H. *The Freudian Robot: Digital Media and the Future of the Unconscious*. Chicago: University of Chicago Press, 2010.

Lopatto, Elizabeth. "Jeffrey Epstein Infiltrated Science Because It Was Ready to Accommodate Him." *Verge*, September 19, 2019. https://www.theverge.com/2019/9/19/20870858/jeffrey-epstein-science-philanthropy-donation-prestige-mit.

Lucas, George. *Law, Ethics, and Emerging Military Technologies: Confronting Disruptive Innovation*. London: Routledge, 2023.

Ma, Junzhao, et al. "Sex Robots: Are We Ready for Them? An Exploration of the Psychological Mechanisms Underlying People's Receptiveness of Sex Robots." *Journal of Business Ethics* 178.4 (2022) 1091–1107.

Marcuse, Herbert. *Eros and Civilization: A Philosophical Inquiry into Freud*. New York: Vintage, 1962.

Mathews, Chris. "Manga, Virtual Child Pornography, and Censorship in Japan." In *Applied Ethics: Old Wine in New Bottles?*, 165–74. Hokkaido: Center for Applied Ethics and Philosophy, 2011.

McArthur, Neil, and Markie L. C. Twist. "The Rise of Digisexuality: Therapeutic Challenges and Possibilities." *Sexual and Relationship Therapy* 32 (2017) 334–44.

Millar, Isabel. *The Psychoanalysis of Artificial Intelligence*. Basingstoke: Palgrave Macmillan, 2021.

Nagayama, Kaoru. "Lolicon Manga." In *Erotic Comics in Japan: An Introduction to Eromanga*, 117–36. Translated by Patrick Galbraith and Jessica Bauwens-Sugimoto. Cambridge: Cambridge University Press, 2021.

Niemeyer, Kenneth. "Elon Musk Says the Risk of Advanced AI Is So High That the Public Needs to Know Why OpenAI Fired Sam Altman." *Yahoo News*, November 20, 2023. https://www.yahoo.com/news/elon-musk-says-risk-advanced-195118901.html.

O'Neil, Cathy. *Weapons of Math Destruction: How Big Data Increases Inequality and Threatens Democracy*. New York: Crown, 2016.

Richardson, Kathleen, and Charlotta Odlind, eds. *Man-Made Women: The Sexual Politics of Sex Dolls and Sex Robots*. Cham: Palgrave Macmillan, 2023.

Shea, Mark. "Is There a Sinister Side to the Rise of Female Robots?" *BBC*, August 7, 2023. https://www.bbc.com/future/article/20230804-is-there-a-sinister-side-to-the-rise-of-female-robots.

Softley, Iain, dir. *Hackers*. Los Angeles: MGM/United Artists, 1995.

Sophia the Robot. "Sophia the Robot & Loving AI Participant." *YouTube*, August 22, 2018. https://www.youtube.com/watch?v=ZhKcaea34RQ.

Sparrow, Robert, et al. "Do Robots Have Sex? A Prolegomenon." *International Journal of Social Robotics* 15 (2023) 1707–23.

Strait, Megan K., et al. "The Public's Perception of Humanlike Robots: Online Social Commentary Reflects an Appearance-Based Uncanny Valley, a General Fear of a 'Technology Takeover,' and the Unabashed Sexualization of Female-Gendered Robots." Paper presented at the 26th IEEE International Symposium on Robot and Human Interactive Communication (RO-MAN), Lisbon, Portugal, August 2017.

Urwin, Rosamund. "Feminist Porn Director Erika Lust: Why Are My Sex Films Feminist? Because I Treat Women as People." *Standard*, September 30, 2015. https://www.standard.co.uk/lifestyle/london-life/feminist-porn-director-erika-lust-why-are-my-sex-films-feminist-because-i-treat-women-as-people-a2.

Wadhwa, Vivek, et al. "The 'God Complex' in Silicon Valley." *Wall Street Journal*, April 8, 2017. Audio. https://www.wsj.com/podcasts/the-god-complex-in-silicon-valley/a17337f1-ad37-4720-9922-771b6dd7680e.

CHAPTER 3

Aquinas, Thomas. *Summa Theologiae*. Translated by Black Friars. Kindle ed. Claremont, CA: Coyote Canyon, 2010.

Augustine of Hippo. *The City of God*. Vol. 2 of *Nicene and Post-Nicene Fathers*, First Series. Edited by Philip Schaff. Translated by Marcus Dods. New York: Christian Literature, 1887.

Brandmüller, Walter, et al. "'Dubia' of Two Cardinals." *Holy See*, July 10, 2023. https://www.vatican.va/roman_curia/congregations/cfaith/documents/rc_con_cfaith_risposta-dubia-2023_en.html.

Bretzke, James T. *A Morally Complex World: Engaging Contemporary Moral Theology*. Collegeville, MN: Liturgical, 2004.

Cary, Liam. "To Bless or Not to Bless: On the Vatican Declaration Fiducia Supplicans." *Diocese of Baker*, February 9, 2024. https://dioceseofbaker.org/to-bless-or-not-to-bless-on-the-vatican-declaration-fiducia-supplicans.

Congregation for the Defense of Faith (CDF). *Notification on the Book "Just Love: A Framework For Christian Sexual Ethics" by Sr. Margaret A. Farley, RSM*. Vatican City: Libreria Editrice Vaticana, 2012.

Connors, Russel B., Jr., and Patrick T. McCormick. *Character, Choices & Community: The Three Faces of Christian Ethics*. New York: Paulist, 1998.

Curran, Charles. *The Catholic Moral Tradition Today: A Synthesis*. Washington, DC: Georgetown University Press, 1999.

———. "Catholic Social and Sexual Teaching: A Methodological Comparison." *Theology Today* 44.4 (1988) 425–40.

Farley, Margaret. *Just Love: A Framework for Sexual Ethics*. New York: Continuum, 2006.

Freud, Sigmund. *Civilization and Its Discontents*. Edited and translated by James Strachey. New York: Norton, 2010.

———. *The Future of an Illusion*. Translated by James Strachey. New York: Norton, 1961.

Jerome. "Letter 48." In *Nicene and Post-Nicene Fathers*, Second Series, edited by Philip Schaff and Henry Wace, 6:68–78. Translated by W. H. Fremantle et al. Buffalo, NY: Christian Literature, 1893.

John Paul II. *The Redemption of the Body and the Sacramentality of Marriage*. Vatican City: Libreria Editrice Vaticana, 2005.

———. *Veritatis Splendor.* Vatican City: Libreria Editrice Vaticana, 1993.

Jonsen, Albert R., and Stephen Toulmin. *The Abuse of Casuistry: A History of Moral Reasoning.* Berkeley: University of California Press, 1990.

Kierkegaard, Søren. *The Concept of Anxiety: A Simple Psychologically Orientating Deliberation on the Dogmatic Issue of Hereditary Sin.* Edited and translated by Reidar Thtomte. Princeton: Princeton University Press, 1980.

———. *Fear and Trembling: Dialectical Lyric by Johannes de Silentio.* Translated by Alastair Hannay. London: Penguin, 2003.

Lacan, Jacques. *Anxiety.* Translated by A. R. Price. Seminar of Jacques Lacan 10. Edited by Jacques-Alain Miller. Cambridge, UK: Polity, 2014.

———. *The Ethics of Psychoanalysis 1959–1960.* Translated by Dennis Porter. Seminar of Jacques Lacan 7. Edited by Jacques-Alain Miller. New York: Norton, 1992.

———. *Identification.* Translated by Cormac Gallagher. Seminar of Jacques Lacan 9. Dublin: Lacan in Ireland, 2010.

———. *The Object Relation.* Translated by A. R. Price. Seminar of Jacques Lacan 4. Edited by Jacques-Alain Miller. Cambridge, UK: Polity, 2020.

Mahoney, John. *The Making of Moral Theology: A Study of the Roman Catholic Tradition.* Oxford: Oxford University Press, 1989.

Paul VI. *Humanae Vitae.* Vatican City: Libreria Editrice Vaticana, 1968.

Strong, James. *The Exhaustive Concordance of the Bible: Showing Every Word of the Text of the Common English Version of the Canonical Books, and Every Occurrence of Each Word in Regular Order.* New York: Eaton & Mains, 1890.

Tan, Nancy Nam Hoon. *Resisting Rape Culture: The Hebrew Bible and Hong Kong Sex Workers.* New York: Routledge, 2021.

Tillich, Paul. *The Courage to Be.* New Haven: Yale University Press, 1963.

———. *Dynamics of Faith.* New York: Perennial Classics, 2001.

———. *The Spiritual Situation in Our Technical Society.* Edited by J. Mark Thomas. Macon, GA: Mercer University Press, 1988.

CHAPTER 4

Anzaldúa, Gloria. *Borderlands/La Frontera: The New Mestiza.* San Francisco: Aunt Lute, 1999.

Cha, Theresa Hak Kyoung. *Dictee.* Berkeley: University of California Press, 2001

Chavoshian, Ali, and Jung Eun Sophia Park. "Listening Not in Spiritual Direction: Lacanian Inkling." *Presence: An International Journal of Spiritual Direction* 25 (2019) 5–12.

Cixous, Hélèn. "The Laugh of the Medusa." *Signs* 1 (1976) 875–93.

Culpepper, R. Alan. *Anatomy of the Fourth Gospel: A Study in Literary Design.* Philadelphia: Fortress, 1983.

Duke, Paul D. *Irony in the Fourth Gospel.* Atlanta: John Knox, 1985.

Eckhart, Meister. *The Essential Sermons, Commentaries, Treatises, and Defense.* Translated by Edmund Colledge and Bernard McGinn. New York: Paulist, 1981.

———. "Sermon Nine (pf 9, Q86,QT 28, Evans II, 2)." In *The Complete Mystical Works of Meister Eckhart,* edited by Maurice O.'C. Walshe, 88–90. New York: Crossroad, 2009.

———. *Sermons and Treatises.* Edited and translated by M. O.'C. Walshe. 3 vols. London: Watkins/Element, 1979–1987.

Lacan, Jacques. *Écrits: A Selection*. Translated by Alan Sheridan. London: Tavistock, 1977.

————. *The Language of the Self*. Baltimore: Johns Hopkins University Press, 1956.

————. "Logical Time and the Assertion of Anticipated Certainty." In *Écrits*, 161–75. Translated by Bruce Fink. New York: Norton, 2006.

————. *Les Non Dupes Errant*. Translated by Cormac Gallagher. Seminar of Jacques Lacan 21. Dublin: Lacan in Ireland, 2010. http://www.lacaninireland.com/web/wp-content/uploads/2010/06/book-21-les-non-dupes-errent-part-2.pdf.

————. *On Feminine Sexuality: The Limits of Love and Knowledge*. Edited by Allen Miller. Translated by Bruce Fink. Seminar of Jacques Lacan 20. New York: Norton, 1975.

————. *RSI 1974–1975*. Translated by Cormac Gallagher. Seminar of Jacques Lacan 22. Dublin: Lacan in Ireland, 2011. http://hdl.handle.net/10788/179.

————. *The Sinthome*. Translated by A. R. Price. Seminar of Jacques Lacan 23. Edited by Jacques-Alain Miller. Cambridge: Polity, 2016.

Lacan, Jacques, and Russell Grigg. "Geneva Lecture on the Symptom." *Analysis* 1 (1989) 7–26. https://search.informit.org/doi/10.3316/informit.461141126692223.

Lao-Tzu. *Tao Te Ching*. Translated by Stephen Addiss. Indianapolis: Hackett, 1993.

Loos, Amanda. "Symbolic, Real, Imaginary." *Theories of Media*, 2002. https://csmt.uchicago.edu/glossary2004/symbolicrealimaginary.htm.

Maybee, Julie E. "Hegel's Dialectic." *Stanford Encyclopedia of Philosophy*, June 3, 2016. Revised October 2, 2020. Edited by Edward N. Zalta. https://plato.stanford.edu/entries/hegel-dialectics.

McGinn, Bernard. "Meister Eckhart: Mystical Teacher and Preacher." In *The Harvest of Mysticism in Medieval Germany*, 94–131. Vol. 4 of *The Presence of God: A History of Western Mysticism*. New York: Crossroad, 2005.

Nicolas of Cusa. *On Learned Ignorance: A Translation and an Appraisal of De Docta Ignorantia*. Translated by Jasper Hopkins. Minneapolis: Arthur J. Banning, 1981.

O'Day, Gail R. *Revelation in the Fourth Gospel: Narrative Mode and Theological Claim*. Philadelphia: Fortress, 1986.

Park, Jung Eun Sophia. *Border-Crossing Spirituality: Transformation in the Borderland*. Eugene, OR: Pickwick, 2016.

Spivak, Gayatri Chakravorty. "Can the Subaltern Speak?" In *The Postcolonial Studies Reader*, edited by Bill Ashcroft et al., 24–28. New York: Routledge, 2003.

Rimbaud, Arthur. *Complete Works, Selected Letters*. Translated by Wallace Fowlie. Chicago: University of Chicago Press, 2005.

Weil, Simone. *Love in the Void: Where God Finds Us*. New York: Plough, 2018.

CHAPTER 5

Alexandre, Michelle. *The New Jim Crow: Mass Incarceration in the Age of Colorblindness*. New York: New Press, 2012.

Felluga, Dino. "Modules on Lacan: On Psychosexual Development." *Introductory Guide to Critical Theory*, January 31, 2011. https://www.cla.purdue.edu/academic/english/theory/psychoanalysis/lacandevelop.html.

Foucault, Michael. *Discipline and Punishment: The Birth of Prison*. Translated by Alan Sheridan. New York: Vintage, 1995.

———. "Panopticism." In *Foucault Reader*, edited by Paul Rabinow, 206–13. New York: Pantheon, 1984.

Hook, Derek. "Towards a Lacanian Group Psychology: The Prisoner's Dilemma and the Trans-Subjective." *Journal for the Theory* 42.2 (2013) 115–32. http://dx.doi.org/10.1111/jtsb.12005.

Lacan, Jacques. *Anxiety*. Seminar of Jacques Lacan 10. Edited by Jacques-Alain Miller. New York: Polity, 2014.

———. *Desire and Its Interpretation*. Seminar of Jacques Lacan 6. New York: Polity, 2019.

———. *The Four Fundamental Concepts of Psycho-Analysis*. Edited by Jacques-Alain Miller. New York: Norton, 1981.

———. *Identification*. Translated by Cormac Gallagher. Seminar of Jacques Lacan 9. Dublin: Lacan in Ireland, 2010.

———. "Logical Time and the Assertion of Anticipated Certainty." In *Écrits: The First Complete Edition of English*, 161–75. Translated by Bruce Fink. New York: Norton, 2006.

"Lacanian Graph of Desire." *Freud Quotes* (blog), July 2015. https://freudquotes.blogspot.com/2015/07/lacanian-graph-of-desire.html.

CHAPTER 6

Alisherovna, Umida. "Discourse in Modern Linguistics." *Journal of New Century Innovations* 26.5 (2023) 123–28.

André, Mark. "Otherness of the Body." In *Lacanian Theory of Discourse: Subject, Structure, and Society*, edited by Mark Bracher, 88–128. New York: New York University Press, 1994.

Bailly, Lionel. *Lacan: A Beginner's Guide*. New York: Oneworld, 2009.

Beckett, Samuel. *Worstward Ho*. London: Calder, 1983.

Fink, Bruce. *The Lacanian Subject*. Princeton, NJ: Princeton University Press, 1996.

Johnson, T. R. *The Other Side of Pedagogy: Lacan's Four Discourses and the Development of the Student Writer*. Albany, NY: State University of New York Press, 2014.

Lacan, Jacques. *Desire and Its Interpretation*. Translated by Cormac Gallagher. Seminar of Jacques Lacan 6. Dublin: Lacan in Ireland, 1959.

———. *Les Dupes Errent Part 1*. Translated by Cormac Gallagher. Seminar of Jacques Lacan 16. Dublin: Lacan in Ireland, 1974.

———. *Écrits: The First Complete Edition*. New York: Norton, 2006.

———. *On a Discourse That Might Not Be a Semblance*. Translated by Cormac Gallagher. Seminar of Jacques Lacan 18. Dublin: Lacan in Ireland, 1971.

———. *On Feminine Sexuality: The Limits of Love and Knowledge*. Translated by Bruce Fink. Seminar of Jacques Lacan 20. New York: Norton, 1999.

———. *Psychoanalysis Upside Down/The Reverse Side Psychoanalysis, 1969–1970*. Translated by Cormac Gallagher. Seminar of Jacques Lacan 17. Dublin: Lacan in Ireland, 1970.

———. *Transference*. Translated by Cormac Gallagher. Seminar of Jacques Lacan 8. Dublin: Lacan in Ireland, 1961.

Verhaeghe, Paul. *On Being Normal and Other Disorders: A Manual for Clinical Psychodiagnosticus*. New York: Other, 2004.

Zwart, Hub. "Lacan's Dialectics of Knowledge Production: The Four Discourses as a Detour to Hegel." *Foundations of Science* 27 (2022) 1347–70.

CHAPTER 7

Agamben, Giorgio. *The Coming Community*. Trans. M. Hardt. Minneapolis: University of Minnesota Press, 1993.
———. *Homo Sacer: Sovereign Power and Bare Life*. Translated by D. Heller-Roazen. Stanford: Stanford University Press, 1998.
———. "No to Bio-Political Tattooing." *Le Monde*, January 10, 2004. https://ratical.org/ratville/cah/totalcontrol.pdf.
———. *State of Exception*. Translated by K. Attel. Chicago: University of Chicago Press, 2005.
Benjamin, Walter. *Critique of Violence*. Translated by E. Jephcott. Cambridge, MA: Belknap, 1979.
Badiou, Alain. *Being and Event*. Translated by O Feltham. New York: Continuum, 2006.
Bion, Wilfred. "Attacks on Linking." *International Journal of Psychoanalysis* 40 (1959) 308–15.
Corradetti, Claudio, and Oreste Pollicino. "The 'War' Against Covid-19: State of Exception, State of Siege, or (Constitutional) Emergency Power?: The Italian Case in Comparative Perspective." *German Law Journal* 22.9 (2021) 1060–71. https://ratical.org/ratville/CAH/totalControl.pdf.
Dickens, Charles. *A Tale of Two Cities*. New York: Dover, 1999.
Engels, Frederick. "On the History of Christianity." *Neue Zeit*, 1894. https://www.marxists.org/archive/marx/works/1894/early-christianity.
Feuerbach, Ludwig. *The Essence of Christianity*. Translated by M. Evans. London: Trubner, 1881.
Foucault, Michel. *The Birth of Biopolitics*. Translated by A. I. Davidson. New York: Palgrave Macmillan, 2008.
Francis of Assisi. *The Writings of St. Francis Assisi*. Translated by F. K. Esser. Rome: Franciscan Archive, 1999.
Fromm, Eric. *Marx's Concept of Man*. Translated by T. B. Bottomore. New York: Frederick Ungar, 1961.
Goethe, Johann W. *Faust*. 2nd ed. New York: Norton, 2001.
Hitchens, Christopher, et al. *The Four Horsemen: The Conversation that Sparked an Atheist Revolution*. New York: Random, 2019.
Lacan, Jacques. *Écrits*. Translated by Bruce Fink. New York: Norton, 2006.
———. *Feminine Sexuality*. Translated by J. Rose. Seminar of Jacques Lacan 21. New York: Norton, 1982.
———. *The Four Fundamentals in Psychoanalysis*. Translated by A. Sheridan. Seminar of Jacques Lacan 11. London: Hogarth, 1977.
———. *Freud's Papers on Technique*. Translated by John Forrester. Seminar of Jacques Lacan 1. New York: Norton, 1988.
———. "On Psychoanalytic Discourse—The Capitalist's Discourse." Lecture delivered at the University of Milan, May 12, 1972. Translated by J. Stone. https://lacanianworksexchange.net/wp-content/uploads/2023/07/Microsoft-Word-Milan_Discourse2.pdf.

———. *The Other Side of Psychoanalysis*. Translated by Russell Grigg. Seminar of Jacques Lacan 17. New York: Norton, 2007.

———. *The Psychoses*. Translated by Russell Grigg. Seminar of Jacques Lacan 3. London: Routledge, 1993.

Marx, Karl. *Critique of Hegel's Philosophy of Right*. Translated by A. Jolin and J. O'Malley. Cambridge: Cambridge University Press, 1970.

———. *Economical and Philosophic Manuscripts of 1844*. Translated by M. Milligan. Moscow: Progress, 1959.

———. *The Gotta Program*. New York: Socialist Labor Party of America, 1920.

———. *Ludwig Feuerbach and the End German Classical Philosophy*. Translated by W. Lough. Moscow: Progress, 1962.

Marx, Karl, and Frederick Engels. *The Holy Family or the Critique of Critical Critique*. Moscow: Foreign Language, 1956.

Schmitt, Carl. *Political Theology: Four Chapters on the Concepts of Sovereignty*. Translated by G. Schwab. Chicago: University of Chicago Press, 2005.

Spinoza, Baruch. *Theological-Political Treatise*. Cambridge: Cambridge University Press, 2008.

Wolf, Richard. *The Sickness Is the System: When Capitalism Fails to Save Us from Pandemics or Itself*. New York: Democracy at Work, 2020.

Žižek, Slavoj. *Event: A Philosophical Concept Through a Journey*. New York: Melville, 2014.

CHAPTER 8

Anderson, Gary A. *Charity: The Place of the Poor in the Biblical Tradition*. New Haven: Yale University Press, 2013.

Barrett, C. K. *The Gospel According to St. John: An Introduction with Commentary and Notes on the Greeks Text*. 2nd ed. Philadelphia: Westminster, 1978.

Bauckham, Richard. *Gospel of Glory: Major Themes in Johannine Theology*. Grand Rapids: Baker Academic, 2015.

Beasley-Murray, George R. *John*. 2nd ed. Word Biblical Commentary 36. Nashville: Thomas Nelson, 1999.

Beirne, Margaret M. *Women and Men in the Fourth Gospel: A Genuine Discipleship of Equals*. JSNT Supplementary 242. New York: Sheffield Academic, 2003.

Bennema, Cornelis. *Encountering Jesus: Character Studies in the Gospel of John*. Colorado Springs: Paternoster, 2009.

Brant, Jo-Ann A. "Husband Hunting: Characterization and Narrative Art in the Gospel of John." *Biblical Interpretation* 4.2 (1996) 205–23.

Brown, Raymond E. *The Community of the Beloved Disciple*. New York: Paulist, 1979.

———. *The Gospel According to John I–XII*. Anchor Bible. Garden City, NY: Doubleday, 1966.

Bultmann, Rudolf. *The Gospel of John: A Commentary*. Translated by G. R. Beasley-Murray et al. Philadelphia: Westminster, 1971.

Carson, D. A. *The Gospel According to John*. Grand Rapids: Eerdmans, 1991.

Coakley, J. F. "The Anointing of Bethany and the Priority of John." *Journal of Biblical Literature* 107.2 (1988) 241–56.

Collins, Raymond F. "'Who Are You?' Comparison/Contrast and Fourth Gospel Characterization." In *Characters and Characterization in the Gospel of John*, edited by Skinner W. Christopher, 79–95. London: Bloomsbury T&T Clark, 2013.

Conway, Colleen M. "Gender and the Fourth Gospel." In *The Oxford Handbook of Johannine Studies*, edited by Judith M. Lieu and Martinus C. De Boer, 220–36. Oxford: Oxford University Press, 2018.

———. *Men and Women in the Fourth Gospel: Gender and Johannine Characterization*. Atlanta: SBL, 1999.

Culpepper, R. Alan. *The Anatomy of the Fourth Gospel: A Study in Literary Design*. Philadelphia: Fortress, 1983.

Downs, David J. *Alms: Charity, Reward, and Atonement in Early Christianity*. Waco, TX: Baylor University Press, 2016.

Fehribach, Adeline. *The Women in the Life of the Bridegroom: A Feminist Historical-Literary Analysis of the Female Characters in the Fourth Gospel*. Collegeville: Liturgical, 1998.

Freeland, Charles. *Antigone, In Her Unbearable Splendor: New Essays on Jacques Lacan's The Ethics of Psychoanalysis*. Albany: State University of New York Press, 2013.

Glasson, T. F. *Moses in the Fourth Gospel*. Naperville, IL: Alec R. Allenson, 1963.

Green, Deborah A. *The Aroma of Righteousness: Scent and Seduction in Rabbinic Life and Literature*. University Park: Pennsylvania State University Press, 2011.

———. "Soothing Odors: The Transformation of Scent in Ancient Israelite and Ancient Jewish Literature." PhD diss., University of Chicago, 2003.

Haenchen, Ernest. *John 2: A Commentary on the Gospel of John, Chapters 7–21*. Edited by Robert W. Funk and Ulrich Busse. Translated by Robert W. Funk. Philadelphia: Fortress, 1984.

Harvey, Susan Ashbrook. *Scenting Salvation: Ancient Christianity and the Olfactory Imagination*. Berkeley: University of California Press, 2015.

Hoskyns, Edwyn. *The Fourth Gospel*. London: Faber & Faber, 1947.

Kesel, Marc de. *Eros and Ethics: Reading Jacques Lacan Seminar VII*. Translated by Sigi Jöttkandt. Albany: State University of New York, 2009.

Koester, Craig R. *Symbolism in the Fourth Gospel: Meaning, Mystery, Community*. 2nd ed. Minneapolis: Fortress, 2003.

Kurek-Chomycz, Dominika A. "The Fragrance of Her Perfume: The Significance of Sense Imagery in John's Account of the Anointing in Bethany." *Novum Testamentum* 52 (2010) xx.

Lacan, Jacques. *The Ethics of Psychoanalysis 1959–1960*. Translated by Dennis Potter. Seminar of Jacques Lacan 7. Edited by Jacques-Alain Miller. New York: Norton, 1997.

———. *On Feminine Sexuality: The Limits of Love and Knowledge, 1972–1973*. Translated by Bruce Fink. Seminar of Jacques Lacan 20. Edited by Jacques-Alain Miller. New York: Norton, 1999.

Lee, Dorothy. *Flesh and Glory: Symbolism, Gender, and Theology in the Gospel of John*. New York: Crossroad, 2002.

Michaels, J. Ramsey. *The Gospel of John*. New International Commentary on the New Testament. Grand Rapids: Eerdmans, 2010.

Moloney, Francis J. *The Gospel of John*. Sagra Pagina Series 4. Edited by Daniel J. Harrington. Collegeville, MN: Liturgical, 1998.

O'Day, Gail R., and Susan E. Hylen. *John*. Louisville: Westminster John Knox, 2006.

Rhee, Helen. *Loving the Poor, Saving the Rich: Wealth, Poverty, and Early Christian Formation.* Grand Rapids: Baker Academic, 2012.

Ruti, Mari. *The Singularity of Being: Lacan and the Immortal Within.* New York: Fordham University Press, 2012.

Saint-Cyr, Viviana M. "Creating a Void or Sublimation in Lacan." *Recherches en Psychanalyse* 13 (2012) 15–21.

Schneiders, Sandra M. "Women in the Fourth Gospel and the Role of Women in the Contemporary Church." *Biblical Theology Bulletin* 12.2 (1982) 35–45.

Schüssler Fiorenza, Elisabeth. *In Memory of Her: A Feminist Theological Reconstruction of Christian Origin.* New York: Crossroad, 1983.

Seim, Turid Karlsen. "Role of Women in the Gospel of John." In *Aspects on the Johannine Literature,* edited by Lars Hartmann and Birger Osson, 56–73. Coniectanea Biblica 18. Uppsala: Almquist and Wiksell, 1987.

Shepherdson, Charles. *Lacan and the Limits of Language.* New York: Fordham University Press, 2008.

Thatcher, Tom. "Jesus, Judas, and Peter: Character by Contrast in the Fourth Gospel." *Bibliotheca Sacra* 153 (1996) 435–48.

Tilborg, Sjef van. *Imaginative Love in John.* Leiden: Brill, 1993.

Winsor, Ann Roberts. *A King Is Bound in the Tresses: Allusions to the Song of Songs in the Fourth Gospel.* Studies in Biblical Literature 6. New York: Peter Lang, 1999.

CHAPTER 9

Baghramian, Maria. *Relativism.* New York: Routledge, 2004.

Baum, Gregory. *Truth Beyond Relativism: Karl Mannheim's Sociology of Knowledge.* Milwaukee, WI: Marquette University Press, 1977.

Benvenuto, Bice, and Roger Kennedy. *The Works of Jacques Lacan: An Introduction.* New York: St. Martin's, 1986.

Congregation for the Doctrine of the Faith (CDF). *Dominus Iesus: Declaration on the Unicity and Salvific Universality of Jesus Christ and the Church.* Rome: Vatican Press Office, 2000. https://www.vatican.va/roman_curia/congregations/cfaith/documents/rc_con_cfaith_doc_20000806_dominus-iesus_en.html

Herre, Rom, and Michael Krausz. *Varieties of Relativism.* Oxford: Blackwell, 1996.

Herrnstein Smith, Barbara. "Relativism, Today and Yesterday." *Common Knowledge* 13.2–3 (2007) 227–49.

Jankunas, Gediminas T. *The Dictatorship of Relativism: Pope Benedict XVI's Response.* New York: St. Paul/Alba, 2011.

Lacan, Jacques. *Desire and Its Interpretation.* Seminar of Jacques Lacan 6. Edited by Jacques-Alain Miller. New York: Polity, 2013.

——. *Écrits: A Selection.* Translated by Alan Sheridan. London: Tavistock, 1977.

——. *The Ego in Freud's Theory and the Technique of Psychoanalysis, 1954–1955.* Translated by Sylvana Tomaselli. Seminar of Jacques Lacan 2. Edited by Jacques Alan-Miller. Cambridge: Cambridge University Press, 1988b [1979].

——. *The Ethics of Psychoanalysis.* Translated by Dennis Porter. Seminar of Jacques Lacan 7. Edited by Jacques-Alain Miller. New York: Norton, 1997.

——. *The Four Fundamental Concepts of Psychoanalysis.* Translated by Alan Sheridan. Seminar of Jacques Lacan 11. Edited by Jacques-Alain Miller. New York: Norton, 1998.

———. *On Feminine Sexuality: The Limits of Love and Knowledge*. Translated by Bruce Fink. Seminar of Jacques Lacan 20. Edited by Jacques-Alain Miller. New York: Norton, 1998.

———. *The Psychoses, 1955–1956*. Seminar of Jacques Lacan 3. London: Routledge, 1993.

Mandelbaum, Maurice. *The Problem of Historical Knowledge: An Answer to Relativism*. New York: Liveright, 1938.

Mong, Ambrose Ih-Ren. *Dialogue Derailed: Joseph Ratzinger's War Against Pluralist Theology*. Eugene, OR: Pickwick, 2014.

Nobus, Dany. *Key Concepts of Lacanian Psychoanalysis*. London: Palgrave, 1998.

Ratzinger, Joseph. "Mass *Pro Eligendo Romano Pontifice*." Homily delivered at the Vatican Basilica, April 18, 2005. https://www.vatican.va/gpII/documents/homily-pro-eligendo-pontifice_20050418_en.html.

———. "Relativism: The Central Problem for Faith Today." Address delivered at meeting of the Congregation for the Doctrine of the Faith with the presidents of the Doctrinal Commissions of the Bishops' Conferences of Latin America in Guadalajara, Mexico, May 1996. https://www.ewtn.com/catholicism/library/relativism-the-central-problem-for-faith-today-2470.

———. *Truth and Tolerance: Christian Belief and World Religions*. San Francisco: Ignatius, 2004.

Smith, Barbara Herrnstein. "Relativism, Today and Yesterday." *Common Knowledge* 13.2–3 (2007) 227–49.

Thurschwell, Pamela. *Sigmund Frued*. Routledge Critical Thinkers. London: Routledge, 2000.

CHAPTER 10

Aers, David. *Community, Gender, and Individual Identity: English Writing 1360–1430*. London: Routledge, 1988.

Allen, Valerie. "Waxing Red: Shame and the Body, Shame and the Soul." In *The Representation of Women's Emotions in Medieval and Early Modern Culture*, edited by Lisa Perfetti, 191–210. Gainesville: University of Florida Press, 2005.

Arnold, John H., and Katherine J. Lewis, eds. *A Companion to the Book of Margery Kempe*. Cambridge, UK: D. S. Brewer, 2004.

Atkinson, Clarissa W. *Mystic and Pilgrim: The Book and World of Margery Kempe*. Ithaca, NY: Cornell University Press, 1983.

Baek, Sanghyeon. *Lacan, Lacaneul Inganhak: Seminar 7 Ganghae*. Paju, South Korea: Hugo, 2017.

Bernau, Anke. "Virginal Effects: Text and Identity in Ancrene Wisse." In *Gender and Holiness: Men, Women and Saints in Late Medieval Europe*, edited by Samantha J. E. Riches and Sarah Salih, 36–48. London: Routledge, 2005.

Bokenham, Osbern. *A Legend of Holy Women*. Translated by Sheila Delany. Notre Dame Texts in Medieval Culture. Notre Dame: University of Notre Dame Press, 1992.

Bullough, Vern L. "Medieval Medical and Scientific Views of Women." *Viator* 4 (1973) 487–93.

Bynum, Caroline Walker. *Fragmentation and Redemption: Essays on Gender and the Human Body in Medieval Religion*. New York: Zone, 1991.

————. *Holy Feast and Holy Fast: The Religious Significance of Food to Medieval Women.* Berkeley: University of California Press, 1987.

Cole, Andrew. *Literature and Heresy in the Age of Chaucer.* Cambridge Studies in Medieval Literature 71. Cambridge, UK: Cambridge University Press, 2008.

Dickman, Susan. "Margery Kempe and the Continental Tradition of the Pious Woman." In *The Medieval Mystical Tradition in England*, edited by Marion Glasscoe, 156–72. Cambridge, UK: D. S. Brewer, 1984.

Evans, Dylan. *An Introductory Dictionary of Lacanian Psychoanalysis.* Taylor & Francis e-Library ed. New York: Routledge, 2006.

Evans, Ruth. "Virginities." In *The Cambridge Companion to Medieval Women's Writing*, edited by Carolyn Dinshaw and David Wallace, 21–39. Cambridge, UK: Cambridge University Press, 2003.

Freud, Sigmund. *Civilization and Its Discontents.* Translated by James Strachey. New York: Norton, 1962.

Gibson, Gail McMurray. *The Theater of Devotion: East Anglian Drama and Society in the Late Middle Ages.* Chicago: University of Chicago Press, 1989.

Kempe, Margery. *The Book of Margery Kempe.* Edited by Lynn Staley. New York: Norton, 2001.

Kesel, Marc de. *Eros and Ethics: Reading Jacques Lacan Seminar VII.* Translated by Sigi Jöttkandt. Albany: State University of New York, 2009.

Kieckhefer, Richard. "Major Currents in Late Medieval Devotion." In *Christian Spirituality: High Middle Ages and Reformation*, edited by Jill Raitt, 75–108. New York: Crossroad, 1997.

Kirshner, Lewis A. "Toward an Ethics of Psychoanalysis: A Critical Reading of Lacan's Ethics." *Journal of the American Psychoanalytic Association* 60.6 (2012) 1223–42.

Knowles, David. *The English Mystical Tradition.* London: Burns & Oates, 1964.

Lacan, Jacques. *Écrits.* Translated by Bruce Fink. New York: Norton, 2006.

————. *The Ethics of Psychoanalysis 1959–1960.* Translated by Dennis Potter. Seminar of Jacques Lacan 7. Edited by Jacques-Alain Miller. New York: Norton, 1997.

————. *The Four Fundamental Concepts of Psychoanalysis.* Translated by Alan Sheridan. Seminar of Jacques Lacan 11. Edited by Jacques-Alain Miller. New York: Norton, 1981.

————. *On Feminine Sexuality: The Limits of Love and Knowledge, 1972–1973.* Translated by Bruce Fink. Seminar of Jacques Lacan 20. Edited by Jacques-Alain Miller. New York: Norton, 1999.

Lewis, Robert E. "Schame." In *Middle English Dictionary*, edited by Robert E. Lewis, 9:595. Ann Arbor: University of Michigan Press, 1988.

Lochrie, Karma. *Margery Kempe and Translations of the Flesh.* Philadelphia: University of Pennsylvania Press, 1991.

McAvoy, Liz Herbert. *Authority and the Female Body in the Writings of Julian of Norwich and Margery Kempe.* Studies in Medieval Mysticism. Cambridge, UK: D. S. Brewer, 2004.

McGinn, Bernard. *The Varieties of Vernacular Mysticism (1350–1550).* Vol. 5 of *The Presence of God: A History of Western Christian Mysticism.* New York: Crossroad, 2012.

Medcalf, Stephan. *The Later Middle Ages.* New York: Holmes & Meier, 1981.

Nichols, John A., and Lillian Thomas Shank, editors. *Distant Echoes.* Vol. 1 of *Medieval Religious Women.* Kalamazoo, MI: Cistercian, 1984.

O'Faolain, Julia, and Lauro Martines, eds. *Not in God's Image: Women in History.* London: Virago, 1979.

Padden, Lisa. "Locating Margery Kempe: An Examination of the Margery of Space and Sexuality in *The Book of Margery Kempe." AnaChronist* 16 (2011) 1–17.

Porter, Roy. "Margery Kempe and the Meaning of Madness." *History Today* 38.2 (1988) 39–44.

Ruti, Mari. *The Singularity of Being: Lacan and the Immortal Within.* New York: Fordham University Press, 2012.

Saint-Cyr, Viviana M. "Creating a Void or Sublimation in Lacan." *Recherches en Psychanalyse* 13 (2012) 15–21.

Salih, Sarah. *Versions of Virginity in Late Medieval England.* Woodbridge, UK: D. S. Brewer, 2001.

VanGinhoven, Bryan. "Margery Kempe and the Legal Status of Defamation." *Journal of Medieval Religious Cultures* 40.1 (2014) 20–43.

Wilson, Janet. "Margery and Alison: Women on Top." In *Margery Kempe: A Book of Essays,* edited by Sandra McEntire, 223–38. New York: Routledge, 1992.

CHAPTER 11

American Psychiatric Association (APA). *Diagnostic and Statistical Manual of Mental Disorders.* 5th ed., revised. Washington, DC: American Psychiatric Association, 2022.

Bion, Wilfred. *Second Thoughts.* New York: Aronson, 1967.

Brazelton, T. B., and J. K. Nugent. *Neonatal Behavioral Assessment Scale.* London: Mac Keith, 1995.

Erikson, Eric. *Childhood and Society.* New York: Norton, 1950.

Fairbairn, W. R. D. *Psychological Studies of the Personality.* London: Routledge & Kegan Paul, 1952.

Fenichel, Otto. *The Collected Papers of Otto Fenichel.* New York: Norton, 1954.

Freud, Sigmund. "The Ego and the Id." In *Ego and Id,* edited by J. Strachey, 1–66. Vol. 19 of *The Standard Edition of the Complete Psychological Works of Sigmund Freud.* London: Hogarth, 1961.

———. "Fetishism." In *The Future of Illusion, Civilization and Its Discontents and Other Works,* edited by J. Strachey, 147–57. Vol. 21 of *The Standard Edition of the Complete Psychological Works of Sigmund Freud.* London: Hogarth, 1961.

———. "Instincts and Their Vicissitudes." In *Collected Papers,* edited by Joan Riviere, 4:117–40. London: Hogarth, 1959.

———. *Three Essays on the Theory of Sexuality.* Translated by James Strachey. New York: Basic, 1962.

Khan, Masud M. *Alienation in Perversions.* New York: Routledge, 1979.

Klein, Melanie. "Notes on Some Schizoid Mechanisms." *International Journal of Psycho-Analysis* 27 (1946) 99–110.

Kohlberg, Lawrence. "The Claim to Moral Adequacy of a Highest Stage of Moral Judgment." *Journal of Philosophy* 70.18 (1973) 630–46.

Kohut, Heinz. "The Two Analyses of Mr. Z." *International Journal of Psychoanalysis* 60 (1979) 3–27.

Lacan, Jacques. *Anxiety*. Translated by Cormac Gallagher. Seminar of Jacques Lacan 10. Dublin: Lacan in Ireland, 2010. http://www.lacaninireland.com/web/wp-content/uploads/2010/06/Seminar-X-Revised-by-Mary-Cherou-Lagreze.pdf.

———. *Écrits*. Translated by Bruce Fink. New York: Norton, 2006.

———. *The Ethics of Psychoanalysis*. Seminar of Jacques Lacan 7. Edited by Jacques-Alain Miller. New York: Norton, 1992.

———. *The Four Fundamental Concepts of Psychoanalysis*. Seminar of Jacques Lacan 11. Edited by Jacques-Alain Miller. New York: Norton, 1978.

———. *Freud's Papers on Technique*. Translated by John Forrester. Seminar of Jacques Lacan 1. New York: Norton, 1988.

———. *Identification*. Translated by Cormac Gallagher. Seminar of Jacques Lacan 9. Dublin: Lacan in Ireland, 2011. http://www.lacaninireland.com/web/wp-content/uploads/2010/06/Seminar-IX-Amended-Iby-MCL-7.NOV_.20111.pdf.

———. *The Logic of Phantasy*. Translated by Cormac Gallagher. Seminar of Jacques Lacan 14. Dublin: Lacan in Ireland, 2010. http://www.lacaninireland.com/web/wp-content/uploads/2010/06/14-Logic-of-Phantasy-Complete.pdf.

———. "Logical Time and the Assertion of Anticipated Certainty: A New Sophism." Translated by Bruce Fink and Mark Silver. *Newsletter of the Freudian Field* 2.2 (1988) 4–22.

———. *Des Noms-Du-Père*. Paris: Seuil, 2005.

———. *The Object Relation*. Translated by A. R. Price. Seminar of Jacques Lacan 4. Edited by Jacques-Alain Miller. Cambridge: Polity, 2021.

———. *The Psychoses*. Translated by Russel Grigg. Seminar of Jacques Lacan 3. New York: Norton, 1993.

———. *La Relation d'Objet*. Le Seminaire Livre 4. Edited by Jacques-Alain Miller. Paris: Seuil, 1991.

———. *The Transference*. Seminar of Jacques Lacan 8. Edited by Jacques-Alain Miller. Cambridge: Polity, 2015.

Levinson, Daniel. *The Seasons of a Man's Life*. New York: Random, 1986.

Mahler, Margaret. *The Psychological Birth of Human Infant Symbiosis and Individuation*. New York: Basic, 1975.

Mahler, Margaret, et al. *The Psychological Birth of the Human Infant*. New York: Basic, 1973.

Piaget, Jean. "Piaget's Theory." In *Carmichael's Manual of Child Psychology*, edited by Paul H. Mussen, 1–18. New York: Plenum, 1970.

Verhaeghe, Paul. *On Being Normal and Other Disorders: A Manual for Clinical Psychodiagnosticus*. New York: Other, 2004.

———. "Perversion II: The Perverse Structure." *Letter* 23 (2001) 77–95.

Winnicott, Donald. *Playing and Reality*. London: Routledge, 1989.

———. "Transitional Objects and Transitional Phenomena: A Study of the First Not-Me Possession." *International Journal of Psychoanalysis* 34 (1953) 89–97.

CHAPTER 12

Abraham, Karl. *Notes on the Psycho-Analytical Investigation and Treatment of Manic-Depressive Insanity and Allied Conditions*. Edited by D. Bryan and A. Strachey. London: Mansfield, 1988.

American Psychiatric Association (APA). *Diagnostic and Statistical Manual of Mental Disorders*. 5th ed., revised. Washington, DC: American Psychiatric Association, 2022.

Aristotle. *Physics: Books I and II*. Translated by William Charlton. Clarendon Aristotle Series. Oxford: Oxford University Press, 1984.

Chavoshian, Ali, and Jung Eun Sophia Park. "Listening Not in Spiritual Direction: A Lacanian Inkling." *Presence: An International Journal of Spiritual Direction* 25 (2019) 5–12.

Fink, Bruce. *A Clinical Introduction to Lacanian Psychoanalysis: Theory and Technique*. Cambridge, MA: Harvard University Press, 1997.

Freud, Sigmund. "Mourning and Melancholia." In *On the History of Psycho-Analytic Movement Papers on Metapsychology and Other Works*, edited by James Strachey, 243–58. Vol. 14 of *The Standard Edition of the Complete Psychological Works of Sigmund Freud*. London: Hogarth, 1954.

———. "The Psychogenesis of the Case of Female Sexuality." In *That Obscure Subject of Desire: Freud's Female Homosexual Revisited*, edited by I R. C. Lesser and E. Schoenberg, 13–33. New York: Routledge, 1999.

———. "Remembering, Repeating, and Working-Through (Further Recommendations on the Technique of Psycho-Analysis II)." In *The Case of Schreber, Papers on Technique, and Other Works (1911–1913)*, edited by James Strachey, 145–56. Vol. 12 of *The Standard Edition of the Complete Psychological Works of Sigmund Freud*. London: Hogarth, 1958.

Freud, Sigmund, and Carl G. Jung. *The Freud/Jung Letters: The Correspondence Between Sigmund Freud and C. G. Jung*. London: Hogarth/Routledge, 1974.

Heimann, Paula. "On Counter-Transference." *International Journal of Psycho-Analysis* 31 (1950) 81–84.

Jacobson, Roman. "Two Aspects of Language and Two Types of Aphasic Disturbances." In *Word and Language*, 95–114. Vol. 2 of *Selected Writings*. The Hague: Mouton, 1971.

Lacan, Jacques. *Écrits: A Selection*. Translated by Alan Sheridan. London: Tavistock, 1977.

———. *The Ego in the Freud's Theory and in the Technique of Psychoanalysis*. Translated by Sylvana Tomaselli. Seminar of Jacques Lacan 2. New York: Norton, 1988.

———. *The Four Fundamental Concepts of Psychoanalysis*. Translated by Alan Sheridan. Seminar of Jacques Lacan 11. London: Hogarth; Institute of Psycho-Analysis. 1977.

———. "The Instance of the Letter in the Unconscious, or Reason Since Freud." In *Écrits: A Selection*, 412–43. Translated by Bruce Fink: New York; London: Norton, 2002.

———. *The Psychoses*. Translated by Russell Grigg. Seminar of Jacques Lacan 3. London: Routledge, 1993.

———. *Les Quatre Concepts Fondamentaux de la Psychanalyse*. Seminaire 11. Paris: Seuil, 1973.

———. *La relation d'objet*. Seminaire 4. Edited by Jacques-Alain Miller. Paris: Seuil, 1991.

Little, Margaret. "Counter-Transference and the Patient's Response to It." *International Journal of Psycho-Analysis* 32 (1950) 32–40.

Marx, Karl. *Economic and Philosophical Manuscript of 1844*. Mineola, NY: Dover, 2007.

Nicolas of Cusa. *On Learned Ignorance: A Translation and an Appraisal of De Docta Ignorantia*. Translated by Jasper Hopkins. Minneapolis: Arthur J. Banning, 1981.

Al-Quran. Translated by Abdullah Yusuf Ali. New York: Tarsile Qur'an, 2006.

Racker, Heinrich. "The Meanings and Uses of Countertransference." *Psychoanalytic Quarterly* 26.3 (1957) 303–57.

Saussure, Ferdinand. *Course in General Linguistics*. Edited by Charles Bally and Albert Secheheye. Translated by Wade Baskin. Glasgow: Collins Fantana, 1959.

CHAPTER 13

Bion, Wilfred. "Attacks on Linking." *International Journal of Psychoanalysis* 40 (1959) 308–15.

Bollas, Christopher. *Catch Them Before They Fall: The Psychoanalysis of Breakdown*. New York: Routledge, 2013.

Freud, Zigmund. *The Schreber Case*. Translated by Andrew Webber. New York: Penguin Classics Psychology, 2003.

Kafka, Franz. *The Metamorphosis*. New York: Classix, 2009.

Klein, Melani. "A Contribution to the Psychogenesis of Manic-Depressive States." *International Journal of Psychoanalysis* 16 (1935) 145–57.

———. "Notes on Some Schizoid Mechanisms." *International Journal of Psycho-Analysis* 27 (1946) 99–110.

Lacan, Jacques. *Écrits*. Translated by Bruce Fink. New York: Norton, 2006.

———. *The Other Side of Psychoanalysis, 1969–1970*. Translated by R. Grigg. Seminar of Jacques Lacan 17. New York: Norton, 2007.

———. *De la Psychose Paranoiaque dans ses Rapports avec la Personnalité*. Paris: Seuil, 1932.

———. *The Psychoses, 1955–1956*. Translated by Russell Grigg. Seminar of Jacques Lacan 3. Edited by Jacques-Alain Miller. New York: Norton, 1993.

———. *Le Sinthome, 1975–1976*. Séminaire de Jacques Lacan 23. Edited by Jacques-Alain Miller. Paris: Seuil, 2005.

Segal, Hanna. "Notes on Symbol Formation." *International Journal of Psychoanalysis* 38 (1957) 391–97.

———. "Some Aspects of the Analysis of a Schizophrenic." *International Journal of Psychoanalysis* 31 (1950) 268–78.

Winnicott, Donald. "Fear of Breakdown." In *1960–1963*, edited by Lesley Caldwell and Helen Taylor Robinson, 523–32. Vol. 6 of *The Collected Works of D. W. Winnicott*. New York, 2016. Online ed. Oxford Academic. https://doi.org/10.1093/med:psych/9780190271381.003.0086.

Index